Journal ir

CW00701671

THEODOR

Translated from the German
by
Alexander Dru

PANTHEON BOOKS

Printed in Great Britain for
Pantheon Books Inc., 333 Sixth Avenue,
New York City

Printed by William Clowes & Sons, Ltd., London and Beccles

To
M. H.
in gratitude for
continual kindness.

PREFACE

The Introduction needs a word of explanation, and perhaps of apology. Haecker's *Journal in the Night* is clear, complete and intelligible as it stands; but Haecker is so little known outside Germany, that this seems the right occasion on which to say something about Haecker's importance. The Introduction is only concerned with that point, with so presenting the intellectual and historical background that Haecker's importance can be seen. There is little, therefore, about Haecker's books individually, a subject which may well be left aside until some of them are translated into English. Instead, there is a summarised account of the movement of thought in which his work took shape. This will, I hope, prepare the reader for the *Journal*, and forestall the misunderstandings that so easily supervene when the perspective is left to chance.

This compressed account includes a number of themes, any one of which might be treated at length. It would have been possible, and even easier, to omit one or another; but the clarity attained by not over-crowding the pages of the Introduction would, I believe, have been fictitious. Haecker's importance as a writer derives from his breadth of view, and this can only be conveyed by pointing out how and where the many themes in his work are related to the movement of thought of which it forms part.

This movement of thought is fashionable at the moment under the name and guise of 'existentialism'; but as a fashion it is a tree shorn of its branches and roots. The aim of the Introduction is, in one respect, to go behind this fictitious simplicity and to stress the historical links that, as a fashion, existentialism seems bent upon ignoring or perhaps denying. When existentialism is considered simply for a year or two he was at last able to realise his ambition, and through the generosity of a friend, went to the University in Berlin. It was there he laid the foundation of a thorough and wide knowledge of ancient and modern literature, though he could not afford to remain long enough to take a degree. On leaving Berlin he went into the offices of an export company, a life that was not made more congenial by being in Antwerp. A year or so later he was again rescued by a friend and was taken into Heinrich Schreiber's small publishing firm in Munich, in conditions which made it possible for him to go on with his studies. From that time, till he was forced to leave Munich in the last year of the war, his life, as far as I know, never altered. He worked in his office during the day, and when he began to write, it was at night. He married late in life, and for the last twenty years lived with his wife and three children in a flat above his office, in a house overlooking the gardens on the further bank of the Isar.

As a young man Haecker's ambition had been to be an actor, until after a long illness, due to an infection of the sinus, an operation left him badly disfigured. It would be difficult to imagine anyone who seemed less fitted for the part he had chosen for himself, though perhaps, by its very incongruity, it suggests to us the mobility of mind and the quick sympathy that lay behind a massive reserve and a disconcerting silence. His silence and reserve were in fact the only surface which he presented to the curious, and he was so lacking in affectation or eccentricity that the most that could be said of him was that he made nothing of himself. Outwardly his life was as ordinary as could well be conceived. He rarely travelled, and took no part in the official learned and literary life that was so well defined in the Germany of that period. Though perhaps here, too, he might have taken a different turn if the Nazi régime had not come at the moment when his books were beginning to have some success, and he had begun to lecture occasionally at the Universities.

Haecker's first essay—*Kierkegaard and the Philosophy of Inwardness*—was published by Schreiber in 1913 as something of a curiosity, for no one had heard of Haecker, and few had heard of Kierkegaard, whose works were only then appearing in German. It was anything but a conventional biography or an impersonal study. The articles which he wrote during the next five or six years, afterwards published under the title *Satire und Polemik* (1914-1920), gave full vent to his contempt for the literary and philosophical pundits of the day of whom probably only Thomas Mann and Rathenau are even names to the English public. The vituperative power of these articles is considerable, and I doubt whether anyone but Karl Krauss, in Vienna, with whom Haecker later became friends, could have surpassed him in violence. There was nothing reserved about Haecker's style, and though he soon afterwards turned his back on 'polemics' for very different fields, what he wrote always had an edge.

The change came in 1920 when Haecker was received into the Catholic Church. For the next few years he wrote little, devoting himself mainly to translations from Kierkegaard and Newman. His introductions and postscripts, together with a criticism of Scheler (which Scheler found remarkable), were published under the title *Christentum und Kultur* in 1927; it was only two years later that he wrote the first short book, from which may be dated the beginning of his work.

Haecker neither wished, nor had the gifts to become a 'figure'. His books were too distant from the German academic tradition, and too wanting in airs and graces, to gain him an audience quickly; they are not easy books to label and it is difficult and dangerous not to be a specialist in Germany. Strangely enough it was probably his grasp of political and social changes and his alarm at the form which the revolution took after the defeat of Germany that carried most weight among Catholics. And here his friendship with Karl Muth, the editor of *Hochland*, should perhaps be mentioned. Haecker's work is not of the impersonal schematic kind which provides the frame-work for a school; and where style is an essential ingredient, the immediate influence is often deceptive. How far his influence took root, how far it may still stimulate and permeate his compatriots remains to be seen.

Haecker had maintained from the first that the Treaty of Versailles was a disaster for Europe, not least because it weakened all the forces that had hitherto done something to contain and limit the Prussian hegemony. And though, as the *Journal* shows, he altered his opinion to some extent, he remained acutely sensitive to the signs of the coming upheaval. Haecker was among the first to discern the real character of the Nazi movement, and his first article attacking its philosophy was published at the time that Hitler came to power. He was arrested a few weeks later and was released only through the help of Karl Muth and Cardinal Faulhaber. From that moment he was a marked man; he was forbidden to speak on the wireless and refused permission to lecture. The death of his wife in 1935 left him very much alone. A letter written in 1939 from Switzerland gives some notion of his feelings at this time.

> I was able to lecture in St. Gallen (in Switzerland) yesterday. The permission was given as a result of an oversight. And in my own country I am not allowed to say one word in public, because my books are having a success and are beginning to have some influence. I have been declared an enemy of the State, a *Staatsfeind*. My name is starred three times in the books of the Police, our tscheka, and my safety is always threatened more and more. I have the feeling and the belief that I am in the hands of God, but I am not on that account freed from anxiety and worry about my children. In a couple of hours I shall be back in Germany, and cannot tell what may not happen. At any rate, once there I shall no longer be able to write the truth.

In the last sentence of his letter is the germ of the book here translated, and in fact Haecker refers in the *Journal* to the change involved in adopting a new form, and compares it to the change when he gave up 'satire and polemics'.

Looking back, it is remarkable how much Haecker could say in his essays that the normally sensitive reader must have recognised as directly applicable to existing conditions, and which the obtuseness of the censors passed over. But with the prospect of war, and of the general catastrophe he foresaw, Haecker felt the need to speak out his whole mind. And so, while nothing could at first sight seem less adapted to his cast of mind than a Journal, it was forced upon him, and he chose it as the perfect vehicle for the testimony he had to give.

The *Journal* was written, like everything else he had written, by night. As much as possible of the manuscript was kept hidden in Karl Muth's house outside Munich, for Haecker had every reason to fear a visit of the *Gestapo*. When at last it occurred, and the police entered his flat, the current pages of the *Journal* lay in a music case on the sofa in his room. Only the presence of mind of his daughter, who caught her father's whispered word *mappe*, saved it from discovery. She ran into the room, called out that she was late for her music lesson, and ran off with the case. Not long afterwards, Hans Scholl, Haecker's friend and the leader of the students who staged an abortive revolt in 1943, was condemned to death. Hans Scholl had noted down a conversation with Haecker in which he had said that above all things Germans lacked humility. This had its humourous conclusion in the interrogation that followed Haecker's arrest. He was asked what he meant by his words, and when he said, 'literally what I said', he was dismissed with the remark: *Ach so, das ist in Ordnung.*

Early in 1944 Haecker's house was completely destroyed during the bombing of Munich. His health had already begun to suffer, and he went to live in a village outside Augsburg. There he was entirely alone. His daughter visited him occasionally from Munich. His eldest son was a prisoner in England. His youngest son Reinhard was sent early in 1945 to the Russian front and was shortly afterwards reported missing. His sight began to fail, and not long afterwards, on 9th April, he died entirely alone.

II.

Dire la vérité, toute la vérité, rien que la vérité, dire bêtement la vérite bête, ennuyeusement la vérité ennuyeuse, tristement la vérité triste: voilà ce que nous nous somme proposé. Nous y avons à peu près réussi.

Le Triomphe de la République 1905
Charles Péguy.

Theodor Haecker belonged to the same generation as Péguy, and both grew up in Péguy's 'monde moderne', the world of 'les intellectuels', of socialists, nationalists, internationalists, in which poetry was an ivory tower and civilisation was already in the grips of the new technology, a world in which religion was wholly irrelevant. However much they differed, they felt their situation to be the same, their paths were in fact the same, their difficulties and problems and even their destinies were not unlike, and in the history of their two countries their places are analogous. And more than that, it might be said that where Péguy left off, cut off in the middle of a sentence, there Haecker, unaware of Péguy's work, picks up the thread.

Charles Péguy's work was a series of discoveries, of brilliant intuitions, set down with painstaking exactitude as a process of 'approfondissement' in which the deepest feeling was of 'fidélité' to truth, and to his human condition. 'La révolution sera morale' he announced, purposely confusing his own and the social revolution, 'ou elle sera rien'.

His search for the truth at times concealed the goal from him—as well as from the readers of the interminable *Cahiers* in which he noted down the world of tradition as it came within his horizon. For it was himself and not Descartes he described when he spoke of 'ce cavalier français parti d'un si bon pas'. The stress which his method laid upon his discoveries—and he defined philosophy as the discovery of a new continent—lent a romantic colour to his vision that falsifies its essential nature. Péguy was neither a reactionary discovering the past, nor a progressive discovering the future; the tradition he perceived was at once older and newer. And if his work is deceptive in this, it is because it was written during the process of 'approfondissement'; the moral and intellectual violence with which he battled his way through the 'monde moderne' left its mark on his final point of view; his 'vérité' was not only dull, obvious and at times sad; we see it as his own.

With the exception of the great unfinished *Cahiers* that were published posthumously* Péguy's work leads up to his return to Catholicism which characteristically he refused to call a conversion; and in the sense that it was the discovery of himself, the understanding of his human condition and not a change so much as a growth, an 'approfondissement', he was right.

Haecker, on the other hand, emphasised the finality of conversion, not so much as a break with the past, but as the attainment of a lasting foundation, the starting point in his life and thought. What he wrote before that date can be ignored. He was received into the Catholic Church in 1920; he published a collection of essays and articles in 1927 and his main work began when he was forty; a work as compact and economical, ordered and objective as Péguy's was straggling, diffuse and repetitive.

Haecker, no doubt, was as conscious as Péguy of having been 'long on the road, slow and obstinate'. 'It may well be' he continues, 'that there are men who find themselves at once; but I am not among them; I had to go a long way

* *Note sur la Philosophie de M. Bergson*; *Note Conjointe sur la Philosophie de M. Descartes*; *Clio*.

round before coming to myself'* The difference between
them lay in the fact that Haecker 'never prized the endeavour above the end, the search above the find'. Péguy
worked his passage; Haecker, as the violence of his first
articles shows, was more impatient for the goal, more
patient of the way.

*   *   *

At the end of his fine study of Péguy, M. Romain Rolland
sums up, saying that 'Péguy's genius was to have been and
to have recognised in himself 'un bon français de l'espèce
ordinaire, et vers Dieu un fidèle et un pécheur de la com-
mune espèce'. As in everything, Péguy was at once struck
by his discovery and by his genius. Haecker neither was,
nor thought himself a 'genius' and gave an almost opposite
account of himself: 'I was very early struck by the thought,
and it has never left me, of how little I myself could contribute to my being and existence; and I drew the conclusion that it was far more important for me to meditate
on the power which created me and sustains me... than
upon the little which I can do. That is certainly connected
with the fact that, from childhood up, I was of a contemplative nature'.

Péguy was not the type to meditate on the little he could
do: he was frankly and naively astonished at his powers,
and when late in his career he became a poet, he was as
dumbfounded as his readers—'ce sera plus fort que Dante'.
But there was a certain ethical strain in his make-up that
shaped his thought more than he understood and prevented
him from freeing himself entirely from the rationalistic
ethics in which he felt enmeshed. 'Contre la morale
catholique' he wrote in an early work, 'seul une morale
socialiste, strictement Kantienne en sa forme' and even in
his last *Notes* this element was not entirely eliminated. It is

*Preface to *Satire und Polemik* 1921.

this ethical turn of mind that gives his poetry its unique flavour.

When Péguy was killed in 1914 he had reached the point where he could no longer have glossed over the question of conversion; the search was at an end. And in fact the unfinished *Notes* and *Clio* suggest a coming change more radical than the whole process of 'approfondissement' as it lies before us in the *Cahiers*. It is with that change, the mature formulation of the contemplative point of view, that Haecker's work is concerned. Péguy certainly saw the problems of his time very clearly, saw the narrowness of the rationalistic interpretations of 'scientific' history. He saw, for example, the confusion that followed when Taine ignored the different 'orders' and explained La Fontaine's poetry in sociological terms and the 'man' in terms of his material and economic existence. But although he criticised and ridiculed the 'enormous conceit' of these 'explanations' he was weak in putting forward his 'humble' intuitive method as the alternative. Having experienced the inadequacy of rationalism and reacted against it, he remained to some degree influenced by its antithetical forms of thought, so that the alternative sometimes presented itself in a form that is not free from irrationalism.

*   *   *

"Apart from 'the faith'", Haecker writes in the *Journal*, "the only choice is between the 'inadequate' and the 'absurd'. Bourgeois Europe chose the 'inadequate', and was followed in this choice by the Fascists. Individual geniuses prefer some 'absurd' or other, usually gnostic in origin, as in the case of Schelling and Scheler, or else of a private nature, like Nietzsche's 'Eternal Recurrence', or Rilke's 'Weltinnenraum'. There is something one-dimensional about the faces of those who chose the 'inadequate' ".

For all their brilliance and truth, Péguy's discoveries are his, and it calls for an effort of mind to disengage them from his grasp—and though he said with some truth to Lotte, his appointed Boswell, 'C'est un renouveau catholique qui se fait par moi', it was a reflection upon what he could do; there was something 'private' about it which interested him quite as much as meditating on the destiny in which he was involved. Péguy had too much genius; he was carried away by his fantasy and his immense dexterity, and delighted in his eccentricities. Yet even his eccentricities have an ethical quality, and his eccentric, drumming, repetitive style, with its angry or ironical emphasis on the obvious, has almost nothing of the 'écrivain' about it. Haecker, on the other hand, is never eccentric and always himself, the difference may perhaps be marked by saying, as Haecker says in the *Journal*, that the paradox is almost always only a way to the simple, harmonious (obvious) truth, though a very significant way. What Péguy and Haecker saw was, in essentials, the same; the way in which they saw it could hardly be more different.

*   *   *

It is at their best that Péguy and Haecker are nearest together, in their regard for the truth and in their faith. 'Sa vraie croyance', Mme. Favre said of Péguy, 'c'était la prière'. That was the source of Péguy's fundamental theme and principle: 'l'insertion de l'éternel dans le temporel'— the fact or data of tradition—

> Et l'arbre de la grace et l'arbre de la nature
> Ont lié leur deux troncs de noeuds si solennels
> Ils ont tant confondu leurs destins fraternels
> Que c'est la même essence et la même stature.

For in the 'monde moderne' nature and grace were not any

longer different 'orders', they were an antithesis. There is
hardly a better example of Péguy's imaginative power, that
flowed from his life of prayer, than his capacity to see nature
and the supernatural once again in the harmony of tradition.
It was as a result of this antithesis—of the antithetical form
of thought that denies the different orders in favour of a one-
dimensional world—that religion had become irrelevant; it
had lost its roots and its links in nature and history and had
become something entirely 'supernatural'—a ghost from the
past. This generally accepted notion was not only the product of Bayle's rationalistic critique of Tradition, but the
consequence of the mechanical rehearsal of the 'evidences' of
Christianity, themselves encased in a rationalistic mould,
divorced (for the sake of convenience) from personal
religion and the life of prayer, and as such abstractions.
In their way the 'evidences' and Natural Theology were
the *preserve* of a cast as distant from Péguy's 'bon
français', as the 'intellectuals' whom Péguy and Haecker
began by opposing with all the vehemence at their
command.

It was in this 'monde moderne,' where natural and
super-natural were separated by a gulf, that Bergson created
such a profound impression. 'He will never be forgiven'
Péguy said, 'for having set us free,' that is neither by the
intellectuals nor by the *ultras*. To Haecker, who described
the philosophy of the period as a process of asphixiation,
Bergson was the man who 'threw open a window and let
us breathe'. But almost simultaneously there occurred the
decisive event in his intellectual development, the discovery
of Kierkegaard's work—and if Haecker did not think in
terms of discoveries, it was not because he did not make
them. Twenty years later, in a critical essay on *Kierkegaard's
Notion of Truth* he wrote: 'I am still too strongly under the
impression which Kierkegaard made upon me as a young
man, to speak of him without gratitude and admiration'.
His conversion was not a break with the past, but the fulfilment of his *fidélité*, and none of those from whom he had

gained an insight into the truth were set aside or forgotten, neither Kierkegaard, nor Hilty nor Blumhardt.*

*   *   *

It was hardly an anachronism that Kierkegaard should have come upon the scene after Bergson, for although his point of view is neither mysterious nor esoteric, his whole mode of thought was obscured by the polemics out of which it emerged. That Nietzsche's work of demolition helped to prepare the way must be evident. But Kierkegaard's delayed action is an excellent illustration of the continuity of thought between the attempt to recover the meaning of tradition which occurred at the end of the XVIIIth century and the movement of thought that recovered itself with the appearance of Bergson—a movement which now acknowledges its origins in Kierkegaard, at least to the extent of adopting his term, existential.

The romantics with whom Kierkegaard had most in common were the failures of the first generation, whose truncated works and fragmentary thoughts were exposed in a wholly misleading perspective by the appearance of the successful and often massive 'inadequate' *oeuvres* that followed. The immediate reaction to the Age of Reason, with its artificial segregation of thought and feeling and its capacity for dispensing with enthusiasm, had released an intuitive perception of the common ground of

---

* *Johann Christoph Blumhardt* (1805-1880) whose life and writings made a great impression upon Haecker as a young man. He studied theology in Tübingen, and took orders. Mörike and David Friederich Strauss were among his friends and contemporaries. His extraordinary spiritual influence in his country parish soon spread abroad, and can only be compared to that of the Curé d'Ars. But his theology was displeasing to authority, and his innumerable cures and miraculous powers were discounted. Neither he, nor his son, who was hardly less remarkable, have ever recived any acknowledgment. *Carl Hilty* (1833-1909) Professor of Law at Bern University—a writer who impressed von Hügel and Haecker and apparently no one else.

tradition and imagination, which was so fruitful in new
vistas and forms of expression, that with few exceptions the
end outstripped the means and was lost in vagueness. The
great example, among these failures, of a mind equipped to
perceive the aim and capable of assimilating the material,
is Coleridge. Newman's 'failure' was to have worked
patiently at the same problem, refusing all the half-hearted
or pseudo-solutions elected by his contemporaries, and only
to have completed in 1870 a work well launched in 1830.
By a curious irony, being twelve years older than Kierkegaard, he lived on ten years after Bergson had begun
writing : no more unpropitious timing could be imagined.*

The aim of the writers who broke away from the rationalism of the XVIIIth century, in some cases hardly more
than an instinct, was the re-integration of thought and
feeling, a unity of life and thought which transferred the
accent from essence to existence. The fact that the XIXth
century fell back again into the same stale dichotomy,
enriched by its scientific discoveries on the one side, and on
the other by the poetic discoveries of the first generation of

---

* What Mr. I A. Richards says of the writers discussing Coleridge
might with equal propriety be applied to those who write on Newman:
they usually "put a ring fence round a very small part of his thought
and say, 'we will keep inside this and leave the transcendental and the
analytic discussion to someone else. ' " Father D'Arcy has observed how
little attention Newman has received from philosophers and psycholo-
gists; he does not mention theologians, perhaps because Newman
emphasised his amateur status. It would have been possible for Mr.
Richards himself to widen his field of discussion, profitably I think,
for in the *University Sermons* Newman added a foot-note to the effect that
Coleridge had forestalled his argument; and then it is evident that the
Grammar of Assent is by no means irrelevant to *Coleridge on the Imagination*.
Recently, Mr. Herbert Read has pointed to the fact that Coleridge
was approaching Kierkegaard's 'either-or', though it would be still
better to say that Kierkegaard on the imagination (especially in
Sickness unto Death) is relevant to *Coleridge the Critic*. In any case
the 'either-or' is apt to be a rather sterile approach to Kierkegaard's
thought. 'Existentialism' is often regarded as a fashion; I hope the
connections suggested by this note will dispel the illusion. Perhaps it is
only a fashion in its attempt to segregate the ideas of Coleridge and
Kierkegaard from their Christianity.

romantics, concealed the importance of Kierkegaard (and of those whose work had similar aims) for nearly a century.

*   *   *

Among the few who saw this clearly, at the time, was Sainte-Beuve, so well situated and gifted to understand the significance of these attempts to grasp the meaning of tradition, and to assess the shortcomings of those who bungled the work. In one of the outbursts in which he excelled, he gave a definition of the *mal du siècle*—as a lack of will—which is by far the best justification for the venom with which he pursued Chateaubriand, and Hugo and the successful romantics, and explains his penetrating admiration of Senancour's 'failure'.

"Parmi les hommes qui se consacrent aux travaux de la pensée et dont les sciences morales et philosophiques sont le domaine, rien de plus difficile à rencontrer aujourd'hui qu'une volonté au sein d'une intelligence, une conviction, une *foi*. Ce sont des combinations infinies, des impartialités sans limites, de vagues et inconstants assemblages, c'est-à-dire, sauf la dispute du moment, une indifférence radicale. Ce sont, en les prenant au mieux, de vastes âmes deployées à tous les vents, mais sans ancre quand elles s'arrêtent, sans boussole quand elles marchent. Cette croissance démesurée de la faculté compréhensive constitue une véritable maladie de la volonté, et va jusqu'à la dépraver ou à l'abolir. Elle aboutit dans le sein même de l'intelligence, qui se glace en s'éclaircissant, qui s'efface et s'étale, au delà des justes bornes, et n'a plus ainsi de centre lumineux, de puissance fixe et rayonnante. On veut comprendre sans croire, recevoir les idées ainsi que le ferait un miroir limipide, sans être déterminé pour cela, je ne dis pas à des actes, mais même à des conclusions. . . . . . c'est une maniére d'epicuréisme sensuel et raffiné de l'intelligence. On ne s'y livre pas d'abord de propos délibéré; on se dit qu'il faut choisir; mais l'âge venant, cette vertu du choix, cette énergie de la volonté qui, se confondant intimement avec la sensibilité, compose l'amour, et avec l'intelligence n'est autre chose que la foi, dépérit, s'épuise, et un matin après la trop longue suite d'essais et de libertinage de jeunesse, elle a disparu de l'esprit comme du coeur."*

Saint-Beuve was taken in, and attributed to Lamennais, not only a full understanding of the *mal du siècle*, but the qualities and gifts, the integration of intellect, will and feeling, that were to fulfill the promise of romanticism in its search for the meaning of tradition. Within three or four years he was obliged to retract, and the terms in which he did so show how clearly he had seen the problem and how deeply he felt the disappointment. Lamennais he admits, was 'beaucoup plus *écrivain* et *poëte* que nous n'avions cru le voir'. In fact he was not very different from Sainte-Beuve's *bêtes noires*, Chateaubriand, Balzac, Hugo. 'Quelle dommage', he wrote a few years later on re-reading his article on Lamartine, 'Quelle dommage que le *sens du vrai* soit si souvent en défaut chez ces hommes en qui prédomine le talent'. That was the theme of *Chateaubriand et son cercle littéraire* in which he so plainly marks his preference for the truth and sincerity of Senancour.† In *Port Royal* he let himself go for the last time on the subject of 'le mensonge de la parole littéraire', and the want of will to bring concept and image together in the truth.

*   *   *

The importance of Kierkegaard's work, so often regarded in its most negative aspects, in its polemic against rationalism

---

* *Portraits Contemporains*: Lamennais.

† As far as I know, Maine de Biran escaped Sainte-Beuve's attention till much later, when his views had already hardened, though even then he took Taine to task for his prejudiced account of Maine de Biran's thought.

and in its impatient dismissal of mysticism (as the antithesis), lies in its attempt to find the meaning of tradition and to understand the truth in relation to man as a spiritual unity of intellect, will and feeling, harmonised or reflected, as he says, in the faculty *instar omnium*, the imagination. This attempt to 'say once again, if possible in a more inward way' what had been handed down 'by the fathers' was guided from the start by a grasp of the irrelevance of religion in the modern world in no sense inferior to Lamennais' *Essai sur l'indifférence*. His own criticism of his work was that there was too much of the *écrivain* and the *poëte* in it.

The greatest fault which a thinker can commit, Haecker was never tired of repeating, was to leave out something, for the errors of over-simplification result in a confusion far more vicious because more radical, than that produced by the mere muddler. At many points Kierkegaard was confused; but he did not leave things out. His faults spring from a different cause, from his often excessive repudiation of the over-simplified alternatives that were proposed to him. His suspicion of 'mysticism' led him in his last pamphlets to take 'honesty' as the final criterion, and almost justifies his German translator in calling him a rationalist. Better known is his sustained attack on rationalism (with special reference to Hegel) and in volume after volume he treated reason to the rough handling that Pascal so admired in Montaigne. In *The Instant* he was 'inadequate'; elsewhere very often 'absurd'. It would be difficult to find these criticisms more forcibly or more justly put than in Haecker's essays; but this did not prevent him from seeing in the problem as stated by Kierkegaard, and in the imaginative attempt to solve it, a world of thought still to be explored. To Haecker, Kierkegaard's work appeared as one of the great and original attempts in the history of Europe to reconcile philosophy and mysticism and to preserve the rights of both intuition and discursive reason.

"Kierkegaard's great existential thesis of 'truth in subjectivity' is one of the vital problems before man and will

remain the source of unrest even in the realms of pure
philosophy. Side by side with the 'philosophy of nature'
and the 'philosophy of life', Kierkegaard's spiritual and
existential philosophy is the task before the future. Its
essence is the *life* of the spirit, the *energeia* of the spirit, a
Ζώγ, a life which is not an *anima mundi*, the life of nature,
but a spiritual life, that of the person in a medium antagonistic to him, which is to say matter, lifeless in his body,
living in his soul. But the task is not what Kierkegaard
thought it to be—himself the victim of a false philosophy—
for he regarded the task as the realisation or actualisation of
a mere probability, and an uncertainty, and to the natural
understanding, even an absurdity; whereas it is an objective
truth, firmly established according to the classical definition
of truth as *'adequatio rei et intellectus'*, a certainty, however
difficult and painful its acquisition and retention".

What Haecker means by 'spiritual man' may be seen
from the following quotation:

"Spiritual man is indeed something other than the
intellectual man, though naturally presupposing him: he
has a whole dimension more, he is the complete man according to the idea of God, a perfect unity, an incomparable
totality, desired by God and longed for by man as *anima
naturaliter Christiana*. Spiritual man is the antagonist of
gnosticism and of the idealism of German philosophy, after
all only a sort of watered down gnosticism. Only the
spiritual man understands the holiness of the body. An
embrace can never be holy to the gnostic. And those who
do not want to insult the creator should be careful not to
insult his creation. The Christian is the enemy of the
world, of the 'world' in inverted commas. And that is not
the 'pure' creation of God, but the product of fallen man
and fallen angels. The world in this sense, the 'world' in
inverted commas, and the man who belongs to it, one might
even say 'man' in inverted commas, that ambiguous fudge
of good and evil, wanting in all decision, not saying 'no' to
anything, is consequently dangerous; metaphysically speak-

ing this 'world' and this 'man' have evil in them as nihilism. The 'man' corresponding to the 'world', sometimes impertinently called natural man, as though he were the product of uncorrupted nature, which exists only in the 'Immaculate', this 'man', outside Christianity, necessarily has in his art a certain nihilism of the feelings. Even love sings and murmurs a melodious Nothing, like *Tristan*; he has a devastating, nihilistic philosophy once away from the privileged philosophy of being as it is found in Plato and Aristotle; he has a nihilistic politics, an apostate politics, because his will is nihilistic and does not will the true end, which is God alone. And it is quite in order and perfectly normal that the three faculties proper to man should have their part in the dangerous, almost mortal sickness of being in the 'world', this 'world' in inverted commas."

The 'almost mortal sickness'—an echo of Kierkegaard's *Sickness unto Death*—is the disintegration of the 'individual', the despair upon which Kierkegaard focussed so much of his attention because he saw in it the opposite of 'faith' as the moment in which man 'begins to exist': when all his faculties are integrated. This despair and nihilism Kierkegaard regarded as the evasion of the problem of existence, a flight into a world of *fantasy* and a lack of *imagination*, in which one or other of the faculties asserts its autonomy at the expense of man's spiritual unity: and it was against 'philosophy' in this sense, whether as rationalism, voluntarism or irrationalism that Kierkegaard fulminated.

The problem of this spiritual unity and its relation to truth is the subject of many of the entries in the *Journal*, some of which have been included although they were incorporated in Haecker's last, and still unpublished book: *Metaphysik des Gefühls*, a metaphysic of feeling. The first outline of the question, so important to a full understanding of Haecker's work, occurs in *Schöpfer und Schöpfung* (his meditations: *Creator and Created*) in a section entitled

Analogia Trinitatis. A passage in that brief excursus gives the aim of his last essay :

"Philosophy belongs by origin to the intellect; and its proper sphere is the sphere of the intellect. Whatever else it may master, it has first to conquer with the help, so to speak, of foreign mercenaries. Its immediate sphere is pure knowledge, and starting from there, it goes on to the knowledge—*always to the knowledge*—of that which is to be willed; and from there it must go forward, a thing it has hardly begun to do, to the knowledge—*always to the knowledge*—of that which is felt. But in the third case the difficulties multiply owing to the new relation of subject to object."

It was in this way that Haecker understood the significance of Kierkegaard's 'truth in subjectivity' as the aim of man whose spiritual unity was not a desperate leap into the absurd, but the attainment and actualisation of objective truth. The problem, he continues, requires a complete thought: 'a complete thought, both abstract and concrete; the thought that grasps knowledge and insight into the universal, together with its knowledge of being—and also a thought that grasps the concrete and the particular, in that it is forever moving between the image that belongs to the senses, and the notion that is purely intellectual, dematerialising the notion and spiritualising the image'.

In this emphasis upon complete thought is to be seen, perhaps, the reflection of Haecker's deep admiration for Newman. It is also noticeable that in his presentation of the need for a new understanding of the relation of subject to object Haecker is concerned with the question that is so much to the fore in M. Gabriel Marcel's work. Perhaps Haecker's position can be best indicated from his statement of principles in the Preface to *Was ist der Mensch?*

"In the long, unnecessary battle between sensualism and reason, between the image and the thought, between contemplation and discursive thought, I am neither a sensualist nor an intellectualist, but a 'hierarchist'. Starting from the senses, and never without them, though not with the senses alone, man reaches thought—and belief. Thought is of a higher 'order' and equally of a higher quality than the image, for the spirit is of a higher order than the senses; and the marvel of the particular creation to which man belongs is that, from the beginning, starting from the bottom, it is both time *and* space: it begins with matter. But he who loves the order of hierarchy, the 'hierarch' we might call him, is only such through love, even in philosophy: he leaves the faults of sensualism on one side, and is not ensnared by its weaknesses; but he does not relinquish the senses, without which he would not be, for he is not a pure spirit, like the angels, and never will be! He flees the impurity of the image, but not the image which he loves eternally and to which he always lovingly returns from the realm of immaterial being that he learns to know weakly in and through the image, although he himself cannot pursue being into those realms. He returns to the image, to the image of his *choice* indeed, for he is master of the image, and pours into it the power of thought and idea, holding it up and sustaining it; for it is he who crowns the image with power and gives it its rights in the spiritual sphere".

I will conclude this section with two more quotations in order to illustrate both the traditional basis of Haecker's thought, and the imaginative freedom which this gave him.

"*Fides quaerit intellectum*, faith seeks and stirs the intellect to the utmost endeavours and assists it. The two are not enemies who can never unite, nor are they two poles for ever apart in stress and strain, as opposites. All such notions are phantasms, woven out of centuries of poisonous heresy, or perhaps just trivial comparisons, words without thought. In any case, such is the sound and true teaching of the Christian religion, as it has been handed down to us in Holy Scripture through Christ and his apostles, and kept alive by the Church."

"Whatever a man says of himself or of others is said by his spirit—but what is it precisely, what power or faculty that gives to things their name?"

"Not his feeling and not his will, however much, however powerfully and often decisively they may enter into it, for the 'human spirit' is always a unity of the three faculties—but his intellect, whose guiding thread and goal is *truth*. The intellect is the light of the spirit—to such crude images are we compelled, even though we may spiritualise them, which is the secret of the mystics!—for it is not given to us to express in positive terms the real essence of the spirit, and we do so in the abstract only by negation: it is *not* material, immaterial; and then again we express it in the concrete through images, upon which there always lies something of the materiality of the sensual life of body and soul, images which in their selectiveness and graduated power are always straining, asymptotically, to capture the 'immaterial'; images such as *spiritus, pneuma,* breath, light, sound. These images and others, are made more intellectual through the spiritual life of man in that they enter into the sphere of comparison and analogy as symbols of the Divine Being. But the furthest limit of the material is reached not in dead abstractions, but vitally through the concrete. The essence of man's cognisant spirit is not immediate spiritual vision, intellectual insight, but thought, which, however, has this very intellectual insight or intuition as its starting point and as its aim and end, spiritual *sight* and vision. And that is why I said that the intellect is the light of the human spirit, in so far as it is knowledge. The essential character of the human spirit is therefore better defined, as far as its being is concerned, as *ratio.* Man is a *rational animal*".

The distinctive feature of Haecker's contemplative cast of mind is his sense of the hierarchy of being. No dualistic philosophy, he asserts, is so false as a monistic system. But what he calls the 'hierarchic' view is neither monistic nor dualistic but trinitarian. And although the *Analogia Trinitatis* first appears where Haecker considers the spiritual unity of man's three faculties, man created in the image of the Trinity, he regarded it in its bearing upon the *analogia entis,* not only as an image with which to further our know-

ledge of man, but as an extension and fulfilment of our
analogical knowledge of being.

III.

> *Ad se ipsum.* Never forget that you could only
> write *Satires and Polemics* (1914-1920) because
> you had promised break off when everything
> seemed at its best, so to speak, when that path
> pleased you most. You had to go a different
> way, that pleased you less. And now the same
> thing is happening again: You have got to go
> a new way, one that pleases you even less.
>   Journal 1939.

The *Journal* is the new form and the new path forced upon
Haecker by circumstances, reluctantly if freely chosen, his
last testimony to the truth and a confession of faith that is
a spontaneous rejoinder to a particular moment in history.
Its uniqueness lies in the fulness of its confrontation of faith
and history and in Haecker's gift of fusing what is so often
separated. The *Journal* is the most direct expression of the
conception of truth which is the subject of his whole work.
    The same *approfondissement* had taken place in both
Kierkegaard and Péguy, but their intuitions, their vision,
remained unfulfilled in a certain measure. This is quite
specially true of Kierkegaard whose last polemics off even
tend to obscure his prophetic insight. Yet from the date
of his conversion, in 1848, he was essentially concerned with
only one idea, 'the witness to the truth' whom—whether we
call him martyr, saint or confessor—he regarded as the
criterion of existence, since in him alone is to be found the
actualisation of 'contemporaneity with Christ'. The notion
of 'contemporaneity' occurs at the very beginning of

Kierkegaard's work as the criterion of the 'stages' or spheres of existence (aesthetic, ethical, religious) and again as the 'either-or', the 'choice' between living 'contemporaneously with oneself' or escaping into past or future and away in fact from the *engagement* which brings time and eternity together.

This conception receives a wider though less deeply anchored and defined form in Péguy's principle: 'l'insertion de l'éternel dans le temporel' with its more direct and conscious bearing on the *meaning* of history and tradition. He was in fact among the first to relate the notion of contemporaneity, so intimately bound up with his life of prayer, to the need of harmonising what he called the Jewish and the Greek 'disciplines'. The real importance of Haecker's work seems to me to lie in accurately perceiving the relation of these two aspects of 'contemporaneity'—though he had not, as far as I know, read Péguy. (It is true that he greatly admired Bloy, whose view of history is substantially the same).

The reconciliation of Greek and Jewish thought and the resulting emphasis upon history becomes in Haecker's hands the manner in which religion becomes relevant, is given its context and its situation in contemporary history. In that sense it would be true to say that the central theme of the *Journal* is the relation of Christianity and culture, or more accurately, a momentous instance of their divorce— the *apostasy* of Germany. The aim of the rest of this Introduction is to indicate briefly and in Haecker's words wherever this can be done, the constituent elements of the point of view from which this theme is treated.

*   *   *

Kierkegaard, Péguy and Haecker are not in the ordinary sense 'difficult' writers; as a general rule it is 'l'esprit de

XXXIV JOURNAL IN THE NIGHT

géometrie' which provides the difficult explanations. Their works are, however, difficult to break into, their approach is unfamiliar; for 'l'esprit de finesse' is essentially inaccessible because it tends at all times to reflect the writer's whole vision or his sense of the 'whole', the *summa*. Their works are therefore like the islands of an archipelago, each personal, distinct and complete, without links with the other, so that there is no 'progressing' from one to the other (from Coleridge to Kierkegaard)—and yet forming a continuous train of thought, a pattern in history. The simplest way of breaking down their isolation is to concede this pattern; and, above all, not to impose upon them the pattern of history which it was one of their principle concerns to break away from.

Once again, this can best be done by stressing the continuity between the reaction against the Age of Reason and the existentialist *volte face*. The two chief points at which the similarity stands out plainly are first, the emergence of a preoccupation with questions explicitly or implicitly theological, and secondly, a marked indifference, or even hostility, to 'historicism'. It is because the problems of man's 'human condition' are theological problems, that existentialism is represented by two camps, the one atheistic, the other Christian; and as though to confirm the truth of this view, Marxism sees in existentialism the one vigorous and possibly dangerous antagonist to its consistent anti-theological conception of man and its 'scientific history'.

The sudden collapse of the romantic reaction into 'historicism' has always been something of a mystery. 'The descent from these cloudy summits of the romantic Sinai', Mr. Christopher Dawson writes, 'to the worship of the Secular State, that Golden Calf in the desert of materialism, is one of the strangest events in the history of European thought, and the philosophy of Hegel remains as a mighty monument and symbol to this spiritual journey into the wilderness'. And in fact the incontinent flight of the romantics, the dismal failure of their promise, is only to be

accounted for if we adopt Sainte-Beuve's analysis of the
mal du siècle and allow that the predominance of 'talent'
over the *sens du vrai* must ultimately be traced to a lack of
will. For what in retrospect appears as a descent from
vagueness to the clear and cogent arguments of the schools
of history, was a retreat from the real problems, the theological preoccupations of a Coleridge and a Kierkegaard.
There followed instead 'the philosophy of history'—still in
inverted commas to Sainte-Beuve—that led to the worship
of the Secular State, first of all identified by Hegel as the
Prussian State, and subsequently by the interpreters of
Marx as the USSR; but it always led to the State as the
central problem, considered from the standpoint of 'progress' or 'reaction' and, as Burckhardt maintained, the
European crisis is a crisis in the idea of the State. This
return to antithetical forms of thought and to the battle of
progress and reaction is the paradox of the romantic
movement, a 'strange event', for in the manner of its return
to history romanticism ultimately lost the meaning of
history.

History became an abstraction, and events were appre-
hended in the laws and processes of culture, economics and
sociology.

*   *   *

The best known account of this strange event is Acton's,
and it is specially instructive because he himself was
involved. In *The German Schools of History* Acton summarises
in masterly fashion the rise of 'the most arduous of sciences'
(the phrase is Fustel's). 'History' he goes on, 'was subor-
dinate to other things, to divinity, philosophy and law; and
the story worth telling would be the process by which the
servant of many masters became the master over them, and
having become a law to itself, imposed it upon others'.

XXXVI JOURNAL IN THE NIGHT

That is an excellent definition of the 'history' against which Kierkegaard, Nietzsche and Péguy directed their polemics and Jacob Burckhardt his irony. It looks at first as though Acton had remembered everything except himself; but in his article on *Döllinger's Historical Work* he recounts the more personal side of the strange event, and it was certainly worth telling.

'Ernst von Lasaulx, a man of rich and noble intellect, was lecturing next door (to Döllinger) on the philosophy and religion of Greece, and everybody heard about his indistinct mixture of dates and authorities, and the spell which his unchastened idealism cast over his students. Lasaulx, who brilliantly carried on the tradition of Creuzer, who was son-in-law to Baader and nephew to Görres, wrote a volume on the fall of Hellenism which he brought in manuscript and read to Döllinger at a sitting. The effect on the dissenting mind of the hearer was a warning; and there is reason to date from those two hours in 1853 a more severe use of materials, a stricter notion of the influence which the end of an enquiry may lawfully exert on the pursuit of it'.

Acton left Munich sometime in 1853; but the description certainly reads like a confession, and if that is so, one might date from those two hours, the birth of the later Acton, the friend of Gladstone who found Newman so difficult to understand. Lasaulx might indeed have provided the link, and it is a letter to Newman that recalls how close was the understanding between master and pupil. 'My old master Lasaulx', he wrote to Newman in the summer of 1861, 'one of the greatest German students, died the other day after expressing the wish that his library should not be sold by auction, but offered first of all to me, and I have bought it, both for his sake and for the excellent books. It will greatly add to the confusion and value of my library, which I continue to hope will one day tempt you to Aldenham'.*

* I owe this unpublished letter to the kindness of Mr. Douglas Woodruff.

There can be little doubt that the change which gradually came over Acton, and the difficulties of the later years, the tension between the scientific historian and the deeply religious mind, can be traced back to, or at least understood in the light of, his failure to carry on the original romantic tradition that he had found so inspiring in Lasaulx, who not only inherited it from Baader and Görres, but was one of its last representatives; instead, Acton capitulated before Döllinger's accurate dates and carefully checked sources.

By a coincidence, which in this context is illuminating, it happened that Lasaulx, who lost a pupil in Acton, gained the one admirer who was not influenced by the rise of 'scientific history', Jacob Burckhardt. Though not mentioned in *The German Schools of History*, Lasaulx is referred to above twenty times in the Introduction to Burckhardt's *Reflections on History*, where there are hardly any other references quoted at all. Burckhardt, in fact, found in Lasaulx's *Essay on the Philosophy of History* no 'authority', but a view of history strikingly similar to his own, which recognised the frontiers of history and the rights of religion and natural theology. For it was because the view of history accepted by Acton threatened the continuity of Europe—the tradition which made room for an organic relation between religion and culture—that Burckhardt and Nietzsche, as well as Kierkegaard and Péguy, rejected it.

Nietzsche's second *Unzeitgemässe Betrachtung*, '*Vom Nutzen and Nachtheil der Historie für das Leben*', he called elsewhere 'We Historians. A history of the sickness of the modern soul'—Nietzsche's 'sickness unto death', in fact. It was written in the last months of 1873 in Bâle where Nietzsche had come under the spell of Burckhardt. Perhaps 'spell' is not altogether the right expression, for unlike Wagner, Burckhardt was not inclined for the role of *Cher Maître*. It was, however, almost the only case in which Nietzsche's admiration did not end in *ressentiment*. His debt to Burckhardt is certainly very difficult to estimate, but it seems fairly safe to say that where 'scientific history' is concerned, he learnt a good deal from Burckhardt, though without grasping Burckhardt's point of view. 'This very extraordinary man', he wrote, 'does not indeed falsify the truth, but certainly tends to conceal it'. It is tempting to suppose that Nietzsche never grasped the implications of the references to Lasaulx without which, no doubt, Burckhardt might be said to conceal the whole truth as he saw it. No doubt Nietzche's mind was already too far formed for him to understand a point of view that allowed for the reconciliation of Greek and Jewish thought and the meeting of Christianity and culture. It will be the aim of the last section to consider very briefly how Burckhardt and Haecker understood the question that Nietzsche answered with the opposition between Dionysius and Christ.

IV.

The Christian and History, published in 1935, though not, I believe, so much read as Haecker's other essays, is in some respects the most important, forming as it were the coping stone of his work. 'An inward reflection upon the essence of history' he wrote in the introduction, 'was no part of Christian Mediaeval Philosophy, and it is therefore all the more important a task at the present time—and that is the apology for this short book'. Its importance for the *Journal* needs no emphasis, and I will begin with some quotations which, I hope, will indicate Haecker's point of view.

"Eternity and time can only come together truly, that is to say in a genuine fashion, corresponding to their nature, and can only be fused in the mind of man, in Dogma. This fusion, this 'meeting' can never be achieved by philosophy and metaphysics alone. In them there is a gulf between the eternal and the temporal, and wherever the restraint and reserve before this mystery (which is the mark of the mind's aristocratic origin) is relaxed and abandoned in favour of some democratic or demagogic opinion, there follows the most murderous nonsense, the fruit of unenlightened feelings with their shameless lack of rhyme or reason . . . . . The fact that such a thing as history exists is a great mystery to metaphysics, greater even than 'being'—which illustrates how far natural metaphysics is from the God of Abraham, Isaac and Jacob, who, to the man of this æon, is in the first instance a God of history and—of faith, for faith belongs to history. The creature always desires timelessness, but never achieves it by flying time in a metaphysical way, in a Hegelian way, but only through the painful *assimilation of time*—the occasion for which is not wanting nowadays. That was the central personal experience of Kierkegaard—an experience, moreover, common to all believers—such is the fundamental significance of the category 'existence' which Kierkegaard threw into the arena of philosophy".

"Can one base one's eternal happiness on an historical fact? Lessing's question, taken up with such passion by Kierkegaard, and answered with the despair of the absolute paradox, was the ultimate historical formulation of the antagonism between metaphysics and history, between Greek and Jewish thought, which are only harmonised in exceptional circumstances, for as a rule the correct relationship is upset at the cost of one or other, so that it even seems as though the one excluded the other—and that has its fatal consequences".

The 'fatal consequences', as Haecker notes, follow, not from a failure to reconcile Greek and Jewish thought (which is rarely achieved), but from the lack of restraint and reserve in face of the ultimate mystery of existence, in this context the fusion of eternity and time—which is to say dogma. Once this restraint and reserve are relaxed, some 'democratic' form of the 'inadequate' is allowed to explain everything, or some 'demagogic' form of the 'absurd' denies all meaning to history. It was the romantic recognition of the role of the imagination (however unclear and cloudy at first) which perceived the mystery and with it the possibility of the reconciliation of Christianity and culture; and it was only when the romantic lack of restraint opened the way for the predominance of talent over the *sens du vrai* that this belief and the will to bring about the fusion, collapsed. It was towards this conclusion that Péguy's intuition was leading him when he discovered the relationship between the Greek and Jewish 'disciplines' and the principle of 'l'insertion de l'éternel dans le temporel'.

There are three conditions, Haecker maintains in *Christentum und Kultur*, in the absence of which the organic relation of Christianity and culture is not possible. First, he says, there must exist a relatively sound and healthy intellectual tradition; second, this must be accompanied by the will to conceive; and third, there must be present, in those who believe, a real strength, the power, that is (and I should say the imaginative power) to *communicate* their beliefs. These conditions are precisely those which Sainte-Beuve lays down in the passage quoted at the beginning of the introduction.

But all these conditions are subject to the central point, restraint and reserve of mind, which might perhaps be translated as integrity. .

*   *   *

'One thing', Haecker writes in the *Journal*, 'one thing has come to full maturity in me, the understanding that I do not understand God, the sense of the *mysterium*. That is what prevents me misunderstanding the things of this world'. It is Haecker's reserve—his 'silence'—that makes him speak of not misunderstanding the things of this world; and that double negative establishes the frontier between the mystagogue, who argues directly to a positive knowledge of things, and Haecker's different claim. The distinction is by no means new, for it is at the very core of tradition itself. In his *Reflections*, Burckhardt marks the same difference when he distinguishes between true and false scepticism. The ground common to both Haecker and Burckhardt lies in the parallel so often used by Kierkegaard between Socratic ignorance and faith, and in his strict identification of (false) scepticism and superstition. That is the first step in grasping the rational basis which Haecker and Burckhardt regarded as the meeting point of Christianity and humanism. The ultimate mystery of existence is the safeguard of truth and knowledge, the only safeguard against the inadequate attempts to explain everything, and the absurd denial of meaning.*

"The theologian is alone in a position to be certain, from the beginning, that the absolute inconceivability of God must, in a sense, be expressed in the relative inconceivability of the world".

Theology, thus understood, is the safeguard of the *Summa*, of the totality of knowledge, and of the independence of its various fields, for otherwise the various sciences all tend to usurp the primacy and, going beyond their charter, try to explain the various 'orders' from within their own 'order'. That is the meaning of Péguy's insistence upon the 'humility' of his 'intuitive method' and his criticism of the 'gigantic conceit' of Taine and Renan who seriously entertained the notion that our knowledge was almost complete—'Mais on voit le bout', Renan said.†

This does not of course mean that theology is the master of history in the sense in which Acton supposed; but the misinterpretation is so ingrained that it is important to reaffirm Haecker's standpoint. The *Journal* is, I think, clear in its rejection of this stout pretension, but I will

---

* The point of view in question is the subject of Sermon XIII in Newman's *University Sermons*.

† Introduction to *L'avenir de la Science*.

quote some of the many entries in which this rejection is affirmed.

"There is a tendency, and God does not seem to be averse to it, to explain the things of this world almost 'totally' and entirely and purely from the immanent laws of nature, from the causality of the *causae secundae*; and what is more to do so on the *whole* field of created being, from physics and chemistry to politics and metaphysics. There is nothing incomplete about it. And in a sense that is a good thing. And then, moreover, it surely makes natural theology a matter of quite tremendous importance?"

In the past, and even in the present, theology has fallen into the error which Acton thought endemic:

"Even in the West, Christian theology has shown a certain cowardice, and a miserable want of understanding of the munificence with which God has endowed created and creative nature and the world with power and energy of its own; and the testimony of history to the fight of the Church against the natural sciences and its representatives and their great discoveries is one that shames us. It arose from a great fear that the natural laws might lead to a proof of the non-existence of God. That is its only, all-too-human excuse".

Ultimately, the weakness comes from attempting to meet rationalism on its own false ground:

"At times the *Zeitgeist* is overwhelmingly powerful. Rationalism for example, was so powerful that it even compelled men who were in essence antirationalists to think and speak rationalistically, at any rate up to the point beyond which it was no longer possible or permissible; for example Pascal and St. John of the Cross, whose mysticism, in so far as he renders an account of it and a justification of it, is the end of rationalism, exhausts it".

The collapse of theology, the failure of the romantic movement (and Hegel began as, and to some extent remained, a theologian), though not endangering scientific investigation immediately, led to the loss of the *summa*, and nowhere is this more evident than in history. When Möhler,

the great Munich theologian died, and was succeeded by
Döllinger the *summa* which had been before the minds of
men like Coleridge and Kierkegaard was in the process of
being sacrificed, unconsciously no doubt, to 'universal
history'. And though Ranke's history became universal
in some measure, it was primarily a quantitative 'Universality'. What was being lost was the unity of history,
and within a short time the universality of outlook, deprived
of the controlling force of unity, decayed into relativism,
and history was deprived of meaning.

It is here that the importance of Burckhardt can hardly be
exaggerated. Burckhardt composed no universal history,
though his *Reflections* have been included under that heading.
But in everything he wrote, and particularly in his *Greek
Culture*, he is concerned with the unity of history framed, as
it were, between the alpha and the omega, between the
origins and the end. 'The philosophers' he says, 'encum-
bered with speculations on origins, ought by rights to speak
of the future. We can dispense with theories of origins, and
no one can expect from us a theory of the end'. Burckhardt
had, in his way, understood as clearly as Haecker the role
of theology; the Jewish conception of history is dominated by origins and end, creation and eschatology;
Burckhardt's study of Greek culture did not lead him to
usurp that function. His 'great theme of contemplation' is
easily defined: 'We, however (unlike the philosopher of
history, whom he dismisses as a centaur) shall start out from
the one point accessible to us, the one eternal centre of all
things—man, suffering, striving, doing, as he is, was, and
ever shall be. Hence our study will, in a certain sense, be
pathological in kind'. His study is in fact concerned with
man's feelings and his imagination.

Burckhardt's view of the immediate future was as dark
as Haecker's, but their point of view cannot usefully be
studied within the framework of optimism and pessimism,
progress and reaction. The spirit, Haecker concludes,
bloweth where it listeth, and to Burckhardt man's creative

faculty the imagination was essentially free;—both believed in man's capacity, to build himself a new house'.

*   *   *

To Haecker, the harmony of faith and reason—however
difficult to attain and retain—was the basis of his belief in
the possibility of an organic relation between religion and
culture which, to be consistent, rationalism and irrationalism
would have to deny. This harmony is the achievement of
'spiritual man' in whom all the faculties, intellect, will and
feeling are integrated. Only this integrity allows of no
premature reconciliations and Haecker was harsh in his
dismissal of the 'Europe and the Faith' theme—'an object
lesson in how *not* to bring Christianity and culture together',
untrue in fact as well as in theory.

Burckhardt's *Reflections* are, at this point, at one with
Haecker's, and he saw in the Middle Ages a period when
religion 'occupied all man's highest faculties, particularly
the imagination' so that it is not longer possible, he held,
to say whether religion influenced culture or culture religion.
But at the Reformation 'religion lost touch with a powerful
faculty in man, the imagination' and was forced to *etherealise*
itself (the word is Burckhardt's). Whenever that happens,
and he notes in particular the disintegration which followed
upon the Carolingian renaissance, religion becomes 'rationalism for the few and magic for the many'.

Perhaps Haecker's view of the relation of Christianity
and culture in Europe is best expressed in the entry in which
he says that a conscious apostasy from Christianity is only
possible after a prior return to barbarism. The *Journal* is a
record of his meditations on that event. Péguy's religious
'approfondissement' occurred to the accompaniment of his
reflections on the relation of Socialism to Catholicism in

the Third Republic*; Haecker's faith was tempered during
his last years as he listened to the 'extinct' voices of the
Third Reich. And his sense of the harmony of faith and
reason was so deep and strong that, as he felt himself plunged
into a new dark ages, he described his own state as being
'the dark night of faith', for his faith had become wholly
contemporaneous.

The *Journal* is Haecker's most personal work, though not
perhaps his most representative. Haecker's importance is a
different matter; and in conclusion I will note briefly
wherein, as it seems to me, it lies.

It is a fact, curious at first sight, that for a long time past
the relevance of Christianity in the modern world has almost
invariably been brought home by those writers who are
furthest from the traditional defence, who overlook or
disregard or even deny the harmony of faith and reason.
Tradition, in that sense, is itself irrelevant. Once again,
Kierkegaard is the classic example. It even appears as
though, in modern times, men desired an irrational religion,
or were content to despair of the possibility of the harmony
of faith and reason.

'Dieu est mort, mais l'homme n'est pas pour autant
devenu athée. Ce silence du transcendant, joint à la perm-
anence du besoin religieu chez l'homme moderne, voilà la
grand affaire aujourd'hui, comme hier. C'est le problème
qui tourmente Nietzsche, Heidegger, Jaspers.'†

Does it even torment M. Sartre? What this seems to
mean is that our rational, notional apprehension of God
is dead and fruitless, and that the scientific demonstrations
of natural theology are 'irrelevant'—because they do not
elicit from 'transcendence' anything but silence. That is
certainly inevitable, for an impersonal question cannot

* Le mouvement de *dérépublicanisation* de la France est profondément
le même mouvement que le mouvement de sa *déchristianisation*—C'est
ensemble un même, un seul mouvement profond de *démistification*.
Notre Jeunesse.

† Sartre—*Situations I.* pp. 153.

elicit a personal 'answer'. Haecker notes in the *Journal* the difference between a philosophy whose starting point is doubt and one whose starting point is wonder, and that difference might be stated epigramatically in the form that doubt being impersonal receives no answer.*

It is writers like Pascal and Kierkegaard, like Bloy or Péguy, who convey to the modern world the relevance of religion because their arguments and apologies, though the opposite, at times, of traditional, are led by a strong gust of feeling: the paradox, the 'choice', the 'leap' concern the whole man and involve all his faculties: intellect, will and feeling, in a word what Kierkegaard calls 'spiritual man'. They are primarily concerned with 'the communication of the truth' and not solely with its demonstration, and consequently with the problem of style in its widest sense, with the image as well as with the concept.

Haecker's importance is to have treated this 'grande affaire' methodically from a variety of angles, always from the point of view and upon the principles of the *philosophia perennis*. I say methodically to avoid saying systematically, and yet to emphasise the fact that while he by no means rules out the paradox, he gives it its proper place within the truth. The 'grande affaire' is the reconciliation of philosophy and mysticism which, regarded as rationalism and irrationalism are, of course, irreconcilable; and it is perhaps the characteristic of Haecker's work that it consistently refuses to be drawn into the whirl-pools created by these alternatives: 'Apart from the "faith" the only choice is between "the inadequate" and "the absurd" '.

* *Journal.*

1939

1. Joy untouched by thankfulness is always suspect.

2. Rejoinder: The most powerful means of forwarding the events of the world seems to be stupidity, the stupidity of the Führer, of the Leader, and the stupidity of the led.

3. The extinction of thought is quite horrifying. Someone remarks that man is changeable, but that the German is eternal. And he is quite incapable of drawing the conclusion that in that case Germans are certainly not men.

4. It takes a certain vulgarity of mind, an intellectual coarseness, that is of course moral as well, to believe that the means do not matter, that the 'how' makes no difference, and once that vulgarity loses its sense of shame, people openly declare their belief.

> Tugend und laster
> Scheidet der Knecht
> ——Alles ist Recht*

In fact it is the 'how' which decides the value of a man or of a policy. The revolution brought about by Christianity is in the 'how'.

5. November. The stone of offence, in natural metaphysics, is the mystery. And the danger is either not to see

*Between virtue and vice
The serf distinguishes
——Everything is right.

1

it or to wish to explain it, and thus disturb the hierarchical order.

6. Even the profoundest truth looks flat beside the abyss of revelation. In the last analysis it misunderstands the nature of the understanding.

7. I really have to like an author before I can take up his faults in any detail: all that he might have done better, and so on. In most cases I leave them entirely aside.

8. I have been horrified latterly at the capacity of the human voice, quite apart from what it says, simply in itself, to express the spiritual extinction of a whole people; and not merely individually, but to betray, to express and proclaim it typically, representatively. The voice of the *announcer*.

9. 18th November. A loss in time and for time is a loss one gets over. 'Too late', in this context, comes under the rubric 'humour'. It is quite a different matter when one acts unlovingly towards someone. If that can not be made good in time, then it lies as heavily on one's heart after twenty years as it does after two; for love is a *res aeterna*, and nowhere, if I may say so, is the need for eternity so compelling and so insistent, lest we render existence meaningless. At this point, even the rights and the power of humour are abrogated; and to maintain them obstinately is either a mere pretence, or a sign of depravity.

10. Hypocrisy and shamelessness are the two poles of depravity between which men move. But although Christ's anger over the shamelessness of the money-lenders in the temple was so great that he gave it outward expression, perhaps his anger over the hypocrisy of the Pharisees was not less.

11. It is probably true that the longest stretches of history are marked with the sign of mediocrity; but then again, mediocrity has few heroes and few geniuses. In modern times, one of the heroes of the half-educated, at least as far as the German nation is concerned, was Houston Stewart Chamberlain. He concocted a soup that wrecked the brains of a whole generation of constitutionally enfeebled minds. And with what results in every day life! Good God!

12. It is only natural that Physiognomy should achieve considerable results in the natural order, and in the hands of a person of gifts and experience should yield a considerable accuracy of judgment. But once a man is out of the ordinary, and is exposed to demoniacal powers, or even becomes their tool, Physiognomy misfires—not of course in principle, and in respect of the natural 'being' of the man in question, by no means. But it goes grotesquely wrong with regard to his influence or the role that he may play.

13. A certain longing to be forgotten and hidden is the mark of the contemplative; he alone might take as his maxim, *Λά θε Βιῶτ*. The natural impulse of the man of action is towards fame and reputation and 'publicity'.

14. The moment when an hour is worth a million years or is as worthless, because they are not eternity! For the spirit desires eternity. That is its home. And until it has realised that, it has not really come to itself.

15. The profusion of nature is surely a want, or the sign of a want, or a very inadequate remedy for a deficiency. Thousands of blossoms yield a few fruits, millions of men hardly one genius.

16. 'Will and Truth': what a theme it is! or rather: 'Truth and Will'. It is curious how the will asserts itself against the hierarchical order! Just as though in fact, 'by nature', the will came *first*: How finicky, doctrinaire, and scrupulous to say: 'Truth and Will'. Only listen: 'Will and Truth', how final and masterly it sounds: *The World as Will and Concept.* (Schopenhauer).

17. Rejoinder: If God is all-powerful then it is an unfathomable mystery that a just cause should be defeated. And if that fact is evaded in a sermon on the subject, it does more harm than good. Rationalism is the great enemy of belief, and thus the great falsifier of being.

18. Absolute and continuous satisfaction in a man would be the image of the nothing out of which he is created; an absolute and continuous dissatisfaction, an image of the hell he has chosen.

19. The ends and objects which men set themselves remain, by and large, the same. Revolutions are about the means. God's revelation is a revolution concerning the means which man is to use in order to achieve salvation. Aristocracies are always constituted by the 'how' of life, that is by the means which are, and which are not allowed, by what is and what is not 'done'.

20. When he prays to Christ, it is the privilege of the Christian to be able to pray to the true God by name. That is the 'sign' for today. When anyone nowadays says God, he may of course simply mean destiny, or some awful caricature of 'providence'. But if a man prays to Christ, then he necessarily prays to the Father, who is God, like Christ, and to the Holy Spirit who is God, like the Father and the Son. He cannot do otherwise. Nothing, nowadays, so defines and separates men according to the spirit, as the Trinity.

21. The mystical and symbolical interpretation of Scripture is only possible by virtue of the substantial similarity of all being, by virtue of the formal principle of analogy. Allegory too, which is as a rule a curious mixture of infantilism and rationalism is only possible on that basis.

22. Nominalists, who say it is ultimately a matter of indifference what one calls the divine, are dangerous people. In Revelation, God gives his name: I am who am. Who else shares this name? Can anyone else claim it? Is it the discovery of man? Could a man discover it? And could any man have foreseen that this name was to be illuminated in the Trinity: Father, Son and Spirit? Really, the nominalists are ridiculous!

23. It would be terrible if God were not the God of the exception too.

24. *Rejoinder:* You Christians are so proud that your God is the God of *all men.* But on looking closely one is more likely to come to the conclusion that he is the God of few, and in a terrifying way: of few! The God of the most rare 'exception', the God of the chosen, of the elect. If God wishes a man to search for him, and to find him, he does not give the key of that man's heart and thought to anyone, not even least of all, to anyone who loves the man, or is loved by him. Then a man really has to search in all seriousness, for not to be understood is to be unhappy. But God permits himself to be found, and the certainty that one will be understood by God and indeed of being understood by him, is a flicker of the happiness to come.

25. *Problema:* In the darkness there was a light that became night. He woke up, his eyes and his cheeks wet with tears. He could not remember the dream, though he knew that he had dreamed. And yet from that night on, his life was different. He had received a light, which let him see a whole new dimension of being. But the source of this light is in complete darkness.

26. 26th November. The simplest words are often the most moving:

> Ich hab einen falschen Weg gemacht,
> Ich kenn mich nicht mehr aus
> Ach, immer dunkler wird die Nacht,
> Ich find nicht mehr nach Haus.*

The child's complaint in the fairy story is that of the soul lost in life. The lines came to my mind at my first reading of 'The Ascent of Mount Carmel' by John of the Cross; I was so astonished at the moving simplicity of the poem which, at first sight, gives one no inkling of the depths of the interpretation which is to follow.

27. The apotheosis of physical strength and health leads, first of all, inevitably to contempt of old age, and then, to contempt of wisdom. Such a thing *has never yet* happened in European culture, either before or after Christ. Nor in the East for that matter! It means devastation to the souls of men; that, God will not permit; we may rest assured of that, assured by our faith, for it is the 'Fathers' of the Church who suffered for us and taught us.

28. 3rd December. The great pride of the children of this world is not to be children any more; and for this reason alone they despise the Christian, who is always, necessarily, something of a child. And how could it be otherwise? When one of God's names, revealed by him, is 'father'.

29. O. thinks that the result of all that is now happening will be to show how irrational all being is, and how severed from our thought. But that is too vague. I think that the Germans will *perhaps* learn two things, two things which

---

*I have taken a wrong road,
I no longer know my way,
Oh, the night grows even darker,
I'll no longer find my way home.

are only superficially contradictory: first, that the disregard of 'reason', provided it rests upon a foundation of wisdom and experience, never goes unpunished, and that consequently the world is not in this sense irrational at all; secondly, that the purely materialistic rationalism which rules in Germany today leads to the most gross errors even in the field of elementary psychology, and fails completely where the spiritual life is concerned. Bismarck was not a great statesman, any more than Napoleon, yet he recognised 'imponderabilia', which though far from being 'the invisible' are nevertheless on the borderland. But nowadays!

30. It is safe to assume that the Germans will do everything, both consciously and unconsciously, in order to forget as quickly as possible all that is now said, written and done. The memory of a guilt weighs heavy, it 'depresses'. If he can, man throws it off. But in the success of the operation God, too, has a word to say.

31. 4th December. There can be no question for the Christian but that the significance of outward events varies in the most terrifying degree. By significance is here meant the relation, closer or more distant, of the 'history' of the world to the 'history' of the Kingdom of God. A Christian cannot be of Ranke's opinion, that every age is equally near to God. Or could he, then, deny that Rome under Augustus, Judæa under Herod and Pilate stood in a more decisive relation to the history of salvation than, say, Europe under Napoleon—not to speak of lesser things? The proximity or distance in the relationship does not depend upon the consciousness of men, although it is not to be denied that it could not be entirely excluded from the consciousness of the men of that time. That events now stand in close relation to the history of salvation, is something upon which many will agree with me. And from this it follows, moreover, that the outward events in the life of the individual come under the category of 'decision.'

32. Except for that which is, there is nothing. That is a metaphysical proposition which no one can deny. And if anyone, nevertheless, does so, there is no sense in talking with him. The puff which blows out a candle has more significance than his *flatus vocis*. But then begins the labour of interpretation, then the never resting world of dialogue begins, the dull, distorting mirror of the world of being. *Mundum tradidit disputationi eorum.* (Eccl. 3, 11).

33. The use, as synonyms, of 'to be mistaken' and 'to err' completed by the pleonasm 'to go astray', is one of the many examples of the impoverishment of language which results from muddled speech. Lack of imagination leads to a weakening of thought, and this, once again, prevents the discovery and recognition of this lack, and language becomes ever poorer in images and thought—'to be mistaken' comes before 'to err'. First of all he made a mistake, then he erred. I make a mistake standing, and going along I therefore go on the wrong path: I err.

34. 7th December. *Superbia:* 'I was predestined to the greatest sins' said the devil, and grew even prouder. 'Who is like me'? Perhaps the 'Lamb'?

35. *Ad se ipsum*
From my childhood
When I was imprisoned by the beauty of poetry, where light and water, sufficient unto themselves, were full of brilliance, all the springs dried up, and the eternal melody itself fell asleep. I no longer recall who or what awoke me.

36. *Ad se ipsum* Never forget that you were only allowed to write 'Satires and Polemiks'* because you had promised to break off, so to say, when things were at their best, when that particular path pleased you most. You had to go another way, that pleased you less. And now the same

_____
* *Satire und Polemik*, 1914-1920, published 1922, Haecker's first book.

thing is happening again: You have to take a different path, one that pleases you even less.

37. Curse the image that denies you the word! Pass on! But I want the rest and peace, which are only to be found in the image, and not in thinking. You are a stranger, a wanderer, a pilgrim on earth, so flee the image, that renounces the word.

38. One's astonishment, half tragic, half comic, at coming across a good sentence that one has completely forgotten having written. Poverty and wealth!

39. The measure of confusion will be full to overflowing when sophists write the history of philosophy, Catalinas the history of states and nations, and heretics the history of the Church. In the past, hardly more than a tendency in Europe, it has now become a serious matter.

40. 9th December. On the wireless today a star fell from the firmament of German literature, "their eyes were opened —and overflowed." My God, eyes opened long ago might have flowed, when it fell and was extinguished on a swamp of abuse from a political robot consisting of a baritone voice and lies.

41. I have finished many a song, and been the first to sing it. And now they sing it after me, as though it were anonymous. That is as it should be. Let me thank God, that I am that far. And let me complain to God that I am *only* so far, and can even think of such things.

42. Second Sunday in Advent. When all is over, then of course even Physiognomy will claim to have been right. And indeed God would not condemn the nature which he created, to lie. He is a faithful God, and 'true'—They will be able to point to the photographs and say: How could it have been otherwise, it simply had to happen! And *isn't* everything on the surface? How could people be deceived. And they will make everything appear much simpler than it was.

43. God has spoken in many words through his prophets and through his 'Word'. No man is free to alter these words, but he is free to use them on suitable and, alas, on unsuitable occasions. That was the whole risk. For it would be impossible to calculate the misfortune which is brought about by using a divine saying at the wrong moment, and not using it at the right moment.

44. All the thoughts that keep on breaking through the principal theme are only of evil when they block the way and make it impassable, not when they make for more space or even make it infinite.

45. Christ also died for 'barbarians', but he did not become man as a barbarian, nor did he live among them, or choose his disciples among them. The relapse of civilised nations into barbarism is moreover not possible unless they first abandon Christianity.

46. Psalm 73
Prayer

You have shown us, O God, the essence of evil, its pride and its triumph in excess and to the point of despair. O Lord, many are falling into unbelief; let us ask you, in a spirit of faith, now to fulfil and illustrate the other truth of the psalm, for the consolation of your servants and to your honour.

47. The sun shines upon the just and the unjust. These great primary blessings, the laws which determine and hold creation together are—or seem to be—indifferent to good and evil. Good and evil deeds (corn and weeds) both fall under the law of growth and ripening. These categories and

laws do not belong beyond good and evil, but belong to the primary goodness of creation, which no power, however diabolical can change.

48. 17th December. All our knowledge is received, in the first instance, through our senses, but we soon begin to suspect that things and truth are originally in the spirit. And according to Revelation (Eph. 3, 15) we are told that all fatherhood is in the image of God, that all fatherhood takes its name from God, who alone is really 'father'. I was thinking today, how can one compare the hardness and the hardening that is in the senses, to the hardness and hardening of the heart and the spirit? And all the presentiments of my youth, and its unconscious, but deeply felt platonism, suddenly awoke. It seemed to me almost a revelation when I wrote: How impoverished is your spring, a miserable image of the heart within me; but then you do not know the winter of despair in my soul.

49. The Germans too want to be a nation 'like others'. But without success. They can only be much worse than the others. They are the abhorrence of the whole world. The Prussian leaven has soured the whole nation and falsified its mission.

50. Looking with a certain contempt upon Christianity, you observe that it has no philosophy, no metaphysic. But is that not an error? The Christian's metaphysics is—that he eats God.

51. In order to do justice to the spirit of Europe a philosopher must know the chief European languages, ancient and modern, and their different images, in order to free his thought from them, and in order not to lose himself in any particular one.

52. 15th December. To equate 'impulse' and 'instinct' with the will, as though it were a conscious impulse only, is vague, confused. No instinct can be dominated by itself, though even the strongest instinct can be dominated by the will. Will is spirit. There is no sense in saying: will is instinct, to which spirit (consciousness) is added. It is something completely and absolutely new in itself. Will is spirit—its flame, just as intellect is its light.

53. Nietzsche, Wagner and Houston Stewart Chamberlain are in fact mainly responsible for the present condition of the German mind. It is they who move the doers, and the evil-doers. Wagner as a musician, is the least guilty, the impure accompanist.

54. After the war, the aspirations of 'socialism' will undoubtedly be strengthened, yet still without attaining the really decisive strength and power of nationalism. A compulsory solution of the social problem, namely through impoverishment, is ambiguous. Everything depends upon spirit. As men are, some form of enslavement is probable; ingenious or shrewd, or both, favoured by men's inclination to deceive one another—as well as themselves.

55. The greatest and bitterest enemies of Christianity, those who hate it most, fail completely to see one thing: that Christianity arose and always arises anew, differently, utterly differently from their Kingdoms and institutions. A man, an animal, a plant, a machine can only go to pieces or be destroyed within the Order in which they arose. The same is true of the kingdoms of this world, and of the Kingdom that is not of this world—but is *in* the world. What the deadly enemies of Christ's kingdom can destroy, is everything about the Church which is of this world. That may be an astonishing amount, a disturbing amount; so much indeed that it looks like everything. The Kingdom of Christ, stripped of everything, rests upon faith, hope and love. Those are not powers which play a part in this world.

56. Third Sunday in Advent. *Gaudete* ..... Rejoice, and again I say to you: rejoice! Once again, as always, astonishing words. The ever new, original and yet identical explanation which the saints of God give of their 'joy' is a proof of its genuineness, even for those who do not or have not known it. And so, O God, I rest satisfied with the pale and distant joy that your saints know, joy such as the apostle has described it: *Gaudete* ...

57. The man is playing for high stakes. Let us not deceive ourselves! Indeed, the game is so high that only the words of the psalmist fit the case: 'The Lord laughs at them'. But it will fail or pass away unless it breaks into the laughter of insanity—But human laughter is not equal to the task—'God laughs at them'. And then one must remember that Germany is not exactly the country in which the ridiculous kills; on the contrary, the ridiculous acts as a sort of preservative.

58. To Konrad Weiss* on his 'Konradin von Hohenstaufen'

Whose song but yours returns unto itself
As oft as yours, till all that's lovely must
Perforce into abundance overflow,
And lose itself where naught is never lost?
None struck so true into the heart of pain
That it still beats while making fair lament.
Yes, falconry's a Hohenstaufen art!
A marvel in lean days! Hail, Konrad Weiss!
Will nevermore this world's deep wound be healed,
Is there no peace in God? Must he still rock
The cradled world? Was not Christ born for us
And rose again? Alas, O Konrad Weiss!

* One of the most important contemporary poets, who died in 1940. *Konradin* was his last work. *Die Kleine Schopfung* published by the Insel Verlag is probably his best known poem.

59. Anyone who is not horrified by the man has nothing in him either of God, or of the devil.

60. It is normal that a Nobody should want to become Somebody in the world. There is nothing to be said against it; it is nature. But how seldom it is that this Somebody should then strive to become Nobody—before God, although that is the only path if one is to reach God. The same thing is true of this Nobody, as of the 'nothing' of the *Summa*. There is a difference between the nothing *before* the *Summa*, and the nothing *after* the *Summa*. Only a sophist can deny it. Someone might perhaps say that this is the very place for the most diabolical *superbia*. Perhaps, but it is a danger one must take upon oneself.

61. The proper distinction between genuine guilt and innocence is one of the great and unavoidable tasks of the future. To say that natural necessity is guilt may produce just as much misfortune as the contrary, and may lead to the absolute denial of guilt. It must be admitted that we live in great ignorance and uncertainty.

62. Once Again: Konrad Weiss

> Whose song but yours returns unto itself
> As oft as yours, till all that's lovely must
> Perforce into abundance overflow,
> To lose itself in nothingness, its aim?
> None striked so true into the heart of pain,
> That it breaks out in lovely loud lament.
> Yes falconry's a Hohenstaufen art!
> Music of home, and of the Swabian, Weiss.
>
> Will God's deep wound, mankind, be never healed?
> Has God Himself no rest, must he still rock
> The cradled world because it will not sleep?
> Was not Christ born for us and rose again?

If he comes not today, will he *not* come
Then at the last?   Is this some tragic mime?
Must we remain without a holy hymn
Because we wait and no Redeemer comes?

Does faith lie dead, and withered all our hope?
Are hatred reason, love delusions then?

63. A 'Grammar of images' is a philosophical undertaking
worthy of a young man, if he could carry the burden of
knowledge already accumulated. The first thing to meet
our eyes is boundless confusion, and the first requirement
would be to bring about order, perhaps with the help of the
co-ordinates: body, soul, and spirit. (That in itself is an
instructive example of an image which is substantially
inadequate, but helpful by analogy). The images derived
from the sphere of the body are naturally far from being the
most numerous, although nowadays augmented by the
quasi-images of technical thought. The broad middle is
occupied by the rich images of the soul, that is to say
of life.

64. 27th December. The most aristocratic contempt is
undoubtedly the philosophical, that is to say intellectual,
contempt of Heraclitus. Political contempt is as a rule only
the contempt of the greater for the lesser scoundrel, *because*
he is the lesser.

65. To 'dispute' with God is either the beginning or the
end of faith. But it always presupposes a tendency to faith.

66. The most primitive attitude in a great war is this:
that one side is absolutely right and the other absolutely
wrong. The thing becomes more difficult and problematical
as doubt allows us to see that right and wrong may be
shared. But it does not really carry one much further. It
stops short at a more or less clever objectivity and neutrality,

which is practically harmless if one lives in the eighteenth century, and the war is in Turkey or China. But nowadays things have come much closer to us and to one another. And here begins the distinction of principles and teachings and theories. A nation whose centre is a miraculous image of the Mother of God may commit the most horrible and horrifying atrocities, but after bitter expiation it will be victorious over a nation whose centre is a rationalistic heretical capital, whose fidelity and honour is thoroughly hypocritical and false. As a private individual, Constantine the Great may well have committed more sins public and private than Julian the Apostate. But the Christian had every reason to wish victory to the former and destruction to the latter.

That is the last thought of the year.

*

*

1940

67. The world in its being is beyond the power of human understanding to survey clearly. Anyone who does not see that, or denies it, can only be left alone, to go his own way. Yet many who, at a pinch, agree, nevertheless demand that the system of a philosopher should be absolutely clear in its survey—though it is only the spiritual image and representation of the world, itself impossible to survey. Still, they are not entirely wrong: To be able to survey clearly is one of the essential demands of the mind, and to this the philosopher must do justice. Only he must recognise his boundaries as human and keep to them.

68. There is a deal of pride in the demand of Kierkegaard's thought, to be faithful always, in all circumstances, to his idea. The idea may only be human, after all—and then how weak and how untrue the demand would be. And perhaps when he is no longer true to it, in pain and shame, he is pursuing God's idea. Then he will have learnt humility, and through it reached victory.

69. There is an honourable irrationalism which is ultimately just the capitulation and respect of human *ratio* before the divine. But there is also an ignoble irrationalism —to which the youth of present day Germany tends—which tries to use 'destiny' to conceal and stifle the voice of conscience and to deny that there is logic in the consequences of crime. It is all very easy, and does not come within measurable distance of the sophoclean conception of tragedy.

70. 2nd January. There is only one sermon to preach today, the triune God; do not get involved in anything else. With that alone you will be able to discern the spirits of men, and compel them to reveal themselves. Never tire of repeating it: Father, Son and Holy Spirit. The Christian God is the Trinitarian God. They call their devil or their idol God, too, and sometimes even 'the all-powerful'. But they do not call him Christ, whom they hate or despise, and they do not call him 'Spirit'. How should they, since he proceeds from the Father and the Son?

71. Immortality *is* in love. It is love which first makes it intelligible and, what is more, desirable. Without love immortality would be frightful and horrible.

72. *Loneliness. An image* . . . . in the night he dreamed. An angel called the name of all those remembered by one single soul with love. That lasted an infinite time. At first it left him indifferent, it disturbed him, he yawned, he laughed contemptuously. Then he grew restless, and he began to wait for the sound of his name. He grew unspeakably sad, and he wept. That lasted an infinite time. His name was not called, and the voice became silent. The sudden silence was like a clap of thunder, and woke him. He found his pillow wet, but his eyes were hot and dry and burning as though his tears had dried up for ever.

73. I am often uncertain and almost blind where things, events, books, sciences are concerned. I only begin to see their worth, or worthlessness again when I look at the people whom they influence.

74. In that part of the history of Christian Europe which is the history of Germany, this war might, and I hope will be the end of the hegemony of Prussia, which had in fact reached its height at the beginning of the war.

75. To the perfection of being there belongs its knowledge of itself, and so too, to the 'perfection' of evil. It is good that evil should 'know itself'. It is certainly difficult to attain clarity at this point, and perhaps impossible. Thought becomes confused.

76. Indiscriminate work is a very uncertain remedy against *ennui.* The one sure means of dealing with it is to care for someone else, to do something kind and good.

77. No one is master of the effect of his sentences, and often one is not even responsible for their good or bad effect. Often enough what is right has the reverse effect upon the perverse; and what is perverse in itself acts rightly on the right-thinking.

78. Man, it seems, is not equal to setting up a just social order on his own. He is hardly able even to perceive the two principles upon which he has to build, namely that men are *equal* and *unequal,* and consequently that he must be true to both principles. As a rule he prefers the easier way and takes only one as his starting point: either equality, or inequality. The result of this one-sidedness is always a catastrophe. But even if the necessity and the validity of both principles are recognised theoretically (and this is still far from being the case) the immeasurable difficulty only begins in applying the principles in practice. And I am of the opinion that at this point man cannot, of his own strength, reach a satisfactory conclusion. He needs illumination, the immediate help of God in prayer and in leadership.

79. Christians are once again becoming the minority that 'does not count'. Undoubtedly they will distinguish themselves from other minorities that 'do not count' by the fact that they will be persecuted nevertheless.

80. To many, war is a satisfactory alibi before the world, even though not before one's conscience or before God.

81. When one thinks how difficult it is even for a Christian, even in thought, to leave revenge to God, one can imagine what is going to happen soon in Germany. What will the victor of this war do? Unless he leaves revenge to God, both war and victory are lost.

82. Intercession is difficult and in fact impossible to man, without grace. Two things are necessary for true intercession. If I am to intercede for a man before God, I must love him. Otherwise it is mere empty formalism. But in the moment I intercede for him, I must not want anything from him for myself. And that is difficult, even if I love him.

83. Variations on one and the same theme, that Nature brings off times without number, so happily, so surprisingly, and so perfectly that the boredom of the *semper eadem* is drowned in the astonishing *idem per aliud,* come very hard to the conscious artist, man. They are rare, and most often found in music. There are two rocks between which the art of variation has to navigate: the theme in its original form should be neither too apparent nor too obscured. Furthermore: the variation must itself be something new and surprising in a deeper sense. On the other hand the theme in its identity must be contemplated (heard) immediately (by one who is trained, of course), and not merely painfully arrived at.

84. I am not in the least afraid of playing with words that are free from the *Word,* or of killing time that is without eternity.

85. Why, when they hate the Cross, do they talk of a crusade against plutocracy, why not a *Hakenkreuzzug,* a crooked-crusade? Why not a new language for a new thing, if it is new?

86. I came across the following sentences in a 'thriller': 'Now, instead of everything going right for him, everything

will go wrong for him! And he, too, will begin to make
mistakes'. (In English in the original). Could a certain
aspect of what is happening today in the history of the world
be made intelligible in words clearer than these?

87. It is difficult enough to know one's way about in one's
own thoughts; how much more difficult where one's
feelings are concerned.

88. Many men find it difficult to believe that God can
forgive. The Prophets were always having to repeat this
very thing. David was a man after God's heart, not least
because he quite simply accepted God's forgiveness of sin
as a fact, nor did he on that account overlook the seriousness
of sin and the necessity for penance. The intellect as such
is absolutely unable to bring us understanding of the forgiveness of sin, and the will can only do so in a political
sense. It is only with love that it can be conceived.

89. 2nd February. A letter from the Franciscan who gave
the last sacraments to Konrad Weiss and who talked with
him on St. Stephen's day shortly before his death, about
my verses thanking him for *Konradin.* What a pleasure to
have given pleasure!

90. My eyes are skinned for men who could make peace
after this war, but I find none. The peace of death is what
they can all make, but the peace of life! If God can no
longer guide men's hearts as he guides the raging torrent,
then all is up. Am I without faith, hope and love? No!
But it is night, a night, however, which is both salvation
and asylum, sent, as it were, by light. A complete lack of
understanding, and yet one which is sent, so to speak, by
the understanding. Not one which it disavows, or is dis-
avowed by it.

91. The religious man wishes to know the God he has to
serve and who helps him, by name. The 'philosophical

mind' believes that this is unnecessary and unneedful. He is content, or only dares to speak of anonymous 'divine powers'. That is what Pascal meant by *Dieu d'Abraham, d'Isaac et de Jacob—non des philosophes!* The Christian knows the names of God: Father, Son and Holy Spirit.

92. What is the most difficult thing for men? Measure: 'the golden mean'. And this is true in theory, in teaching as in practice, in doing and acting. And that makes one despair that things will go better after this war. Those with a sense of measure will not have the power to make the peace, and those who have the power will make peace without 'measure'.

93. The Germans have a 'natural' disposition for religion. And for that very reason they can only be united religiously. They could only be so in the Catholic faith and its unity. There is consequently something painfully unreal and untrue about public invocations of God on official occasions. It is something done with a bad conscience. And we shall never get away from that, though ever so many among us were to be true friends of God, or even followers of Christ— as individuals!

94. *Propaganda:* In spite of a gigantic weight of lies the things of this world still function for an astoundingly long time without breaking to pieces; they almost seem to be strengthened. It is a mysterious and awful fact, and a great temptation to the spirit, to doubt the decisive significance of the truth in regard to the events in this world. But it is only a temptation: deep inside the spirit of man there is an assurance that lies destroy a man, and also a nation.

95. It is a serious business to form a doctrine, a view of the world, a *Weltanschauung*, out of the average 'natural' aspirations of this 'world'. Nor is the seriousness of it lessened because the world is comic and ridiculous in its new

'teachings' and its new styles. Anyway, to be ridiculous is
no danger in Germany, and certainly not fatal; and then
everything 'false' is essentially ridiculous! Even the Devil
is in certain respects comic and ridiculous. The most
important thing, and this is what is new, is to construct a
'doctrine' inductively upon the factual practice of evil men,
and to provide it with authority and sanctions. For example,
justice without love, complete mercilessness and so on.

96. 13th February. What strikes coldest in one's heart is
the spiritual state and the behaviour of the German Judges.
They condemn a man to prison for standing a Pole a g˙ass
of beer. That is really frightful.

97. To make God responsible for all and everything may
of course be the blasphemy of a sinner and a demon, or it
may be the praise of an angel or a saint. In fact, a creature
must ultimately reach the point at which he throws every-
everything upon God. On the other hand there is the
inescapable demand of the free spirit to be autonomous and
consequently to bear the responsibility for everything he
does. But how can the two aspects be harmonised unless
the created spirit becomes *divine?*

98. The spirit of man that always longs for a new expression
of the old, remains in the direct line of God's creation that
unceasingly creates new individuals, new expressions, that
is, of the same 'kind'. The mechanical copy is just about
the most inhuman, and what is more the most ungodly thing
that can be imagined.

99. 20th February. Altmark: Running amok in lies.
How childish it is to want to save Europe from destruction
by changing governments and economic policies. Only a
complete change of sentiment and conviction and of heart,
a Μετανοεῖν can help us. And 'Prussia', certainly, is the
great hindrance.

100. The inconceivability of God lies before my silence and behind all my words. Could I but express it in my own words, I should be a great writer.

101. Patriotism lies in the nature of man and is something so self-evident that any exaggeration or emphasis is only painful or ridiculous, and smothers it instead of sustaining it.

102. There is no one who cannot imagine something more perfect than he is and than he was. That may be one of the proofs of his imperfection. But is perfection necessarily capable of imagining something less perfect? And would that be a proof of its perfection?

103. Ultimately, after all, we are made for happiness which is, so to say, the normal and the certain. The Church declares that certain men whom she names by name—her saints—are, with unquestionable certainty, in heaven. She does not say of any man, that he is quite certainly in hell— not even Judas, the betrayer of the Lord. She says it only of the Devil, over whom she has no jurisdiction.

104. Rejoinder: God created the grass-hopper and the shark and the wasp (a beautiful animal) and the flea and the louse and the bug (more beautiful animals!) Would he have created them if he had not taken pleasure in them? And you expect to understand this God? How silly that is! He places the world's destiny in the hand of a gipsy, a knife-grinder, a ham actor, a buffoon, or, in case I am going too far (and I don't want to say too much), he uses him as an instrument. That takes some understanding! The only explanation would seem to be a certain constraint upon God!

105. Woe to the poor man who has no other prayer but: Lord help thou my unbelief!

106. 'Heaven and earth will pass away, but my words shall not pass away'. If anyone believes that to be true, then he believes at the same time that it is God who said it. Those who know anything about words know how ridiculous it is for a *man* to appeal to the everlastingness of his words.

107. If anyone were to have doubts about God because he could not conceive Him, he would simply not have faith. For that is the beginning of faith—when a man cannot conceive Him.

108. 24th February. The voice of the Wolf as the voice of providence. That is how it proclaims itself, shouting about the *Herrgott*, the favourite word of the German blasphemer. And it ends with a quotation from the great German heretic, Luther: And even if the world were full of devils . . . . Oh, how he mocks his own, and knows not how. A German destiny indeed. But only wait a year! A whole long year in blood and filth!

109. There are writers, unlucky men, whose quills adorn others, but not themselves.

110. 25th February. The German *Herrgott-religion*—for so we may call it after yesterday's speech—begins to take shape, vaguely of course, because that is what it is. It undoubtedly has something in common with Mohammedanism, for at a pinch it is monotheistic, and absolutely anti-trinitarian. It is much less universal than the religion of Islam, makes no claim to be so, and could make no such claim; on the other hand it is 'fanatical', as dervishes ought to be, but then again unimaginative, dry, Prussian: 'A fanatical sense of duty' its ideal, the most frightful and horrifying that mankind has ever seen. The principles of the German *Herrgott-religion* go far beyond those of the English 'plutocrat's-religion'; it accepts the success of a deceit, a betrayal, of murder or violence as a proof of the *blessing* of the German *Herrgott. Success* alone makes any action, however monstrous, blessed.

'By their fruits ye shall know them'. In the German *Herrgott-religion* Christ's words are given a different sense. It is not the tree which bears good fruit which is good, and the tree which bears bad fruit which is bad; but the tree which bears fruit whether good or bad is good, and the tree which bears no fruit is bad—and what indeed is the purpose of the fruits which are visible only to heaven, which an adherent to the German *Herrgott-religion* does not, and cannot see.

111. The temptation of those of little faith: 'Perhaps he is the instrument of God, and *we* are disobedient, rebels against God's will'. Seven years of success *are* after all a sign from God!' Patience, patience, and in this hour, read the psalms, in this long hour, which is granted with such sublime generosity to evil, in this anxious hour.

112. The interlarding, combining and mixing of the lowest personal interests and the highest vital interest of public life has surely never before been so successfully managed by a party, both consciously and unconsciously. The solution in fact was a super-human task. Only war, after all, which is certainly something of a divine judgment, could solve the problem. Perhaps!

113. One must be careful of asserting that such a thing has never been, excepting as regards quantity, and mass, for that may well be true; but in other things one must be careful. And so I cannot tell whether there was ever a time when such great power was granted to evil. However that may be, it is a curious age. As for the *means* of power in this world, everything is in the hands of evil. God has given it a free hand on a grandiose scale. Yes, to the very limits, beyond which even the just would despair.

114. Because the fulfilment of mankind will only be complete in an unknown period of time, in an objective continuity certainly, though the continuity will not always be

conscious and subjective, nor in a direct line, but zig-zagging
and spiralling about, it follows that individual races, and
individuals themselves experience things and have to adopt
an attitude towards them for which there is neither analogy
nor comparison in the immediately preceding years, though
no doubt in earlier times. We today, in Germany, understand the first Christians much better than the Christians
of the Middle Ages at their peak. We also understand them
incomparably better than the Christians of the Middle Ages
could or did understand them.

115. I am to be master of my thought, my will and my
feeling! In all truth, is there anything more mysterious than
such an *I?* What is it then? With what, through what is it
to be master over thought, will and feeling, if it is to be with
and through thought, will and feeling? Or is there something
else above these three, something simply indescribable? The
inaccessible essence of being, the person, having 'power', who
is 'powerful'?

116. 28th March. If a man paints Christ, he paints the
second person of the Trinity who became man. That is the
first principle for a Christian painter. All other questions
are to be considered in that light. The first person of the
Trinity is not to be painted. That one may make no image
of him remains true, now as formerly. The third person of
the Trinity the Holy Spirit, is represented in the form of a
dove, according to revelation, for reasons which to us are
inscrutable. The second person really became man. So that
the image of the second person must be the picture of a real
man. That allowed and allows for many conceptions.
Signs and symbols belong in a different order. We are
speaking of images.

117. None of Christ's contemporaries appears to have felt
the need to possess a drawing or a painting or a statue of
him. But undoubtedly the desire soon awoke and was

satisfied, and so it has gone on from that day to this, in ever changing styles and conceptions. Nor will it ever cease. And I only note it for the painter's sake, and because of his difficulties—the painter of today, in the west, who not only has to bear the weight of a tradition two thousand years old, but has to come to terms with it. In no instance is he any longer a 'naïve' artist, that is out of the question. Anything attempted in that direction bears the stigma of unreality, and of untruth if not of mendacity.

118. The gospels and the letters of the apostles moreover, do not give the artist the very slightest hint about Christ's outward appearance, except perhaps for his age and the indirect information that he behaved like other men of his time and certainly did not stand out as original in any outward sense or desired to draw attention to himself. The first reason for this is that it was not in the character of the time to attend at all to the eyes or the hair or the nose of a person in a story. Nor is anyone so described in all the gospels. The one exception is, to a certain extent, Christ himself, since he talks to one of his disciples, quite in general of course, as a typical Hebrew, even externally. And that presupposes that one was quite clear as to what the type of a true Hebrew was.

The second, deeper reason why nothing whatsoever is said about Christ's appearance in the gospels, is that his spiritual being put his physical appearance in the shadow for those who were moved and believed. Naturally it was there, even in its effect; and that spiritual being, action and speech did not have just any appearance, but had a quite definite one, of that there can be no doubt. The writers of the gospels were deeply moved and believed: it was the spiritual aspect which penetrated, outshining the psychological and the physiognomical effect. Though it was there. Men who were not affected, who did not believe, of which there were many, many more, could more easily have observed the outward man. They could have 'made a report', they could have registered a photographic impression. But more on this point later: I have a theory of my own.

119. 31st March. I often wonder whether the world would not be more understandable if there were no animals in it, for it seems to me that they are the most un-understandable of all things. Writing at night, I have often contemplated moths and fantastic green flies for hours, gazing as into an abyss. I can stand for hours in front of an aquarium with my understanding motionless. And then there is the suffering of animals. But what does it really mean: 'understanding'? For I always have the impression of being much further away from a thing I 'understand' than when I don't understand.

120. When I think back to the hours spent writing, and all its happy side, the curious mixture of unmerited inspiration (brain-waves) and most intensive personal activity, its quite incomparable joy and pleasure, then it almost seems to me that it is a life worthy of eternity and unendangered by the disgust that would certainly follow the prolongation of any other mental or physical pleasure.

121. A world catastrophe may serve many purposes. As an alibi before God, for example. Adam where art thou? 'I was at the world war'. Only it's a coarse excuse. Others search for an alibi in their own consciences. Adam where art thou? 'I was with my conscience—does it not belong to me'! That is the subtlest way of all of avoiding action.

122. Many a man thinks to satisfy the great virtue of moderation by using all his shrewdness and bringing all his experience to bear upon limiting his pleasure to his capacity for pleasure. But simply by the fact of setting enjoyment as the end, he has radically violated the virtue.

123. When dare a man say everything about God and
about his ordering of the world? When he loves God—
that, the Old Testament teaches us. When I see a man do
t without love, it sends a shiver down my spine.

124. The attributes of God in which a Christian believes
are hard for the human understanding to acknowledge.
[t is well that he should freely recognise this. The difficulties
do not always remain the same. God's allpowerfulness and
ove are, as a rule, the points in question. Certain facts
known from our vision and knowledge of this world must
be used, in their analogical sense of course, and that right
carefully. In a darkened room, shut in, I cannot see the
sun-lit earth. From a height I perceive things which I
doubted on the level. My natural knowledge grows and
matures, and with time I acquire insight and so on.
Why should a man, better, more blessed than me, not
have less difficulty in the matter of allpowerfulness than
I have?

125. Beware of the terrible light-hearted simplifiers—both
theoretical and practical. They create the most hopeless
confusion imaginable, in the long run. Omit something,
and you bring about a disorder infinitely more disastrous,
than that produced by the mere muddler.

126. The belief in an evil power, in the devil, in the Prince
of this World, has much declined in the last centuries. It
s the remedy for many distorted forms of belief, but its
use is a delicate matter, for inevitably it leads people to a
false view of the world. The state of this world simply
cannot be understood if we omit the power of evil. This
dangerous conception has slipped in even among Christians
—as a result of an omission. Evil is forced back into
nature', and becomes 'comic' (a war, for example, is a
comic event), and even into the 'demoniacal' powers of
nature, this side of good and evil and there conceals itself.

Then the state of this world is seen to depend on the all-powerfulness of an all-loving God, and on original sin and the sins of mankind. But that is not an adequate basis; man, in this case, is over-rated, over-valued. He simply has not got the power to disrupt the world, to make it as it is. A man to whom this sort of faith has been taught, and it is certainly not the Christian faith, might justifiably fall away upon a closer and clearer consideration of it, or again his soul might sicken. He would have to look upon God as either without power or without love. Man cannot get away from good and evil, either by the most violent anathemas, or by watering it all down—something always remains, even when good and evil are degraded into useful and useless.

127. The most radical denial of the need of redemption in this world seems to me to lie in the phrase, 'the eternal recurrence of the same' (Nietzsche). Logically it represents a fantastic confusion of thought, since quite evidently everything points in the very opposite direction. Theologically, it is at an infinite distance from God, and it turns everything upside down. At this point discussion is no longer possible.

128. One of the more difficult things to determine is the degree of corruption and the number of false principles with which the nations put up and the length of time they endure before the catastrophe comes. Usually, it lasts longer than one thinks. Comparisons with individuals and with families easily lead one astray. And those who furthermore believe that God has the destiny of nations in his hand, will take the greatest care.

129. How I started, when the deadest voice of the Reich (Goebbels) ended his speech with the words: 'Praised be . . .' He even paused—could he have forgotten himself, have dropped back into memories of childhood? But he continued 'Whatever hardens us'. That, of course, is in line. The

religion of the German *Herrgott* is the religion of the 'heart
of stone'. They will be beaten, they will be ground to
powder, and then they will once again desire a heart of
flesh and blood.

130. 5th April. 'The eternal recurrence of the same'.
Psychologically it is precisely his fear of a repetition that
fascinates a man's spirit, hynotises him, so that in order to
attain peace, he throws himself into this abyss of nonsense.
A hellish affirmation of the horrible. I thought at one time,
light-heartedly, that this matter could be answered with
scorn and contempt. But at this point ridicule loses its
power. The world is very much deeper. Ridicule does not
go deep enough. It is a form of rationalism, and it, too, is
shallow.

131. 6th April. To the man who believes that there is
such a thing as a blessing, and that it is of the greatest
moment, and is linked, by and large, to certain conditions
which the recipient must fulfil, by fulfilling the laws of God,
to this man the immediate future is shrouded in darkness.
For things are happening upon which God's blessing
cannot rest.

132. Rejoinder: 'And so one may say that ultimately you
only believe in God because you are convinced that the
devil exists, and that he has power'—Yes, that is how
things stand, although you express yourself rather
crudely. In point of fact, I should deny the existence of
God if anyone were to insist that there were no evil spirits,
infinitely more powerful than man, and that the whole
frightful misery of mankind lay purely and simply in its own
sinfulness and in the imperfection of nature.

133. One begins to philosophise with wonder. But
then, too, philosophy ends in wonder. Is this wonder
perhaps a sign that the spirit of man is created? For

why, otherwise, should being be in wonder at itself, at being?

134. It seems to be reflective rather than immediate thought and knowledge, that lead to doubt and to rebellion against God. I have suffered much both spiritually and physically in my life. But only once did it end in doubt about the righteousness of God and in an attempt at rebellion; and then it was the mercy of God which restrained me, so that instead of the curse that was on the tip of my tongue, I stammered out the blessing of Christ: Blessed art thou, Simon son of Jonas, for thou believest. I can remember the night and the room well. But it was the presence of a reflective element which brought things to a head. For weeks I had been expecting the unbearable pain (I had no narcotic at the time, not even aspirin); and so, too, on that night. It is quite another matter when it comes to seeing the misfortune of others, children suffering, for example, or hearing reports of concentration camps, battle areas and so forth. Then my understanding is brought up against quite other difficulties. When my son Reinhard was a year old, and for weeks on end had attacks of croup every night, almost choking to death, everything became dark before my eyes, for I could not and cannot see in this the faintest glimmer of reason, it is utterly unintelligible. Man has no immediate consciousness of the innumerable generations that preceded him or of those that are to follow. Ten or a million are all one. Everything that a generation experiences in the way of misfortune happens, where immediate consciousness is concerned, just once. And yet it happened and happens probably for millions of years. That is reflective knowledge. And it creates difficulties. It puts the unanswerable question: why this endless repetition of unspeakable misfortunes through thousands of generations? That is where faith has to fight its hardest battles. And it can be seen that reflection, where the stream of knowledge always runs thin, is its greatest opponent, and its most dangerous one.

135. 'Mockery' has many levels. It can even be affectionate, but it can be as poisonous as hell. It does not exist in the fullness of love, except possibly as a means of education and aimed wholly at the good of the object of laughter. But that is rare. A healthy pride and an honest contempt for what is base may make use of mockery, even though they may prefer to remain silent. Mockery is the favourite weapon of *Schadenfreude*, a sign of its base origin. And sometimes it is only a mask, concealing a poor, sad, unhappy and broken countenance. Man, unlike the angels is so changeable. Weakness is one of mockery's favourite targets, man's real weakness, and God's apparent weakness. God, in all three persons, was and is mocked daily. Why do the great and powerful of this world *fear* mockery and the mocker? It would be inexplicable if they were certain of their power. But they are not. There is a weakness in them, and if none other then in this at least, that they are anxious lest they lose their power.

136. 'On the seat of the mockers', as it is called in scripture, sit the lost souls, those who hate God and man and themselves. But even there, nothing is final. One day they may stand up in order to fall down on their knees and adore what they once mocked.

137. The fame of this world vanishes like smoke. That is true enough. But this, too, must be realised, and made real. That is to say, a man must acquire and possess this fame and *then* recognise that it is nothing and leaves his soul empty. Only then is the saying true. Those without fame only say half the truth, and the other half is a lie. Even a nothing in this world must, so to say, become body. In this world every truth must have a body or receive one.

138. There can be no neutrality towards God. That is a simple and intelligible proposition. Now, if man is God, or the immediate emanation of God, then sooner or later, he will say, according to the measure of his power: no one can be neutral towards me.

139. 9th April. The Germans stand by the words of their beloved teacher, Martin Luther, *pecca fortiter—mentire fortiter*. And since the whole of Europe lies, and they lie *fortiter*, they are successful, at least until someone no longer lies.

140. The most hopeless misunderstanding: he does not see what I see, and I do not see what he sees.

141. There are many people who do not deny that the things of this world are symbolic, but they hold that *that which* things signify, *that which* they symbolise is *nothing* real or capable of determining our actions. Is that not poor logic?

142. It is of the nature of things that they might equally be other than they are, and that is more astonishing than they themselves. And that is what makes *time* and *not* space the inmost problem of our being.

143. Kierkegaard's thesis that the prevailing category of the demoniacal is the 'sudden' has been demonstrated to the full in recent times.

144. 'To be master of one's fate' is a crude expression which needs first of all to be interpreted in order to yield its truth. How should I be master of something which as a rule is not in my hands?

145. Being presupposes nothing but itself. That is both clear *and* revealed: I am who am—that is certainly true. And so it is not a will without being, so to speak, which first creates being. Will *is* in being, so that one can undoubtedly say: being wills itself. That is true of absolute being and of God. It is otherwise with created being. As being it presupposes the divine Logos and as existence, the divine will. Only in the case of created being can one speak of a primacy of divine will.

146. The truly philosophical spirit is a contemplative spirit. It is not captivated by the things that one can change, but by those, precisely, which cannot be changed.

147. Love is the *fulfilment* of the Law, not its destroyer. It is hierarchical, not anarchical. And because it is the fulfilment, its violation is the real sin. A man will be measured by his love.

148. "Science" (Wissenschaft), necessarily uses a positive, historically developed language from which the element of 'chance' is not excluded,* on a level of general understanding. Not so 'wisdom.' Wisdom has a much more inward, deeper 'language', mysterious in its essence, and related to silence. But what has the scientific method to do with silence? It must speak in the simplest sense of the word. More than the half of wisdom, however, is in silence.

149. In this world and in this aeon evil is often cured by evil, provided only that one is careful that Beelzebub who drives out the devil does not remain behind, doing his work. Hypocrisy can be expelled by shamelessness, and human nature can once again find its balance in the slow labour of salvation. Hypocrisy is of all conditions the most hated of God, according to scripture. And in the last centuries hypocrisy has ruled European politics. It looked as though the various dictators intended to supplant it by shamelessness, and so bring men to their senses and set them on the right path. That was an illusion. For in the meantime hypocrisy and shamelessness have signed a shamelessly

* For example, the word Academy, derived from the name of a garden where Plato taught.

hypocritical pact in the name of these dictators, against which only a martyr can be victorious. Perhaps the great outpouring of grace is to come that Blumhardt hoped for in his old age, longed for, prayed for and perhaps foresaw.

150. All great gifts are one-sided and pretty well exclude the others. As always, human nature is limited. The man who possesses the highest gifts in the hierarchic order, does not necessarily possess the lower gifts. On the contrary! Because they were the chosen people, the Jews had the highest gift in the hierarchic order, the gift of religion, but to the exclusion of all others, with the one exception of poetry, and then only in the service of the divine. It was only later, and after they had crucified Christ, that they became 'artists' in the pagan sense, in the sense of the gentiles, the peoples, *gentes*: and then they were only 'talented', though they often had very great 'talents'—and that is a very curious fact, worthy of note. The Jews have never been philosophers, poets, painters, sculptors, architects, not even technicians in an original, fundamental primitive sense, like all other peoples. There, too, they are unlike others.

151. 'He was one of the most widely read writers of his day, and today it is quite impossible to read him, one cannot even understand his success'. That is the hardest thing that can be said of an author, and reveals what *time* is as a counterpoise to eternity.

152. What is the secret of German military power? Who can say? The incapacity for leisure and enjoyment? The complete adaption to the 'world'? The extinction of every metaphysical need, so clearly revealed by every official German voice? Does it belong to the providential vocation of the Germans for the *Reich*, which remains theirs even though they ignominiously betrayed their trust?

153. 13th April. Snow and rain. What about the German *Herrgott*, the 'stony-hearted God'? Is he really a demon scorning his adepts, not allowing a single blade of grass to grow in this extraordinary spring? Or are the slow mills grinding, are the mills of the true, eternal, trinitarian God grinding more quickly?

154. Rationalism and irrationalism are both the fruit of pride. Where the one sees the other is blind—thus do they contradict one another. Rationalism sees, rightly enough, that ultimately things must be understood, and are reasonable, but in its pride, thinks that reason itself, that is to say human reason, is the measure of all things: and that what it cannot understand is simply non-existent. Irrationalism sees very well that things do not fit into reason, and yet they *are*. But thinks, in its pride, that things are irrational in themselves, even to the divine reason.

155. The worst of poverty—today at any rate—the most galling and most difficult thing to bear, is that it makes it almost impossible for one to be *alone*. Neither at work, nor at rest, neither abroad nor at home, neither waking nor sleeping, neither in health, nor—what a torture—in sickness.

156. Lead us not into temptation! What can this prayer mean, since God certainly cannot tempt any creature to evil? And yet a request simply cannot be so utterly unintelligible to us as to have virtually no meaning at all. We may and must try to give it some meaning. Personally, I interpret it in the following sense: that God should not conceal himself entirely, or for too long, in the ordering of things public and private, in order that the believer may perceive the outward covering of the thread, that is hidden to the 'world'. If God were to withdraw himself entirely, who could keep the faith? According to his promise, he will not do so; but in order to avert this temptation, into which, unlike all others, God himself can lead us, it is taken up into the great world of prayer: 'Lead us not into temptation!' Show thyself! That thy mills do *not* grind *too* slowly! Show us thy love *and* thy justice. Let no one doubt that thou art *the Lord,* let no one despair! Psalm 42.

157. Our first comprehension of the world and of things through human reason and the human senses is far from having been fully explored. We comprehend a great deal, at least as a whole, that needs to be analysed, but must not be 'constructed', for this may lead to the most serious errors. Now, no investigation of any kind can begin without presuppositions. And this is the supposition: first, that what is given contains very much more than appears at first sight. And consequently, no premature simplification! Secondly, that which is given is ordered hierarchically; thirdly, the relation of the parts to the whole is full of mystery.

158. There is no longer a god of war, and in consequence no fortune of war! Mars and Fortuna have been thrown out and the machine has been brought in, working to a fraction of an inch. Man has been so dehumanised that his capacity for error has also been reduced, and may, in practice, be overlooked. 'Lead us not into temptation'!

159. The blossom of a cultivated cherry tree is quite as uncompounded, and direct, and indivisibly 'blossom' as that of the wild cherry. 'Culture' does not destroy immediacy and directness, but enriches, ennobles, and beautifies it. Indeed the immediacy *as such* is more plainly revealed.

160. Of no individual thing can one 'say' *what it is.* Our very first comprehension implies this. We comprehend that the understanding never gets to the bottom of things.

161. One belongs to the world as long as one is more ashamed of a *faux pas,* a display of ignorance, a wrong turn of phrase, a misquotation than of an unloving action.

162. One of the most arrogant undertakings, to my mind, is to write the biography of a man which pretends to go beyond external facts, and give the inmost motives. One of the most mendacious is autobiography.

163. About an author: He gives the appearance of wanting both in his writings and in himself, to hold the balance between faith and doubt, to stand above both and to wait and see who is right. An attitude, indeed, which is only possible to such a strange being as man. God protect him!

164. Rejoinder: The contrary of faith is unbelief, not doubt. Faith and unbelief cannot be in a man at the same time. Faith and partial scepticism may well be present simultaneously, at any rate superficially. A sounding, however, then gives the one or the other: faith or unbelief.

165. A clean and tidy classification which awakens a sense of completeness and of a proper emphasis upon the individual parts, is an intellectual pleasure, though it must not be allowed to cloak the danger of arbitrariness and subjectivism. How difficult it is, in fact, to interpret in any detail, even the most certain, universally valid, objective classifications of being, life and death for example, good and evil, ugly and beautiful, will, reason and feeling! How almost impossible it is to penetrate their interrelationship!

166. Spiritual life and spiritual thought does not mean living or thinking without the body or even against the body, it means living and thinking hierarchically. The new slogan about educating man on 'a physical basis' (*vom Leibe her*) is of course anti-Christian, since Christianity aims to educate man spiritually: it is hierarchical. That it has made many mistakes in education is not to be denied, principally when it became *bourgeois* and, losing all sense of elevation and of the traditional hierarchic doctrine, fell into indolence and heresy. But education 'on a physical basis' only produces animals.

167.   To do one's will leads to satisfaction and to a joy of a quite particular, incomparable kind. It is said: 'Man's will is his paradise'. To do one's own will and to be autonomous is essential to happiness. It is the happy union of God's will and the creature's own will, of the man adopted in Christ. And freedom then is not impaired. To do one's own will belongs to the essence of freedom.

168.   Man cannot deceive God. That is not too difficult to perceive. Nevertheless he always tries to deceive Him. And so one has always to repeat that one cannot deceive God.

169.   Can anything really be done by man unless he does it of his own *will*? If not, then one would have to distinguish between willing and willing. Many a man has to do work which he does not 'will' to do, and that he only does in order to earn his daily bread, or to avoid punishment.

170.   Stars that as things are, are infinitely distant, are flying away from us, so the astronomers tell us, with a speed of 20,000 kilometres a second. Why? They can't say. Some aver that the only alternative would be for them to move in our direction, for they cannot remain where they are, motionless. But why not come nearer? Or are they uncertain of polishing us off as long as the strongest military power in the world gives them to think? Or is it just simply a matter of taste—to fly before this planet?

171.   What more perfect image of the New German than modern military music? Respectable warlike sounds mixed with a dull brutality and a smarmy sentimentality.

172.   20th April. How little truth man needs in order to live, and how many lies! *Nescio, mi fili, quam multis mendaciis*

regitur mundus (I do not know, my son, with how many lies
the world is ruled).

173. Their voices, my God, their voices! Again and again,
I am overwhelmed by all that they betray. Their deadness
is the most frightful thing about them. The stinking corpse
of a *vox humana*! Death, disease and lies, and a solitude
proud of being deserted by God.

Under the hegemony of Prussia, today at its peak,
the Germans have always been driven back more and more,
whether they wished it or not, upon the motto: *oderint dum
metuant.* (Let them hate, as long as they fear!). That leads
to a bitter ending, for the fear will disappear, and the hate
will remain.

174. The world's knowledge is never without pride. And
so its mouth is ever full of contempt, scorn, rejection, and
unfriendliness. And always without joy. It is not as though
knowledge itself were without joy, but the pride embitters it.

175. 21st/22nd April. Everything was so dark in my
life, and God illuminated it. Do not forget it, O my heart!
Do not forget it!

176. Might a just man put God to the proof?—which is
not the same thing as tempting God. The Bible tells in
favour of it. But he may not do so often.

177. I can at any time so sink myself in a thing or an
occurrence that its initial intelligibility is swallowed up by
its essential unintelligibility to my reason.

178. 24th April. During long years of suffering, perhaps
I too have been an occasion for someone to doubt the
righteousness of God, and perhaps at the very moment
when I myself was most inwardly assured of the justice,
and of the love of God.

179. The assurance with which some men draw practical consequences from theoretical truth, as though they were *the only possible ones* would be enviable, if nothing depended upon it (it so simplifies life)—but as things are it is more nearly a misfortune and even frightening, for so much in the end *depends* upon it. It makes a difference, naturally, whether a heretic is burnt or celebrated as an original genius. There are periods when men are sceptical of the deductions which their reason is capable of drawing. Today that is not so. The consequences deduced from the most threadbare 'scientific' hypothesis are looked upon as though they were eternal truths.

180. If the possibility, indeed the probability of a personal immortality could or had to be imparted to men simply through arguments addressed to their reason, then the Christian faith today would be in a desperate position, for it presupposes that we live on, or again one might say that personal immortality is an integrating aspect of the Christian faith. But the probability of a personal future life is not the discovery of reason *ex nihilo*, but is on the contrary based upon a sort of instinct in man, which may certainly be silenced at times, but always comes to life again. It may be drugged by the intoxication of life, by great successes, discoveries, inventions, conquests and by the fog that so easily rises within a man, produced by a certain animal health. When disappointments of every kind, and illness and the infirmity of age and the certainty of an early death lead a man back to that instinct, and he consciously orders his thoughts, and returns to 'the faith'—then the proud and unbending onlookers have a habit of saying: it is their *enfeebled* under standing which makes them capitulate. But that is an undergraduate argument, a superficial and careless way of thinking. In any case, one might with quite as good grounds say that a path which had been closed or blocked to thought had been opened and made free. And furthermore that the eye now sees things that were formerly in mist and fog.

181. This age is not favourable to the eternal. There is no doubt of that. But is that not the rule? So that the men who live in an age favourable to the eternal are exceptions and live in an illusion if they do not know the rule. The old words of wisdom: No rule without an exception, but the exception proves the rule.

182. The *German* Red Cross has as its badge an eagle puffed up with pride, a *Hakenkreuz* for a heart, sitting on and digging its claws into a—cross, the red cross. They *have* to reveal themselves!

183. Short dialogue: It must be a dispensation of Providence that the gramophone record should have been invented for an age when the human voice is of such great significance and betrays so much. By their voices ye shall know them! How easy it will be for the future historian to judge, if only he has the records at his disposal, and plays them!

But to whom, my friend (to how few), is given the gift of discerning voices. (Karl Krauss possessed the gift in a remarkable degree). And then is it given to Historians? Do not overrate it! At the present time the gift seems hardly to be widespread. How would it have been possible, otherwise, for it all to have happened?

That is no doubt true; and yet the disease in question, resulting from a reversal of the hierarchic order, was the reason for the sudden appearance of these voices, their success and the failure to recognise them—this specific disease, I maintain, can and will disappear (to be replaced, no doubt, by another) and then everyone (even the historians) will suddenly *hear* the horrible disease and the depravity of the voices, their emptiness and their 'possession'—and that is no contradiction—the spiritual stupidity and dumbness in the bellowing mask. Only believe me, it is the work of Providence that there should be *records.*

184. Compassion without love does exist. It is certainly not worth much, and is often paired with baseness and depravity. It is often the 'fury' whose 'heart of gold' beats loudest for "our dumb friends". But there is also love without 'compassion', in the ordinary sense, for physical suffering. This may make a man seem cold and hard and even cruel, although he may show great compassion where spiritual misfortune is concerned. And .naturally, that too is not right. The most difficult thing of all for man, is a sense of measure.

185. The gods of the Germans decorate themselves, roll their eyes and bellow—no wonder they are called barbarians.

186. 27th April. The Germans will not be conquered by the strength of man. They are the strongest and most frightful people on earth. They will be conquered *by God himself*, alas, and probably without noticing it.

187. Athanasius the Great said of the Emperor Julian, who was persecuting him to death, and whom he barely escaped, that he was 'a cloud which would soon pass by'. Less than two years later the cloud had vanished. Today things are different. Perhaps because there is no Athanasius. We must wait. Watch and pray!

188. How sad age would be without the joy of the young over which to rejoice. But that, too, is only melancholy without the hope of salvation.

189. What the preachers of Christ's words need is surely a new voice, and a different manner. A 'style' is always necessary. Neither Peter, nor Ambrose nor Augustine nor St. Thomas, nor Newman can have spoken just as they thought, or without thought. But the style current now has surely become a quite shapeless, rusty old container? Both unnatural and contrary to nature, as well as unspiritual. A painful, false note, enough to make a man of the present day run away. Is there not a correlation between evil will, erroneous thought and forced or false feeling (and what may it be?) But my sight is feeble; I cannot follow the threads, I only confuse them, or lose them.

190. I have long maintained that to find out where a concept or a word really belongs is properly speaking a philosophical task. It is something much more than etymology as it is usually treated, which is only a valuable scientific help towards a properly philosophical knowledge of the different elements.

191. 29th April. Richard Wagner, 'Siegfried's death' on the wireless. What a magician! Genuine barbarism, shaped to the ears and moulded to the style of the bourgeois *salon* of 1880 (they still exist today, in 1940). No wonder he is regarded as the musical prophet of the incomparable barbarism that rose up out of the decaying bourgeoisie.

192. Short dialogue: A: Good and evil undoubtedly correspond best to the sphere of the will, true and false to thought; that is where they are at home. But what about feeling? At the moment I do not see any attributes that corresponds to it in the same way. Perhaps the nearest would be genuine and sham, only they go with true and false; or friendly and unfriendly, which again, are related to good and evil. How curious it is. Feeling is the most difficult sphere of man's being to penetrate.

B: That is perfectly true, simply because feeling is so inward, and in spite of its wealth, so inarticulate. It is the 'mode' of the very heart of being itself. Willing and thinking are more distant, and are directed outward in the very manner of their activity: they always have an object. Feeling is, so to say, the first primary mode of being, of *complete* being as spirit. It refers to being itself, and to the condition of being. Everyone knows that immediately. Only the reflective philosopher could make a mistake and go astray as you seem to be doing, my friend. True enough, as you say, good and evil belong immediately to willing, and true and false to thinking—therein you are undoubtedly right. And then, you maintain, feeling has no such immediate attributes, and by looking far afield you fail to find what is so near at hand, all too near, as it would seem. What then does being want to be, being in its highest manifestation, in the person, what does it want to be? It wants to be happy, and God, the source of all being is happy and blessed.

Indeed, just as good and evil refer to willing, and true and false refer to thinking, so happiness and blessedness refer to feeling.

193. A scandalised question: Does God let Hitler do his or His will?

194. 30th April. There is one thing that has come to full maturity in me: the understanding that I do not understand God: the sense of the *Mysterium.* That prevents me from misunderstanding the things of this world.

195. The darkest hour of faith: when every human standard and example fails one. Everything is nonsense.

196. The one holds he is guilty of everything, another that he is not responsible for anything. Both are wrong, nevertheless the former is nearer the truth.

197. 1st May. The right of what is established seems to be relatively simple. Seems, I say; at least that is how men behave, even though in truth it is far from simple. But it is not so easy to formulate the right to conquest and the right of the victor. There is disagreement upon the very first principals. Has every man who is alive the right to live by the mere fact that he is alive? Or is this right determined by his situation, or by his capacities, or his qualities? Do men and nations, in principle, exist for one another or are they against one another? Does the right of the stronger take priority over the right of the weaker? If the concept 'stronger' were simple, and that of 'weak' too, then one might erect the proposition upon the basis of nature, where it seems to hold good, at least as far as appearances go. In actual fact, however, both concepts are so ambiguous, that it is possible to grant a certain meaning to paradoxes such as 'strength in weakness' and 'weakness in strength'. In this aeon there is an impulse to conquer, and from this it follows that there is also a right; but who can formulate it? It cannot be formulated, except prophetically. Of course, as long as a conquest happens peacefully, the right of conquest creates no difficulty; and where there is no wrong, there is naturally right. Only when, in addition, it involves war, do the problems arise, and man alone cannot answer them. The Jews were given the right by God to conquer Palestine and to wipe out nations or deprive them of their rights. We may take it that these peoples were degenerate, and had forfeited their right. The same might be assumed of the Inkas of Mexico, and even of Carthage, or the Abyssinians of today. But the proof does not always hold good. A great war is certainly always a sort of judgment of God. And the right of the victor resides in the fact that he puts through His will. That appears to be his purely formal and absolute 'right', no matter whether his will is just or unjust.

198. 2nd May. Kierkegaard's category 'the sudden' came to my mind all at once, today, in the garden. Quite suddenly, like lightning, a big black bird (a blackbird) flew into the bush of brilliant white blossoms, at which I had been gazing for some minutes sunk in thought. And then, suddenly, my contemplation was disturbed, and my thoughts confused.

199. With practice a man can accustom himself not to deceive himself any more and to be honest with himself. He may even be able to bring it to the point at which he can deceive himself as little as he can deceive God. And then, certainly, no one can deceive him.

200. Perhaps the Germans have made themselves into a sort of spiritual *cul-de-sac* as a result of their apostasy. So far and no farther! A blank wall—in front of it a little music still flowers, a few nature lyrics, some family affection, and above all a perfectly functioning bureaucracy, hard work and—worst of all—military efficiency.

201. Separated from the mood in which they are spoken and from the voice that speaks them, words often lose half their power and significance. Some poets, indeed, have the gift of bringing the mood to life again, but the voice, the lovely or the hideous voice, they cannot recapture. The historian of the future, however, will find in the gramophone record a source of primary importance for European history at the present time which formerly only the contemporary historian possessed when he himself could *hear* the active participants.

202. Old people often say and write things which they look upon as wisdom and profound teaching, while others, not indeed always the hearers, but the readers, speak of commonplaces, banalities or even twaddle. Very often both are right in their way. The 'words of wisdom' of old people may be banal in themselves, but they are wise because of the depths of feeling and *memoria* from which they spring, and because they themselves are wise. But they are easier to see or to hear than to read.

203. It has always been recognised that the crown is an essential part of the *Imperium.* That has been understood in modern times by England, by Napoleon, by Wilhelm

D

and by Mussolini. The gipsy seems not to know it. But perhaps it will occur to him later. He will design one for his own use, and as impossible as himself.

204. Consider well that if we Christians were so wrong that our religion meant nothing real, and was nothing but invention, imagination, phantasy, nevertheless after two thousand years we ourselves would be *a reality* by reason of our intellectually complete system, through the power of our faith and the life in our saints, which made us into Gods.

205. The proposal of a 'neutral aesthete': Why not let those thorough Germans build the motor roads in Europe, and organise the post and the railways and the fire brigades? We will look after art and the things of the mind! For of course we must remain neutral.

206. The strongest and most immediate unity is created not by the same thought or the same will even, but by the same feeling (the same *memoria*), in and upon which thought and will rest, from which they spring and in which they leave their traces.

207. The choice between falling into the hands of God and into the hands of men, costs me no agony of indecision. I wish to fall into the hands of God, however frightful it may be. That is how I have understood every serious sickness, full of thankfulness in suffering. What it means to fall into the hands of men, I tasted for just half a day—on 20th May 1933*

208. Hilty maintains that a German world hegemony could only be justified upon the basis of the innate virtues of fidelity and purity (he appeals to Tacitus). Fidelity and

*On this date Haecker was arrested by the Gestapo for the first time and interrogated about his article on the *Hakenkreuz* which was about to appear in the *Brenner*, a periodical published in Innsbruck.

purity 1940! Fidelity? How in the world is fidelity possible after the apostasy from Christ—except as a farce and a caricature, as a horrible sort of gangster fidelity full of nauseating romanticism. And purity? In a state proclaiming a naked stud morality in the place of marriage.

209. 'If the Hottentots were to become Christians today, they would still not be able to build the German Cathedrals', says Herr Rosenberg, and thinks it is an argument in favour of the racial doctrine and against Christianity. My God! There has not been such a depth of idiocy in the west in two thousand years. Indeed we are agreed, Herr Rosenberg: the Hottentots would not build any German Cathedrals, nor French ones for the matter of that—certainly not. Not even the Letts could do that, Herr Rosenberg: but a Hottentot, and even a Lithuanian can become a saint and become blessed.

210. 10th May. The invasion of Belgium and Holland: yesterday the *Frankfurter Zeitung* wrote that strategically an attack on Holland would be a mistake and nonsensical! Why did it write that? From conviction? Simply out of ignorance and stupidity. How can there be conviction in Germany, when it is a sea of lies and is lost. Was it said tactically? Strategically a mistake and nonsensical! Is there a single idiot in the whole of Europe who does not know that Germany wants the Dutch coast? And so why?

211. In the wars of this world, man fights against man, not good angels against bad; even though it sometimes seems, and perhaps really is so, above and beside men. But the principal thing is: man fights against man, and as men they are roughly alike, but they may be very different where their mission is concerned, and as instruments.

212. Not every war is a judgment of God. But one can, for example name the following: Greeks against Persians,

Rome against Carthage, the West against the Huns and the Turks. And today, what are the Germans—after their apostasy? Are they not . . . . .?

213. Insults are thoroughly human because there are things which are human *and* insulting. Insults can only be misused because they can be rightly used. They are rightly used when language does not otherwise do justice to the thing, when the thing simply cannot be fully recognised without an insult. The Son of God, made man, used the most terrible insults of his time and people against the Pharisees.

214. The man who strikes the balance of the virtues is by no means mediocre. The rifleman who hits the centre of the target is no mediocre shot. And when he hits the bulls'-eye doesn't he hit the middle of all the rings?

215. The German *Herrgott-religion* must, nevertheless, distinguish itself from the religion of law of Jehova, for better or for worse. For worse, without a doubt: today the announcer with the dead German voice on *Deutschland-sender* (O what the Germans have sent us, what a mission!) made known the will of the German *Herrgott's* elect. It is not: an eye for an eye, a bomb for a bomb, but: five bombs for one!

Technical progress has made man's two weapons super-human and consequently inhuman: it has transformed the word into the press, and the sword into the cannon. The frightful thing is, that (without the direct intervention of God) this necessarily favours the wicked, who make un-scrupulous use of them.

216. It can now be seen that it is precisely the claptrap, which seemed so harmless as such, that calls forth, supports and maintains crimes and horrors on an unprecedented scale.

217. Whit Sunday. 12th May. The fate and thus the task of the German Christian is without parallel in history to which he might cling, it is even without the remotest analogy which, on a different level indeed, might serve as a guiding thread. He is alone! Everything that he feels, thinks and does has a question mark to it, questioning whether it is right. The leadership of Germany today, and of this there is not the faintest doubt, and it cannot be evaded, is consciously anti-Christian—it hates Christ whom it does not name. We are making war against peoples and States which although often only euphemistically Christian could not in any single instance be called definitely anti-Christian. And one cannot therefore avoid recognising the fact, that over and above being a war of power—it is a war of religion. And we Germans are fighting this war on the wrong side! We are, as to the majority, making war as willing slaves, and as to the minority, as the unwilling slaves of a government that has apostatized, strong in the passion of its despair and in its despicable subjects, and all of us, the slaves of slaves without honour—*ruimus in servitutum* (are rushing into slavery). From the very beginning, the repeatedly successful trick of these inhuman beings, sent to plague Europe, has been to combine, more or less, the special interests of their basely impulsive, greedy natures, intellectually speaking soulless and half-educated, with the true and genuine wishes and claims of the German people, combining them by an unprecedented skill in the art of lying. The climax of this hellish art has now been reached. Who does not love his country and his people *by nature?* There are innumerable people who love it more than their fathers or their mothers, their wives or their children, their brothers or their sisters, which is why it is always dangerous and almost a crime to over-excite this love. And who, then, will not *instinctively* wish his country to be victorious in a war? But: we Germans are on the side of apostasy. That is the German position. Today is Whitsunday, but my spirit is heavy, and the shadow of affliction is upon it. For I must live, whether the apostate is victorious or defeated, and with him—no, that is not true: the German people will be beaten, but not struck down and wiped out. The one ray of light in my mind is this: it is better for a people to be defeated and to suffer, than to win and apostatize. But if it were to be victorious? I should not then give up my faith. I can always pray: Lord, help thou my unbelief!

218. Almost everyone loves their country, and I have not the slightest regard for those who are proud of it, like our Führer. But how many love God at all, not to speak of loving him with their whole heart and their whole soul? That is what makes it so easy for the seducers to lead a people into the sin of apostasy; to turn the phrase, *my country right or wrong*, which at least recognises the difference between good and evil, into the simple apostasy: 'what serves the nation is good and right'.

219. If a satirist were to imagine that he had to carry on his work for centuries, endlessly, then he would be in hell. I am speaking, of course, of the satirist who is a real man. Karl Krauss once said to me: there must be an end; I think he wrote it somewhere. And he meant it in all seriousness. I think he did not wish for immortality in the Christian sense. Hence my fear of satire; though I was not without gifts for it and, what is more dangerous, enjoyed it and took pride in it.

220. The uniqueness, the natural election of the Greeks, manifests itself among other things in the fact that in theoretical philosophy there will always be Platonists and Aristotelians, and in practical philosophy stoics and epicureans; for they incorporate attitudes of mind which exist and will exist at all times, among Christians as well. On the other hand, there will not always be Cartesians, or Kantians or Hegelians, or even Schopenhaurians, and Nietzscheans. They have had their day.

221. 13th May. God will give victory to those who best subserve his end, which is the Kingdom of God, now, but above all in the future. Who that is, only God knows beforehand, and those in whom he wishes to confide. Who knows, perhaps God will decide in favour of the empire which once again allows the martyr to stand out in his original, visible form. And that would not be the democracies. We know nothing. In the beginning of its existence the Church was set in an empire that created martyrs. Whether the German apostates are to take over this task once again, and assume all the consequences, we do not know.

222. Rejoinder: We must learn to keep every eventuality in sight. To say, if this, that or the other happens, I should despair, is certainly not a Christian standpoint. No doubt, Kierkegaard knew perfectly well that it does not lie solely in the power of man's will not to despair, but in the grace of God. That is certainly true. Prayer then, is always the principal weapon.

223. There were probably many believers in the 16th century who believed that the hope of the Church stood or fell with the fate of Spain. And perhaps many despaired when the Armada was defeated, and heretical England triumphed. That is not of course comparable with what is happening now, any more than Napoleon's victory would have been comparable with Hitler's victory. Those are not comparisons, one must work on a much larger scale. In antiquity the victory of the Greeks over the Persians, the victory of the Romans over the Carthaginians (the victory of the Romans over the Greeks is secondary, the main decision had already been reached), and in Christian times, the victory of the Christian west on the fields of Catalonia over the Mohammedans. No other analogy stands up to it. It is no longer a war within the religion of the West. It is a war *against* the religion of the West on one side, on the

German namely. O, but do we know that so clearly? Is that, too, not known only to God?

224. A 'general rejoicing' and a 'general sorrow', by which is meant the joy and the sorrow of the 'nation' or of the 'State', can never satisfy more than the *middle* region of man's soul. It has heights and depths which are untouched by this feeling, unless it is sick and has fallen away from God.

225. A friend of Scheler's said to me: I have always thought you were unjust towards Scheler. It is true that he said that you had the art of saying things publicly to him which were meant *only* for him, and which he alone understood rightly. That is, of course, something I cannot judge. But I think that you sometimes come very near to impugning his *bona fides* as a thinker. I hope you will not question mine, if I explain the following to you. I always find your priests just about as stupid as possible, and using expressions and phrases that do not deceive my ear, when they announce that 'God permits evil'—and what evil. I always regret that I cannot put these priests before a concrete case, and study their faces. A child is slowly tortured by its parents and dies. And since God sees all things, does he not also see that he has permitted it, to use your *terminus technicus*, in order, perhaps, to achieve something good thereby, which would not have been possible previously. What would a powerful man be (and, to you, God is allpowerful) who stood by and permitted it? A monster, don't you agree? And God is—love! You and your religion have never been able to explain this and so many other frightful things—for example the absolutely useless suffering of animals which according to you do not have immortal souls and are guiltless—more humanely and divinely, more ethically and rationally, more soothingly to rebellious feelings than Scheler: namely that God permits such things because for the time being at any rate, he is still powerless. Can't you see that you are the slanderer of God, you who

maintain that he allows a child to be martyred, lets millions of animals suffer, *although* he could prevent it; and not us, who say God *cannot* change things, because he is imprisoned in a divine process, which some day *perhaps* will attain its end in the omnipotence of the Good.

226. It is not only in an objective sense that the voice which is *Deutschlandsender* is *in*human; it is a mockery of the supernatural life and the trinitarian God. That is for the moment (18th May) the only reason why I think that God will not let this pest win; but his Will be done! I believe, I can no longer lose my faith, but: God, help thou my thought!

227. It may be that the monumental cowardice of some German Catholics and Protestants, trying to get rid of the inward pest by means of outward events, will lead, as a punishment, to hundredfold increase of this Pest, and what is more through outward events. Then it will be a case of *mourir pour Dieu seul!*

228. The faces of our Generals and officers reproduced in the papers are all of a thoroughly uniform vitality, clean, and stigmatised so to say, not by passions but by thoroughness (Tüchtigkeit), often enough handsome in a disagreeable sort of way, and in an absolutely terrifying way, metaphysically *empty*. I have only to look at those photographs to hear their voices, identical with the voice of the announcer of Germany's 'mission', and that is the only thing which makes me doubt their victory, for in fact they have the faces of conquerors.

229. *Qua* soldier, the German soldier is the strongest and most frightful in the world because he does not need to know what he is fighting for, and in point of fact, under the Prussian hegemony, never hás known. It does not occur to him to ask. He is simply hypnotised by his favourite calling, for which he has an immense talent. And even the most depraved creature can catch his imagination at this point, and lead the nation into the direst suffering with absolute certainty. But it doesn't matter. The German soldier will continue to function immeasurably better than his machines, themselves quite good enough.

230. The paradoxical state of the world can be seen from the fact that scoundrel helps scoundrel more than the good, the good.

231. 19th May. Today the voice of the automat proclaiming the 'German Mission' announced one of the thoughts of its Lord and Master. The verve and the fighting spirit of the German soldier, as he overran Belgium and Holland can only be compared with the power of the Revolutionary armies that overran the whole of Europe and spread the ideas of the French Revolution. These ideas are antiquated; the future belongs to National Socialism. It is very strange what can be said in times such as these, and it seems as though it were a matter of complete indifference *what* was said, at least in respect of the *truth.* Let us see: the ideas of the French Revolution were liberty, equality, fraternity. These ideas were stolen from Christianity, and in some measure falsified and poisoned. But in themselves, they were ideas capable of arousing enthusiasm, and rightly so, understandably, for they are human. But now what are the ideas of national-socialism? Without any doubt, the exact opposite. Inequality in the place of equality, for the whole movement goes back to an Essay by Gobineau on the Inequality of Races. Unfreedom instead of liberty, for the Führer decides *everything,* even in science and art and above all what comes first in man, in religion and faith. Not fraternity, but enmity, for there is *one* race, which is superior to all others, to whom it certainly cannot show fraternity, and there are even races, like the Jews and the Poles, which compared racially with the 'Arians' are *sub-men,* certainly not brothers. These then are the ideas which we are bringing to the people of the world. And in their enthusiasm they will hardly recognise themselves. Though to pretend that our soldiers are good soldiers where these ideas are concerned is a fantastic contention.

232. Everything seems to be topsy-turvy: and it is harder to bear victories than defeats. But what is upside-down and who? That too is difficult to say. For if one attaches a disproportionate weight to external things, it robs them of weight and balance, and everything is topsy-turvy.

233. Nations, it is said, are just big children. True, but they are also evil! And with leanings towards great crimes, which is why they so often follow great criminals. They are 'naturally' stupid, and feel uncomfortable in the presence of great cleverness. Their favourites must indeed be shrewd, but at the same time stupid.

234. Vergil, the friend of Augustus, the greatest Emperor of the Empire that is the model of all Empires; Vergil who was so often able to express his horror of war, would today be silenced in a concentration camp. That is one of the characteristics of this accursed *Reich*, which by its express apostasy from 'the Faith', has fallen infinitely below an adventist paganism.

235. *Tantum dic verbo*—say but the word—said a Roman Captain to the Son of God made man. And now the Prussian Generals say it—but to whom! Even the standard of military honour is contained in the standard of Christ.

236. Victory and defeat are categories of human life in this aeon, and correspond to joy and sadness. But the victory of the good is not the same as the victory of evil, and the defeat of good is not the same as the defeat of evil. In the joy of the one lies perhaps the justice of God, and in

the other case, the hatred of hell. In the sadness of the one there lies perhaps the peace of God, which is above all reason; and in the other the despair of hell.

237. Does not the Cross of Christ stand threateningly before every Christian in this form: that in the end Christ was looked upon as the enemy of his people? This war is the end of all National Churches desiring to be Christian.

238. The Catholic Church is very far from having recognised the treasures of knowledge (and above all the knowledge of *time* in so far as it is related to the Kingdom of God), and still less has it assimilated all the knowledge that has been brought to light by men outside the Church, who loved Christ with their whole heart. Catholic theologians have behaved very poorly towards men like Blumhardt, Hilty and Kierkegaard. They cannot even see the pure gold shining through the dust of heresy—they only see the dust. And that is a great pity!

239. 22nd May. France has many saints, which is to say that it is a country of prayer, for only a country where many people pray produces many saints. At the present time there must be many praying in France. But perhaps it is laid down that they will not be heard—for the present! The Church knows that in most cases public prayers are not heard, but she seldom ventures to say so.

240. How peace is to come, in any sense resembling the *pax romana*, I do not know. To me, that is utterly obscure. The most probable thing, it seems to me, is a state of exhaustion. But no peace!
    Culturally a frightful desert. Everywhere. Most of all in Germany. Southern Germany and Catholic Germany is prussianised, irretrievably perhaps, and so destroyed. In Italy, Fascism is a roller that levels everything flat. Will England and France follow? America is unfortunately, as it

seems to me, too young a country. But I may be mistaken.
Ultimately that is a matter of indifference; for the decision
does not lie there. Perhaps there will be none, none at all.
Lord, help thou my unbelief!

241. 23rd May. The unalterable law of 'the world' is
that evil is fought with evil, and that the devil is driven out
by Beelzebub. And so long as that remains unaltered,
Christianity is not victorious.

242. It is often said that the mark of the German is his
refusal to compromise. But up till now I have asked in
vain for examples. What about religion? There is no such
thing as German atheism in the uncompromising form in
which it exists in latin countries. The Germans still have a
sentimental divinity of woodland and stream, a lyrical,
rutting divinity. In the same way there is no such thing
as frank materialism in German philosophy—it is all
second-hand—though there has always been a halfway-
house philosophy, a 'biological' philosophy, a *Lebensphilosophie*.
In the Christian life the religious Orders have always been
uncompromising. Yet not one of the great religious Orders
was founded in Germany, not to speak of the really strict
ones. It is something quite different, I think, which has led
to this undoubtedly false assertion. It resides in the main
in an inebriated sense of the vast, and this prevents thought,
hinders right thinking based upon a natural and supernatural sense of measure and proportion, given to us by the
philosophy of Aristotle and Plato and in the supernatural
by the Church. Hence the fiasco of German mysticism in
Eckhardt. And on a different plane, in the field of political
struggles, the reason why these struggles are so poisonous
and violent is not because there is purity in this will to
realise an idea recognised as true, without compromise, but
because there is an incapacity, clouded by feeling, to see
or to hear the right on the other side. It is very often
stupidity, and nothing more.

243. Are the Germans not lacking in two great and related yet not identical qualities, and is this not the reason why their history is wanting in the very deepest colours? *Générosité* and *magnanimitas!* For the first we have no German word at all, it is a specifically French thing. For the second we have a resounding word; *grossherzig*, large-hearted. But it is more a matter of German longing than of a German reality. The German is not *généreux*, or at least very seldom; and then it is a miracle. That is why there are no great lovers in our literature and history—for *générosité* is the gate to great love, to natural as indeed to supernatural love!— With us it exists neither in reality nor in poetry. The only exception might be Goethe, and he is a great European rather than a great German. We have not got the great lovers that all other European nations have, though they make our hearts beat faster. Nor have we the great saints; there were no saints at the Reformation, such as Thomas More and Fisher; and they were both *généreux*. *Magnanimitas* is a political virtue: Augustus is its great representative figure, and Vergil its incomparable poet. I think that some of our Mediæval Emperors shared in this virtue; and later the Habsburgs knew it. The powerful Prussians, and what comes from them today, are all 'small-minded', the opposite of large-hearted. And France dishonoured herself in Versailles because it was small-minded, and is at this moment doing penance for it, though probably only 'for a time'.

244. It is not every man who can be the 'scourge of God'. Even Attila had to be *chosen*. The vanity of mankind is mysterious and indestructible. The 'scourge of God' is proud of it, not so much of being 'the scourge of God' as of the title.

245. Behind the frightful grimace of this world, there are so many unhappy men. And now that you are old, you should never forget that!

246. The Tower of Babel is always being built, and after its destruction those who were building it will always say, to the end of the world: 'We only missed by a hair's breadth. It was only a very minor mistake, otherwise we should have been successful'—or: 'It was sabotaged, the Christian poison . . . .'

247. The little whore called history in Germany today, for sale to the feeblest individual, exploited by those without honour who support the ruling clique, is not 'history'. Although one might at a pinch, say that history was 'made' in Germany today, history is no longer 'written' in Germany. That will happen elsewhere, or if it happens *in* Germany, then it will be written *by* others.

248. Ever since men ceased to believe in eternal life, we have had history in the place of the Judgment, history which is not finished but flowing on, and which, if there is no Judgment, will flow on for ever, into nothingness or the Eternal Return of all things—history, then, is the last court of appeal. And the paradox is that history is suddenly to be truth itself, justice itself, honesty itself! But history is written by men, who either speak the truth, or lie, are just or unjust. That is why history, humanly speaking and without the guidance of God, is a very questionable matter. The Gospel narrates the betrayal by Judas and the denial by Peter with absolute objectivity. That is something quite impossible in a purely human Party. Present day history, an episode let us hope, certainly lies more than was ever the case before. If God did not have other ways and possibilities, despair nowadays would be an understandable way out, assuming always that man was concerned about the truth. The most painful experience of those who seek the truth is: that to the majority of men, the truth is just about the most indifferent thing of all. Yet that is not quite right. They do, in a way, desire the truth, but they are afraid of the effort it requires. And so they believe the lies that are told them, not as lies but as the truth. That is easier.

249. À propos the 'uncompromisingness' of the German. I do not believe in it. Not at least in any failure to compromise where the development of a clear idea is concerned. 'Clear' is the operative word. That is where my principal objection arises. Uncompromising and clarity are related, and that is what the German mind lacks, except in the relatively low sphere of technical matters. Though even now, everything is not quite clear. What characterises the German, what he has in a pre-eminent degree is: *Eigensinn,* self-will, obstinacy. The history of the Reformation is only too full of it. And Michael Kohlhaas is a purely German figure. And his creator!* Self-will is the absolute enemy of love, and above all of the love of God. Self-will and sanctity are utterly incompatible.

250. 26th May. If I were to die today (and since the 14th March† I no longer fear death as such, on the contrary, how welcome it would be!), were I to die today, replete with sadness and melancholy, like all those of this world who are mellow and ripe with years, seeing only darkness ahead, the return of the *dark ages* in fact—I should not die in despair. It seems as though nothing could now rob me of faith. May it remain so! O God, may it remain so! If I were to die today, in complete disagreement with the ruling spirit of the people to whom I belong, I should not die in despair, and might not that be a *témoignage?* For today one may surely be sad, may one not? Is that not so? Difficulties I may have, and live under a cloud, but I also have an infallible method: when the difficulties become too great I throw myself upon God who is inconceivable. The inconceivableness of God hides me. Not it alone, of course,

---

* A story by Heinrich von Kleist the motto of which might be *fiat justitia pereat mundus.*

† The day of Haecker's arrest.

but God's grace. It bears me up upon the abyss. I should not die in despair. More I will not say, for I would not lie. And I also see the hour when I shall no longer *be able* to lie.

251. When I am told that the German youth of today, the official youth, know nothing of two thousand five hundred years of Christian and adventist history, know nothing of it, do not wish to know anything of it and cannot be moved by it, I know it is true and I am sad. But when I am told that there is none among them who in his inmost being is moved by it, then I feel cheerful once again, for I do not believe it, and it is not true. They exist, and they are the aristocracy of the youth of this country. They will live under a cloud, as I do. But they will stand in the glory of an eternal light, as I shall do. And they will know it, as I too do.

252. I never cease to wonder at our capacity to wonder; My wonder is inexhaustible for wonder. Why do we feel a sense of wonder? Does it not presuppose that the mind which marvels is in a sense a stranger to the 'being' in the presence of which it marvels? A perfectly normal man may fall to wonder at things which are strange and unusual to him; but he does not wonder at everyday things and the customary things with which he has grown up. Philosophy begins with wonder at the usual, everyday thing, but does that not imply a gulf between 'being' at which I wonder and me, who am in wonder? Me! Who and what am I? Do I not belong to 'being'? So that—what is it that makes me wonder, ultimately, if not I myself? Who is it then, that wonders. And one's thought is engulfed in a sense of giddiness. Is it being that wonders at being? Does God, in fact, wonder? And these are but the reflections of the impotence of our understanding, in face of the inconceivability of being.

253. *Rejoinder.* One can never tire of wonder......O, yes, I do, when I receive no answer.

254. Pain sometimes pulls a man together, so that he should not dissolve in pleasure; for just as in the end pleasure is a solvent, pain draws one together. And looking round one often finds that the naturally pleasure loving individuals are exposed to the severest physical pain. There must be a certain natural compensation at work here.

255. Rejoinder: Whatever makes you complain that Justice is wanting in this world? Is it not perfectly just that, when it has dominated long enough one nation's lie should be exchanged against another nation's lie? And so it goes on. That is 'just', and the world needs nothing more.

256. After the war certainly, perhaps even *during* the war, the social Revolution which is moving towards the complete extinction of the bourgeois order, will no doubt keep nationalism down to some extent. In any case, it had passed its zenith with the German madness of a natural, racial Elect. Even were Germany to be temporarily victorious, it would relinquish the principle of nationalism still further in favour of the Imperial principle.

257. 29th May. In the heart of which nation has God placed the mysterious, hidden certainty and expectation of victory? I do not know. And yet this is the nation which will be victorious, so that it does not matter what it may portend in other respects.

258. Ultimately it is the Kingdom of God which is at stake, and the war is about the 'faith'. And to which people, factually, will the commands of the Trinitarian God be given? It will receive the leadership of mankind from God, quite regardless of what race it belongs to.

259. 31st May. It is because the ultimate and the highest cause of this war is the hatred of Christ and the Kingdom of God, that Mussolini's policy is so disgusting and

despicable. Simply for the sake of his romantic Imperium
he supports the Reich of Antichrist. Mussolini, it is said,
will attack today or tomorrow. His European name is—
Betrayal.

260. Who takes the sword shall perish by the sword.
Every *Reich* will perish by the weapons with which it was
founded and sustained. The weapons of Christ's Kingdom
were, in the beginning, and must remain: faith, hope and
love. Go to it, then, all of you who wish to conquer
the Kingdom of Christ, and you are many today,—go
to it: with the weapons of faith, of hope and of love: the
Kingdom of Christ will lie at your feet. You will have
conquered!

261. Nowadays, can anyone in Germany who is not a babe
at the breast express his immediate feelings directly? Are
they not immediately snuffed out at their very birth by that
frightful apparatus called Propaganda? Are they not
deformed, or better still twisted out of the true with lies
into a 'national feeling', an artificial product, claptrap!
What inhuman results are bound to follow!

262. If this war is just a war between 'Plutocrats' and
'Have-nots', between Capitalists and Socialists for the goods
of this world, or their division, then in an insane way it is
laughable, and of course criminal, to heap up mountains
of corpses for such a matter. But I do not believe it. Wars
like this are fought for higher things.

263. The man who explicitly does not believe and does not
will to believe (for the will to believe belongs to believing)
in an eternal life, that is to say in a personal life after death,
will become an animal, an animal being which among other
things, man is. Man is 'planned as spirit', as Kierkegaard
puts it, but that includes the immortality of the soul. Whoever relinquishes that also gives up the spirit of man.

264. Those who give up all spirituality and consequently life after death, can only regard marriage as a stud. And that is what the German state does officially, without any shame whatsoever. And they think the hegemony of the West will fall to them? But, my friends, then it would simply not be the West any more!

265. One is constantly allowing oneself to be impressed by German thoroughness and their superficial decency, forgetting the German *Herrgott-religion* that lies behind it, that is certainly an abomination to God! I martyrise a whole people and then call heaven to witness, and shout on the wireless, when a couple of my people are oppressed (perhaps!—it may of course be a lie), and I *believe* in my right to do both (the average German does). Has the like ever happened before? I don't believe it. It is an appalling degeneration, or is it perhaps 'our norm'? Then let each one of us do penance! *Mea culpa!*

266. That things first of all sound right, and that dissonance comes afterwards—is the first principle of my philosophy. And so: Good comes before evil, Truth before the lie, and the beautiful before the ugly. That is my whole philosophy.

267. 'Terror' is the discovery of fallen spirits. It is a spiritual weapon of the soul aimed by evil against good and evil, a weapon which is not, consequently, like material arms, indifferent in itself, but which is evil in itself. It may not be used by good men, it cannot be used by them, because it makes them themselves evil. Terror is the discovery of anarchical spirits. It is the weapon of anarchists, using this word as the opposite of those who believe in hierarchy. For those are the two poles: Anarchy against hierarchy. The kingdom of antichrist is essentially anarchical.

The 'organisation' of Anarchy and Terror is sometimes deceptive. At the present time, in Europe, Terror is organised by the 'Germans'. (It is difficult nowadays to speak of Germans and not of the 'Germans'). The gift of organisation is to a certain extent 'natural' to the German: it must be related to their vocation (betrayed) for dominion and for the *Reich*. It is really the German organisation of Terror which makes it so frightful.

268. 'Fear ye not'. Almost all the messages of the angel of God to man begin with these words; and today they have acquired a special significance. 'Abyss calls to abyss', the hellish abyss of organised terror awakes in us a sense of the heavenly terror, of the divine 'fearlessness'. We live in the night of faith, and it is our only light. To him that is, whom God has led so far that he grasps it in prayer and peace, which is above all reason.

269. Everything has *its* time, but in the *same* time; that is much more difficult to grasp or even to perceive in general, than that *everything* has *its* place, though in *one* space, for that is only a weak analogy of the first, a flat, one-dimensional analogy of the depths of the individual rhythm of time within 'contemporaneity'. Every musical time has *its* time, but within the time of the rhythm and the melody: another feeble image.

270. 1/2nd June. Newman's theory respecting the strange coincidence of natural events at particular moments, as signs of divine providence, came to mind as I read that the weather was misty. That is how the Cardinal, were he still living, might have understood it: an angel smoothed the channel which is normally rough at this time of year, and spread the darkness of mist and fog over the sea at the same time. And so ten thousand were saved.

271. To the German Herrgott-religion: Your Priests are lyrical, emotional, or technical in their activity rather than theological. From time to time one must explain their Credo to oneself. The German *Herrgott-religion* does not promise eternal life or the resurrection of the body. That much is certain. It appears however to promise the eternal continuance of the German people. And that of course, is pure nonsense. This planet had a beginning, and it will also cease to be. It is really astonishing that the Germans, so proud of their science, should swallow such nonsense. I can believe something, the ultimate sense of which is concealed from me. And as a Christian, I do so. But I cannot believe something that has no meaning at all. The German *Herrgott-religion* proclaims that whatever serves the people is right (law). This proclamation is affirmed in countless speeches and written works. It is not, of course, so meaningless, new and original as the first proposition. It is quite in line and consonant with the Human, the All-too-Human. What is new is the radical way in which this self-evidently false axiom is put into practice, the undiluted shamelessness and the boundless hypocrisy. In all other cases, nations are *either* shameless *or* hypocritical. The combination of the two was not to be foreseen, but it has been achieved. In his own sphere the German *Herrgott* is not illogical. For example in the teaching on marriage and sexual morality which he imposes upon his believers. This, too has been made perfectly clear by its preachers, both in public and secretly, as clearly as the conception of law. The best one can say for it is that it reduces man to an animal, it is a stud-farm morality. The soul of a spiritual man, it consumes with disgust. It remains to be seen if there are any spiritually minded men among the Germans. The Catholic Church will have to watch out that the fruitfulness which its teaching on marriage inculcates, is not confused with the animal fertility of the German *Herrgott*. They mix like fire and water.

272. It is quite conceivable (a subject for comedy) that a man who alone, among many, correctly foretold a disaster, in which he himself is involved, should get pleasure from his suffering because he was right, because he *knew* it. It is

curious how universal man's will to be right is, to have been right. How does it arise? Perhaps it implies that he values knowledge, *simply as knowledge*, a fact which does not otherwise come to light among men.

273. The Germans will not, like the Greeks and Romans, write their own history. The Germans have made it impossible for themselves to write that history. Since the Reformation, and still more so since the apostasy, they can only write party histories, necessarily full of lies. I have always said that Prussia is a provincial thing, even though it develops for a moment as it does now, into a monster. And being provincial, Prussia does not write its own history itself.

274. *Le mieux est l'ennemi du bien*—'The better is the enemy of the good', is a sentence concealing great suffering and very many difficulties. This epigrammatic, this almost sad expression of the objective situation, and of the fact that there exists at the same time a good and a better between which a man is free to choose, may easily lead to confusion and to misunderstanding. The better is not, in itself, and in the sphere of pure being, the 'enemy' of the good (they are ordered hierarchically, peacefully, compatibly, one beside the other), but only in the transposed and comparative language, which is the language of the will and its struggles, where man can rise from 'the good' to 'the better'. There are many to whom this represents the very essence of tragedy, indeed of 'Christian' tragedy; but that is only a confusion of terms. The young man who did not follow Christ's invitation to seek the 'better' in the place of 'the good' is not a tragic figure. The mystery goes deeper, and lies beyond the conception of 'guilt' which belongs to tragedy, lies in the sphere of 'love' itself and its unfathomableness, in the growing sacrifices through which it descends into itself. God would have been 'good' even though the Eternal Son had not become man, God would have been 'good' even though the Eternal Son made man had not been

sacrificed on the Cross. And the man who discovers that the better is the enemy of the good is on the track of this divine love—and not of tragedy.

275.   German idealism, in Kant and Fichte, is a Prussian affair. Schelling belongs elsewhere; he was a spontaneously speculative mind and a gnostic. Hegel too was originally a great speculative mind, but as happened again and again with so many south German minds, he became infected with Prussianism and was corrupted. Prussian idealism took the heart of flesh and blood from the German and in its place gave him one of iron and paper. The German heart is now a material all of its own, of paper and iron, claptrap and act. That is really the 'inhuman' quality of the German as a Prussian product.

276.   The association of duty and claptrap is what really dehumanises man. It is a characteristic Prussian-German discovery. It is twofold in its consequence: a man does his duty for the sake of claptrap, or: his duty is no more than claptrap. Both things happen today. But there is still some sound sense in the world and it will defend itself with both hands against this inhuman conception. Even Frederick II's words about being the servant of the state was a mere claptrap. He was much more honest when he admitted that he fell upon Silesia out of vanity and longing for fame. As far as Prussia is concerned, it is enough to make the very concept of duty hated, to make people forget its truth and its justification.

277.   Dictatorships are *always* a 'feverish' condition. We know from the life of the individual how long a fever can last. The same thing is true of the moral life of a people. It is not the norm.

278.   My impression is strengthened as time goes on, that the Germans and the Jews have something in common which is not found elsewhere among European peoples. *Only* a German Christian can cut himself off from the immediate destiny and the immediate history of his people, as the Jewish Christian has always done, from the beginning down to the present day, without cutting himself off from it spiritually and in respect of the history of our salvation— on the contrary: the importance of this cannot be exaggerated. But it is hardly noticed. Even on the natural plane there is an analogy to this fact. It is only among Germans that so many thinkers of distinction, on the purely natural plane—and that is to say without the Christian love of the true Christian—have taken up an attitude violently antagonistic to their own people, beginning—and how significant that is—with Luther, and continuing with Hölderlin, Schopenhauer, Nietzsche.

279. This war confirms my thesis that quantity creates a kind of quality. Twenty thousand tanks are not merely arithmetically more than two thousand tanks, they are something *other*, and they act as a quality. It is as a result of this quality that the Germans are at present winning. Only one ought to recollect that *no* other quality is so easy to imitate as this one, even in its effects. It is the lowest form of quality, somewhere between quantity and quality.

280. It looks as though victor and vanquished were alike intoxicated with the thought that this is the greatest battle in the history of the world. Never was the primacy of quantity in this technical age more clearly demonstrated *ad oculos*, nor indeed the meaning of *vanitas vanitatum* more clearly shown.

281. The hour of evil is the hour in which the devil does greater 'miracles' than God.

282. A curse on every wish that blurs the sight, paralyses the tongue, cramps the hand and prevents the truth being seen, said and written.

283. Apart from 'the faith' the only choice is between the 'inadequate' and the 'absurd'. Bourgeois Europe chose the 'inadequate'; and was followed in this choice by the Fascists. Individual geniuses prefer some 'absurd' or other, usually gnostic in origin or nature, like Schelling and Scheler, or of a private nature, like Nietzsche (the Eternal Recurrence) or Rilke (Weltinnenraum). The faces of those who chose the inadequate as a religion are, so to say, one-dimensional. They themselves talk of health and harmony. One cannot deny that at the moment a tremendous effort is being made with the help of the religion of the inadequate, the religion of 'this world', to master the life of man and to lead it. Ultimately the attempt is a battle against God, and the most terrible decision He could make would be for the attempt to be allowed to succeed—that would be the end of Europe.

284. 14th June. Entry into Paris. If the Germans were real pagans they would surely feel something like fear of the envy of the Gods. But they are worshippers of the 'inadequate' and find it perfectly in order. Or am I mistaken? Has God not yet deserted us?

285. 'To say what is' is difficult indeed when being is transitory. And what being is not except the being of God, that we do not know? The most lasting, the truest, and the nearest expression of reality is ultimately: everything is transitory—and its variations.

286. I entertain no doubt that the religion of the most primitive peoples is of a depth unplumbed by comparison with the German *Herrgott-religion*, which has never been equalled for blasphemous shallowness and simple brutishness. Behind every primitive religion there is always something, a fullness that has not been plumbed, through which man has not seen. Behind the German *Herrgott-religion* there is vacuity, emptiness and nothing else, the same unending nothing which was, moreover, at the back of German idealism, only that its façade made a finer impression. And of course the German *Herrgott-religion* has its own voice, the voice of the announcer of the 'German mission'—the *Deutsche-sendung*.

287. It is always a good thing to meditate from time to time on the commandments, general and particular, of the *Herrgott-religion*. Thus: Whatever is useful to the German people is Right; cannons rather than butter; the individual is nothing, the people everything; there is one race, of which the German people is the mind and the heart, a race that has created *out of itself* everything that is great and good in the world. That is the gospel which the heavily armed missionaries of the German *Herrgott-religion* have to bring to all the peoples of the world.

288. Nothing is so successful, visible, direct, quantitively calculable, and consequently capable of being foretold, as technical progress, the daughter of mathematical science. 'Success' is the accompaniment of technique. The nation which devotes itself to technical progress is successful. Probably, or even certainly, it can only be bought at the cost of the loss of one's soul. Man is *quodammodo omnia* (in a sense all things) and so too a machine. Theoretically and philosophically *l'homme machine* is a French discovery, but it has been realised in practice to the furthest limits of possibility by Prussian Man who was victorious over the German.

289. 'Success', in so far as it can be calculated, included in one's reckoning, and is therefore a 'gain' which has been earned, is the exact contrary of God's blessing, which is, in an absolute sense, *gratis*. No worldly, or demoniacal copy is possible, or can ever hope to replace it. A blessing is visible, even naturally, but it appears as it were visibly out of the invisible, whereas success is the result of something visible. While success is explained away in the reckoning, a blessing is always a mystery. Success is part of nature, it is almost the product of nature, prepared and arranged by man as *technique*. A Blessing is divine. The least successful of men and peoples may be blessed by God, and the most clamorous success may be a curse. And the confusion of these two things and concepts has today produced the most terrible confusion of mind. The 'prophetic' voice of the Church is dumb, as though her prophetic office were suspended. Does that too belong to the hour of evil? And every individual man is left to fumble his way through the night. Success is not simply a blessing, nor is failure simply a curse. Nor is the reverse true, as Christians have often thought.

290. If Christ did not rise from the dead, then Christians, in the words of St. Paul, are fools. That is the brutal formulation given by the Jew, who cannot imagine happiness without relation to the body. And with that he is probably nearer the reality of being than the idealistic European, who as a Christian would naturally also regard himself as lost and deceived if Christ did not rise again from the dead. Yet he would no doubt express himself differently from the fleshly Jew: If Christ did not rise from the dead, then God does not exist—then Christ is God, and we too are Gods, and better than all those who have been held as such—to that extent we are not deceived, for what is the pleasure of seventy years compared with our idea? Or again, he might say: even though God were still to exist, he nevertheless treated Christ shamefully, and so Christ is *greater*. But how despairing it all sounds, the Jew as well as the Greek—if Christ did not *rise again*. *Et resurrexit!*

291. The German *Herrgott-religion* is a 'Weltanschauung' this side of every true religion, and of every true metaphysic. In this it is nearest of all to Islam, although Mohammedanism had a primitive belief in immortality. The German *Herrgott-religion* is also a child of German idealism, which in its turn was an offspring of the German heresy. In Kant it immediately reached a high point, and continued with Fichte, Hegel and their lesser followers. Schelling, a gnostic, and Schopenhauer, a disciple of Indian thought, were both metaphysicians. But they are both without influence on the *Herrgott-religion*. As a substitute for the first principle of religion (which is the love of God) it has a conception of honour run mad, and as a substitute for true metaphysics, the first principle of which is Being and the primacy of the spirit, it has an infantile mystical conception, *Blut und Boden*, blood and soil.

292. 23rd June. The soul of the man who only has ears for the noise of these times will soon be miserably impoverished. He will soon be found to be deaf to all reasonable language.

293. *Rejoinder:* The men of today, my friend, feel the need of salvation far less than the man of two thousand years ago. They even find life in hell quite bearable, because they do not see that it is hell, do not feel the need of salvation. How should they feel any need for salvation? Who still thirsts after justice? They drink injustice like water, they even taste it like good wine. Who still hungers after truth? Lies are their daily bread, and they cannot live without it. And as with truth and justice, so with purity and love. And then: they only believe in this life, they do not believe in the immortality of the soul. And in the last extremity salvation is immediately to hand: death, freely chosen death, or as it used to be called, self-slaughter. The age, my friend, is not propitious for a religion of salvation.

294. To taste the happiness of an hour, and the hour itself, as time, as duration in the past, is a thing of age, and not for youth, unless it is that a man is predestined to an early death.

295. When a man perceives that the person he is talking to simply cannot see the things about which he is talking, then he should stop talking.

296. Man's power is great. Wherever he goes, he alters the face of the earth. He cannot certainly put out a star, or set another alight. But I am careful in denying the possibility that some day cosmic forces may be used. There is a great deal to be awaited from that quarter.

297. Two thousand years of Christianity ought finally to have inculcated the lesson that power, of whatever kind, is not the means by which to make a man a Christian. It is contrary to the will of God, though he may at times wish a man to seize the kingdom of God by power. In the first instance violence is done to man's freedom; in the second, a man exalts and magnifies his own freedom. And freedom is what is in the balance! It is in the mode of freedom that God created man, and how much more so the Christian, the *homo spiritualis.* How gently God, the *all-powerful,* handles the free will of his saints! Until he has led them to an inexplicable union with Him. And he can only lead them once they have given him—their will. God desires the *Will* of man.

298. The richer Being is, the more images it requires for its description and the more inadequate every particular image is. The art of rightly using images is indeed rare. Some writers are all too logical and rationalistic, the image is drawn down to the last detail, as though an image (of speech) had to coincide in every detail with the thing it purposes to represent. A great error in the language of imagery, for often just a couple of strokes, one or two colours of the appropriate image are enough, and express the whole genius of an image. Others, inferior writers, are just bunglers producing a daub: a donkey serves not only as the image for a horse but for a lion.

299. The command to love: thou shalt love God with thy whole heart .... creates such great difficulties for the philosopher of this world that there are many who hold it to be nonsensical. Love cannot be commanded, compelled, they say, and of course they are right. If anything must come 'from the heart', must be free and without cause, so to speak, it is love. It is driven away rather than enticed by a command. But the obligation of the first and principal commandment is above all else an objective command, at least in the first place; it demonstrates the divine order, it asserts: the right and true relation of man to God is love, and indeed love from the whole heart, with the whole mind, with all one's strength. And in fact an obligation may be understood in several ways. On the basis of this eternal order and of this eternal being as it should be, the individual man can do a great deal subjectively without doing the impossible, or doing under compulsion what can only be done freely: loving. The commandment does not say: thou shalt love under compulsion, which is impossible in the sense that one can work under compulsion; the commandment is that thou shalt love. That is perfectly in order, it is an order which can only be overturned because it is based upon freedom. It is certainly to be observed that if love without freedom is neither possible nor real, neither is freedom possible or real without love. The love of God is a spark in the heart of man, a natural disposition, something in fact which he does not make himself. 'To have to' do something always implies that the will is directed either towards 'willing' or towards willing something in particular. In the sphere of freedom, in which love belongs, 'to have to' means that I must make room for freedom, 'prepare the way'. Love itself comes freely, like grace, to which it belongs.

300. *Am deutschen Wesen soll die Welt genesen*—The world shall profit from the Germans—and it is not said for the sake of the rhyme, it is said in all seriousness, it is really meant.

In any case the contrary, so much more probable, also rhymes: *am deutschen Wesen soll die Welt verwesen*—they will corrupt the world. *Salus ex Germanis*, that is what is meant. Not *salus ex Judaeis*. The history of the world, or rather sacred history, is to be overturned. I am horrified when I see and hear to what an extent people underestimate this apostasy. Their attitude to the Christian religion is not simply machiavellian, or napoleonic, or fascist, a purely political attitude, bent upon bringing Christianity under their dominion; no, they mean to destroy and supplant it. *Salus ex Germanis:* A German saviour and bearer of light is to replace Christ. What a good thing he has been photographed so often and that his voice has been recorded. They will bring a moral, a religious, and what is more a material misery upon the world that we can only imagine with difficulty, that only the apocalyptic author on Patmos and here and there one of God's saints has seen in the spirit; all that will be fulfilled, if God wishes to wait. How dark everything is before our eyes.

301. It is not easy to take the principles of Christianity and to deduce how a Christian should behave in a concrete case in order to be, without any doubt, a Christian. For Christianity is not a philosophical problem composed of lifeless, abstract principles. It is, on the contrary, of its very principles that every individual can always be under the living providence of the living God in every particular case —and then there is nothing to deduce, for God is freedom. Nevertheless, it is easier (since deduction is in any case easier than induction), than to argue from the life and acts of, say, our present governors, to their faith. What sort of a faith can these men have? Perhaps one can get behind it by adopting the *via negationis*. They cannot believe in an eternal life, for then they would have to believe in an eternal judgment. Their lives and acts, however, show clearly that they do not do so. Or else they act thus and coerce their real inner belief; that may of course be so.

All that I can and wish to say is that their *public* life and acts presuppose a belief which would lead a man who thinks, and who recognises the demands of logic in the right place, into a lunatic asylum or into some agonising intellectual inferno. Their belief is wholly limited to this world, and with this belief they believe they will prosper, that with it one is the strongest and can command all others, and that to this end *everything* is allowed except the breaking of a certain arbitrary, chance code of honour, changing according to circumstances, and with the exception of a few generalities, applicable to every warlike people: a romantic, barbaric form of infantilism. The metaphysical kernel of their belief in this world, as a substitute for religion, contains the following absurdity: the *eternity* of the German nation in a world which is *not* itself *eternal*. If we believe that, then we shall exactly fulfil what the German *Herrgott* demands of us. That is the belief which is offered to the German people as a substitute for Christianity. Those who do not confess this belief are, at the very least, unworthy of taking part in public life. Our pre-Christian forefathers did not of course believe in any such nonsense. And that is only made possible by the semi-education which sets the standard (if one may use the word) today.

302. Certain words and phrases are acquiring a psychological usage which quite prevails over the original, purely logical, sense. For example, a man says: I heard footsteps and tried to interpret them. But the man who made them was not the one I expected. I was disappointed. Logically that means he was in error and was then freed from it. But in present-day language he says more, namely that he would have preferred the man who, in error, he expected, to the man who actually came. In the opposite case he would have said: I made a mistake, or possibly: I was agreeably disappointed.

303. 7th July. The dove! Companion of the oracular gods in the first dark advent. Messenger of Salvation and

E

sign of the Holy Spirit—shall I fashion my Ode, impressionist in its beginning, theological in its end? Eternity must be morning, noon, evening and night, for how should I do without any one of them? And the voice of the dove: bless us, O powerful Spirit and say: Amen. The clear sayings and the dark contradictions betray the night of my thought and my weakness. Through hearing I came to the word, and through the word to the form: and out of word and form there arose the poem.

304. How sovereign is Pascal's observation which came to my mind as I listened to the announcement of a victory: One could overlook the fact that the youth, Alexander, wished to conquer the world, but at his age Cæsar should have known better. We are now in the process of learning, if it does not drive us mad, the infantile assumptions concealed behind this kind of *Gloria Mundi.* Still, perhaps that is to take the world *trop cavalièrement.* Perhaps God loves those simple minds that give their lives for 'wealth and honour' rather than the proud man who despises the normal life of this world, to which belongs war and conquest. In that there is no doubt some truth, but where the Germans of today are concerned the thing is: what does it profit you to win the whole world and to lose your soul! It is no longer a matter of childishness and youthfulness, but of a sickly infantilism which is at once guilt and punishment.

305. Not every grape is capable of fermenting nobly. A 'culture' is presupposed. Thus in literature there is a certain aristocratic boredom. It presupposes a culture, and its greatest name is Adalbert Stifter.

306. 10th July. And so after all it is possible that a man knowing that he will fall into madness, should nevertheless acquiesce beforehand, and commend his spirit to God before collapsing into the abyss: Lord, into thy hands, into thy hands . . . .

307. There is the dew of tears on all beauty in this aeon.

308. How difficult it is to imagine what man can have been before the fall, not so much, of course, in the abstract, but in the concrete. Moreover the difficulty lies in the fact that the whole of nature would be different, and even in this aeon it can sometimes be different for the Saint: Francis.

309. There can be no doubt: whoever is convinced that only this world exists, that there is no eternal life for the individual person, then as ruler he must see to it that Christianity is stamped out, for it presupposes all that. He must also fight with all his might, with poison and deafening noise, against the merely *natural* longing of mankind for eternal life which was fulfilled through Christ. The doubt remains, however, whether a man can be as absolutely convinced that life is wholly and entirely of this world, as of the fact that England is an island, for example, and whether he does not merely wish it so for some reason or other (often transparent enough). In that case it is not his judgment which is in question, but his intention and his *will* that decides the matter.

310. Spernere sperni (despising contempt) is only possible in God. Every unbaptised (and in the ultimate sense) unredeemed spirit is proud. The subtlest pride is in the humblest. The man who does not want to be noticed, nevertheless wants this to be noticed. And here I can only praise the politicians; they are not so refined.

311. Nature is stronger than culture as soon as culture relaxes its effort for a moment. How quickly a cultivated rosebush goes back to its wild form, and how vulnerable and breakable is the culture of man. And this is the fact that the politicians of today overlook with incredible levity. The very fame they desire presupposes the culture they are

in the process of destroying. And what then of their fame?
O, if only they suspected how quickly men will not only
despise them but forget them. They are fed to the teeth
with them.

312. A politician who knows his job catches men (leaving
aside the crudely material basis of which he is not absolute
master) not so much through honour, which presupposes a
moral person, whereas he needs a mere instrument, 'num-
bers', but rather through the desire for honours or *ambition*
which is among the lowest and most childish of passions.
An ambitious man, desiring honours may perfectly well
be so distant from any conception of honour that he is
capable of the most contemptible and disgraceful actions
towards others. Honour is based upon the hierarchic ordering of the human 'being', that is to say upon the recognition
of that order. If the order is perverted and truth falsified,
then honour is reduced to a miserable and dangerous
caricature of itself. There is a'positive' honour, just as there
is a positive law, a natural honour and a natural law. If
I falsify the natural law with the proposition 'what serves
the nation is right', I falsify honour at the same time, for
honour is necessarily bound up with the preservation of
the law. Whoever subscribes to that false proposition
enjoys the highest honours in the State which proclaims it,
but in truth, in the true and indestructible order, he is
without honour. The State which turns marriage into a
stud *must* in this matter, order the man to seek his honour
in being a bull, and the woman in being pregnant as
often as possible, and in leaving the man who cannot
make her pregnant. Both must commit the most dis-
honourable actions when judged by true standards of
honour.

313. A note on the word 'disillusioned'. The usage of
this word is most instructive philosophically. It assumes
that as a rule a man prefers to be deceived than to be

disillusioned. In a truthful world there would be no such thing as deception, and in a world in which the love of truth came before everything a deception would always be looked upon as a misfortune and disillusionment regarded as a blessing—because it means literally that one is taken out of an illusion. But custom shows that the illusion is nearly always preferred, and the disillusion that follows is unwelcome. The old saying is confirmed: *mundus vult decipi*, the world wants to be deceived.

314. The colossus of mediocrity who himself produces colossal effects, was produced by the German apostasy, is maintained by it, and will be brought to end by it. The password of the archangel Michael is: Who is like God! *Basso* the Prince of mediocrity asks: Who is like me! He is a colossus, colossally destructive, the engineer of a colossal *Reich*, and of a colossal culture. He uses the language of mediocrity, unending superlatives.

315. In 'an evil hour' everything is falsified by oversimplification and false comparisons. Good and evil are alike, success is the criterion of the good and every means is justified.

316. The difficulty with all conversations is that the two speakers do not really understand one another. But although this is true in principle of all men, there are of course differences of degree to be taken into account. A man can only understand another in God. Men do not, however, need to know whether, at the moment they are talking, they have a relation to God. Kierkegaard possessed this 'double reflection' as he called it, all the time he was in conversation —and it is almost equally certain that the other man did not know it. This hindrance, the great hindrance, the fact that men do not really understand one another, vanishes completely when we talk with God—at any rate on one side: we can be absolutely certain that God understands us

completely, better than we do ourselves. It may of course
be that this very circumstance frightens man off, for to talk
with God, as Job did, is exhausting and ends in prayer and
silence. The soliloquy is a special problem. If it does not
end in conversation with God it is very dangerous, more
dangerous than conversation with a real partner. For what
man knows himself? Soliloquising, man often constructs a
false image of himself, or even a wholly unreal partner, and
God alone knows where it all ends, and sometimes the devil
alone knows.

317. All in all, the best things that God has given me
are my nights of solitary writing. An occasion for eternal
thankfulness.

318. 'Nietzsche smashed Christianity to pieces' is the
official reading of the new state-religion. And at that there
is not one of the moderns who has been broken to pieces by
Christ with more merciless mercy. His intellect calcified,
a granite-like stupidity formed itself into an invulnerable
bulwark against the spirit, while the moral structure and
manners were dissolved into a morass that could not be
parallelled in the *Inferno.*

319. How ambiguous things are, what a frightful difference
runs through the whole world! Tears came to my eyes the
first time that I heard that in eternity all tears would be
dried. All! And how my eyes burnt when I heard a man
tell the SS that he had laughed to tears at the last comic
convulsions of the body of a man shot down with a machine-
gun. Is it the same word?

320. One thing the founders of the German *Herrgott-
religion* do not and cannot assert: that Christianity came into
the world through the Arians. One or two little efforts in
that direction soon came to an end. But the Germans, they
say, after having fallen for it in a weak moment, or having

been outwitted, or having violence done to them, ennobled Christianity by building the most beautiful cathedrals and painting the most beautiful Madonnas. Even if that were so, and there were no French, English, Italian or Spanish Christian art—what thinkers! The antipodes of hierarchic, orderly thought! Christianity itself is a lie, the product of degenerate races and of slaves from the Mediterranean pond —but the sons of the German *Herrgott*, managed before revealing their true nature, and the truth of the German *Herrgott* (which is what is happening now) to build 'noble' buildings, and for a time sublimated the Christian lie. They built their beautiful cathedrals for a false faith, which—in their opinion—came from the dregs of humanity, namely the Jews—what will they build for their *faith*? Just look and see, they are building already!

321. Most great men, being egotistical, do not do the will of God and become, for others, a dangerous *cul-de-sac*. Those who imitate them and run after them can suddenly go no further and are all at once at a dead-end. Then some other 'Führer' is needed to draw them in a new direction leading, so it seems, into the open. But after a short run the walls again close in. There is only one who is 'the way'. The way to God is God himself.

322. The ideal of most translators is to write a 'smooth' German. But what if the author in question, whom they are translating, writes an English or Danish by no means 'smooth'? What then? Isn't that a more essential falsification than merely mistranslating a word here and there? Then what is a smooth style in Europe today? The language of newspapers, no doubt! That is the magic of the printing press, its product; and the more it prints the more smooth it becomes, the more liquid, the more watery, the thinner. We seem almost to have reached the point where the European nations only understand their languages in this same 'smooth' style.

323. What remains of the mockery of God but a petrified grin? Mockery is too light to act as a weight, too short to take soundings in the depths of being.

324. It often seems to me that the Vatican has completely and absolutely forgotten that Peter was not only Bishop of Rome, and as such held the primacy of teaching and was infallible, but was also a martyr. But the days of recollection and imitation are approaching and are not far distant.

325. Many thinking Christians consider that what is happening nowadays is not merely hard to understand, but altogether un-understandable. What is to be said of that? *Distinguo.* Considered absolutely, it certainly cannot be understood at all. And in that sense the things which are happening now are no different from any others. *Absolutely* understood, all events vanish in the silent depths of the inconceivability of God. But a relative understanding of everything that happens is always possible, and so too of what is happening today. There are many degrees of understanding, and there are many aspects of understanding. One of them is this: it is being shown on a vast scale that a *Reich* and a peace (Peace is the principal mark of the idea *Reich*) can be based upon the apostate principles of a madman—Nietzsche. For Hitler is an utterly plebeanised version (that is to say German, with a gipsy admixture) of Nietzsche-Wagner. I have always maintained the close relationship of both *anarchical* spirits. And now it is proved in the concrete, of both, in a single expression of will and activity.

326. The freedom of the children of God corresponds to the freedom of the children of Satan, only that these last make a use of their freedom which goes much further.

327. Among men there is a certain joy over the fact that another man sins, falls, and loses something of his personal worth. It is the specifically devilish joy, far more evil than *Schadenfreude*—it is the joy of the devil himself in a man. Ultimately it is the joy of extreme absence of love, and to that extent it is a problem in itself—the problem of how there can be joy in such a thing. The measure of all the good in a man is love, and the measure of all evil in him is absence of love.

328. Overnight, National Socialism has succeeded in reducing the Norwegians, who have been free men for a thousand years, to a form of servitude that has never existed in the world. The nations which were led into captivity by the Egyptians, the Assyrians, the Babylonians were certainly not compelled to assert they were free. And that is precisely what the subjugated nations of today are compelled to do.

329. The racial theory includes the denial of the proposition that the spirit bloweth where it listeth. Just as man *can* become the slave of the machine which he freely created, so, according to this theory, God having once created the Arian, and in particular the German, is compelled and obliged to place the creation of all good gifts for all eternity in his hands. Or more briefly: everything that they do comes from God and is good and right. To a healthy understanding that is of course childish, but then, once and for all, the mark of the Third Reich is infantilism.

330. This is how it starts. When men no longer have the least fear of saying something untrue, they very soon have no fear whatsoever of doing something unjust. I mean this in general, of the teachers and leaders of nations.

331. Where is the thought and the word that I think and say 'at home'? What father bred them, what mother bore them? That is what I want to know, that is the end of my philosophy. The spirit has many abodes on earth and I wish to know them and be the guest of many.

332. Language as such has its perfect spring and summer and autumn and winter, exemplified and exalted in the languages of the different peoples. None of the newer European languages possesses the spring of the Greek language or the maturity of the Latin, in comparable perfection.

333. The essence of modern dictatorship is the combination of one-dimensional, flat thinking with power and terror.

334. Wonder is the qualitative distance which God placed between man and truth. It enables man to find the truth.

335. Philosophy has gained its best knowledge with the method of 'wonder', and the knowledge thus obtained is far deeper, far more valuable than that yielded by the method of doubt. Nevertheless the latter is quite in order, but it is ordered beneath the former. Whereas wonder alone is in place face to face with immediate being, what I can do and the compass of human understanding is quite rightly subjected to doubt. Indeed, when error has become ingrained, the method of doubt is the right one and helps to restore health.

336. It is always at the cost of great errors that the distinction between being and thinking becomes a separation, as though the one could exist without the other. Thinking is or has a being, and everything which is, either thinks or is thought. Nevertheless being is not thought nor is thought the same as being. Being cannot be nothing, but thought can think nothing. Therein lies the superiority of the spirit.

337. It is hard to be forced to do work which one does not like, but it is horrible to be forced to stated times to a stated enjoyment. That is one of the discoveries of modern dictatorship, and that alone shows its devilish nature and its contempt for man.

338. The Germans have dug graves for many nations, and into all of them they will fall themselves. They are digging themselves a 'greater German' grave. Until one comes who *turns back*. There is no other road to peace, except by 'turning back'. But can nations ever turn back? It seems only to be possible to individuals. Have nations ever 'turned back' in history? I know too little to be able to say. But I doubt it.

339. The liberal democracies are perishing or will perish (unless they take the necessary precautions) from a lack of sense of obligation. It is just like a body perishing from lack of vitamins. Everything appears to be there, and nothing seems to be lacking, a mere nothing is wanting, but of a different *order*. The sense of obligation is a power unto itself, seemingly independent of the fact whether it is right or wrong that is binding. Where nothing is 'binding' any longer, there is weakness, the 'lukewarmness' spoken of in the book of Revelation. Where there is no longer any possibility that Christ or his disciples should be crucified God and the devil have lost their rights and wrongs.

340. A man will be judged by God according to the measure of his love. What love? Love of who or what? Now the answer to that is as clear and simple as possible. The Son of God answered this very question, literally, word for word, so to say, so that any evasion is impossible. But love is a transcending power, even though it is disorderly. It has, as it were, a superfluity of the divine within it. And so forgiveness is infinitely closer to a man who commits a great sin out of love for another, than to a man who un-lovingly commits a slight sin. For to be without love is in itself the greatest sin, far greater than any sin which a man can commit, though his love be disordered.

341. Summer. Now that 'he' has 'achieved' so much, it must really annoy him not to be able to control and make something so simple and material, and yet very important, such as the weather. He will certainly have noticed that, though he certainly does not notice that he cannot 'make' a German art, not to speak of a new religion.

342. Naturally it is false to say that *everything* false, and that *only* the false is comic, and that the comic is based entirely upon the false in the sense that it contains a contradiction. On the other hand it would be true to say that there is something false in everything comic.   .

343. The Germans have changed somewhat. They always, it is true, loved the inadequate, but they also loved the inaccessible and all the forms of its expression. That is no longer so: the inadequate is taught and absorbed in the most accessible forms. That is of course only temporary, for Hegel, and there will always be a Hegel, is part of 'eternal Germany'. There is one here now. What bad luck for Heidegger to have arrived on the scene during this *intermezzo*, of all times.

344. I have already lamented in these pages that the philologists who know so much, and have such a talent for learning and acquiring knowledge, then have so little idea what to do with all their knowledge, whereas there are things which I could do if only—alas!—I did not know so little, and had so little talent for finding out the things I want to know. At the moment, for example, I should like to know when 'History' was acclaimed divine judge for the first time. When did all that begin? One can perfectly understand that men laid great stress upon cutting a fine figure in the eyes of future generations, but from that to replacing God, the living and just judge, by such a questionable abstraction as history, always written by partisans, is a long step that can only be understood with difficulty.

Do men wish to be judged by man alone, even nowadays, when they no longer wish to write history objectively, truly, justly, no longer *sine*, but *cum ira et studio?* What happened to bring that about? What was it exactly? And there the Philologist might be able to help me.

345. It is a long time before most men recognise that there is such a thing as the 'irrevocable', and once again a long time before they recognise that they must act accordingly, and for the third time, it is very long before they do so act. And then, moreover, without grace, it would never happen at all.

346. Everything tends to completeness, towards the *whole*, and completes the circle of hierarchy! Thus, what does it mean for a man to be 'spirit'? It means that his thoughts should have 'body', that his body should not merely be a refractory organic or technical instrument of the spirit, foreign to nature, nor even an absolutely obedient instrument; on the contrary, as a body, it should become spirit, so that while there would always remain a difference there should never be a divorce.

347. That the thought looks for the word is a common or garden experience which almost everyone who has searched for a word, claims to have had. And naturally it is true enough, but real spiritual labour, and its adventures too, its conquest of unknown territories begins, without a doubt, when a word is in search of the thought. As a rule a word is both too much and too little for a thought. And in that way it sets thought in motion. In looking for a word to match the thought, the right word is found through reflection, by bringing the word back again to the thought and to thinking. The interchange of thought and language, of thinking and speaking takes place under the dominion of thought. The sphere of man's existence within thought is infinitely richer than his language. He can only express a tithe of his thought. This is absolutely true of the poorest, as of the richest in words, and it is the latter who will see the impotence of language most clearly. And whoever knows this and can express it in such a way that he extols its wealth and in the same breath betrays its want, and when he laments its want allows its superfluity to shine through—is worthy to speak of language.

348. Rejoinder: A rule is, as a rule, good *qua* rule, but beware if it rules out the exception.—But surely that is what it must do, if it is a 'rule', doesn't that belong to the very conception of 'rule'?—Yes, *as a rule;* but there are exceptions.—And here we are, in a circle! What then is the meaning and significance of 'the exception'?—Fundamentally, it is the privilege of God, of the Lord who presides over the rule; it is the primacy of *freedom,* of the *person,* which takes precedence over the compulsion of laws and rules; its meaning is that, ultimately, we are not under the hard and fast, mechanical rule, but under the all-powerful will of God, which is free.—Now what does that mean? Here and there, there is an exception! As a rule God desires the rule of law, even where we men are concerned.—That is not quite certain. Perhaps as a rule, God desires the exception, and we bungle the thing, by following the rule lazily, as a rule, even when we do not will it.—Don't you think your ideas are getting confused?—No, I think they are well ordered.

349. Things which have greatly concerned and bothered one should never be allowed to recur once they are in fact settled; they should be left alone, even in thought. · Those who live predominantly in the realm of memory often offend against this law of prudence. Memories of this kind are as a rule very agreeable, once the real danger has been eliminated. They offer a sort of intellectual pleasure that weakens and unnerves the spiritual life.

350. How early in life a certain knowledge, self-knowledge and forebodings come to a man! Often enough it is only

the weakness of our memories which prevents us noticing
it. I can remember how in my childhood, when I was
about twelve years old, a thought struck me; and as with
other deeply rooted memories, I can remember the very
street, and see myself as very strange, and almost inconceivable, walking along. We were reading Cornelius Nepos
in school at the time, and I liked to imagine myself in the
role of a roman consul or senator; but one day, at the
'Fish Fountain', the thought suddenly struck me—I was
twelve years old—: How strong you would be if only you
stopped playing and turned your mind to 'real' things! I
still have the same inclination towards childish, fruitless
phantasy, though I am 61 years old, and always with the
recollection of that foreboding, not to let an inborn tendency
become a vice, but to make a virtue of it. I have also
found that men without a trace of this kind of phantasy
become irretrievable philistines, hard working, certainly,
and very often successful.

351. In the West there has always existed an intuitive
recognition of the spirit of virginity, realised in the mar-
vellous and beautiful goddesses Artemis and Athene, and
in the paler, and more easily conceivable forms of Diana
and Minerva. No other people had anything approaching
it: the Jews had the 'bridal' virgin. And it was only the
union, natural and supernatural of Artemis, proud and shy,
and of Athene, motherly and wise, and of the Jewish conception of 'bridal' virginity, with the supernatural conception of the Mother of God, that brought forth that
magnificent conception, the Nun. Today contempt and
defamation are poured out from the heart of Europe upon
the Bride of Christ, the natural nobility of the West, and the
whole conception of virginity expressed in Artemis and
Athene; they are all dragged in the mud. And what are
the ideas which are put in their place? Something easier
to realise! The regimented whore and the calving cow! The
idea of perfection in marriage stands in the closest relation

to that of virginity. And virginity is placed above marriage
in anticipation of the state of eternal life. In heaven 'man
and woman' will not cease to be—they are eternal; for man
is created as 'man and woman'—but the propagation of the
species will no longer continue.

352. Men who are 'still waters' often believe with difficulty in the forgiveness of sins, and remain clouded, and do
not get rid of the dirt. Men who are active, who are
'running water', believe in it more easily.

353. Among mortals, it is Plato who found the happiest
images with which to express the being and existence of
man and the world, and in certain circumstances they are
the most dangerous: that the essence of the world is superfluity and want; that there is one power in man which lifts
him to the sun, one that drags him down; that the complete
man is both man and woman; that man only knows the
shadows of the truth—he is really unsurpassed and by
himself, perhaps, no man can surpass him. And why then
are they dangerous? Because they are images of the truth;
not the truth. Because they are only shadows of the truth.

354. If *eternal* life were not free from 'dread', I should not
desire it. But supposing for a moment there was a man in
this life who was entirely without 'dread' (and at the
present time there are many in high places who pride
themselves upon the fact), then I should not want to be that
man. I should indeed 'dread' him.

355. And so you have not done something and not had
something which you thought it impossible not to do and
not to have. It was, you see, possible. The imagination
is often the most stubborn antagonist of a better will.

356. If God himself had not proclaimed that He rested
on the seventh day, and had not ordered men to have one

day's rest in the week, the spiritual man might easily have
been led astray not to rest, and even to look upon rest as
a crime. But it is also said that God *always* acts. And so
perhaps man too can work while he is resting. But that is
only intelligible to the *Homo Spiritualis*.

357. It is usually men with ulterior motives who want to
express Christ's words or the words of the apostles more
clearly. But though their intention may not be evil, they
are lacking in the 'sense of faith'. And that too is by no
means harmless. The 'sense of faith' penetrates the obscurity
of the words of scripture, but it does not *clarify* them.

358. Humour is a finite spiritual sphere while faith is the
infinite. That may be seen from the nature of despair, and
its dialectic. A man in despair, a man that is, who has not
got faith, or has lost it, can perfectly well have a high degree
of humour, even to the point of genius. Shakespeare is full
of examples. The humorous rejoinders of a man in despair
are flung back, as it were, from the walls of the infinite
spiritual sphere which to him are impenetrable, and they
have a particular, unmistakable and sinister ring. The
humorous rejoinders of a martyr like Thomas More at the
moment when his faith looked into heaven strike a very
different note; the *tone* is of *this* world like the tone of all
humour, but it is not the tone of a solitary, 'lost' man, as
in the case of a man in despair; he strikes a chord in which
sounds the heavenly harmony of the seen and the unseen
world. At times the believer may see himself in this world
bereft of every finite possibility, he may be deprived of
humour altogether, even of the humour of despair, and yet
with the eye of faith he will see the quintessence of every
possibility, and of what is for man the impossible possibility:
God himself.

359. No subject without an object, and the reverse, is a
genuinely metaphysical proposition which Schopenhauer,

for example, loved. But that alone does not get one far. One has the right to speak of a sub-objective and even of an ob-subjective. Though perhaps that is unnecessary. I should, however, unhesitatingly speak of feeling as sub-objective. In feeling the fusion and interpretations of subject and object is complete, whereas in the rational-logical the distinction between them, their separation reaches its furthest degree though this is not, consequently, the case in the true concrete thought of reality. The rational-logical is an abstraction. In reality, in real being, the sharpest distinction between subject and object belongs to the will, with the centre of gravity in the object; in feeling it is weakest and weakening, for it runs the danger of placing everything in the subject (the 'name' is noise and smoke). The normal relation of subject and object, so to speak, belongs to pure thought.

360. If the 'authoritarian' States, whose task was a corrective one, continue to commit crimes inhuman and most offensive to God, on this scale and at this tempo, then in no very distant time the age of liberalism will be looked upon as the golden age.

361. 'As if' has its place in human thought; which cannot operate theoretically or practically without an hypothesis. But it is pure sophistry to put forward the thesis, and not the hypothesis, that all our knowledge rests on a hypothesis, on an 'as if'. One sees it at once when instead of saying 'A is A' one simply says: 'it is as if A were like A'. That is absurd. 'As if' has little point in all *essential* knowledge. But that is not true of questions relating to *existence*. It is not senseless to say: 'It is as though God existed', or 'It is as though God were not'.

362. At one moment Ibsen was a great prophet in great and decisive matters, hidden, speaking softly, hardly conscious of his own significance; and that is in the *Master Builder*. The play is more profound and far more important

as a personal tragedy, than as a fable, though even as such it is by no means unimportant. The Master Builder rebels against God and rejects God on the tower of his Church. It all happens, of course, in the style of the 19th century, but is no less clear on that account. One had a drawing-room, or a sitting-room or a front-parlour (three degrees), and even in the last extremity did not forget to behave 'correctly'. The Master Builder was to build no more Churches, but only houses for men, just as Ibsen the poet was to write no more *Brands* or *Peer Gynts* but only social plays, contenting himself with this world. This tragic decision certainly weighed heavily upon Ibsen, and he died in spiritual darkness. But: the rejection of God under the form of not building any more 'unprofitable' Churches, but only 'useful' houses— is a prophecy which was to be fulfilled on a gigantic scale.

363. To require of a man whose calling it is to concern himself with modern literature and philosophy, to consider literature and philosophy *sub specie aeterni* means quite simply that he should not see them at all, for *sub specie aeterni* they simply do not exist. Ought one to require this asceticism from him, if he does not himself wish to exercise it?

364. It is *verboten* to refer to members of the party as *Kerle* 'fellows'. A tremendous change in the language when one thinks that Goethe and Schiller were still 'fellows' and took no offence at it, although the word had already been debased and corrupted by a Prussian King. But really these 'fellows' who now forbids its use, have done more than anyone, by their very existence, to defame the word.

365. When one reads history and the histories of the nations and their accusations one against another, then God has only one thing left to do, and that is—revenge. Is that a task worthy of God? But why all this? What is it all about? Why is the world like it is? For the stupidity of the world, which is certainly undeniable, the stupidity of not seeing what is happening and how things stand, is not after all any explanation of the fact that God allows it to happen; on the contrary, it is the stupidity, which most of all needs to be explained. That is the language of the angered. Every man is angry at times, and before God he is *always* in the wrong. One of the differences between the children of 'this world' and the children of God is this, that the former regard the moments when they are 'tempted' to believe in God as their moments of weakness, whereas the latter, on the contrary regard their weak moments as those in which they are tempted not to believe in God. That is perfectly in order. The former regard themselves as strong, the latter themselves as weak, and God as strong.

366. Thinking is not speaking. It is a very difficult thing to discover and acquire the language of one's own thought. Each separate individual is very likely original in his thought. But between his thought and its fit expression the well established common language stands like an enormous, impenetrable wall, like an all-devouring monster, like a steam-roller levelling everything down. Only the whole strength of love, only a loving strength, and strength joined to humility and devotion can make it personal, and yet in such a way that it remains the common tongue.

367. It could not be said that God loves miracles particularly. They are extremely rare, both in public and in private life.

368. The tragic destiny of the Germans: through grace they received the gift of the *imperium*, 'for nothing'; and they made 'nothing' of it. It has been a terrible falling off, and at that very point, for the sake of the *Reich*. And childish men are destroying it on the plea of establishing it for ever.

369. Tyrants always want a language and literature that is easily understood, for nothing so weakens thought; and

what they need is an enfeebled thought, for nothing keeps
them so firmly in power. When the ideal and the order is
to write an easily understood style, anyone who is difficult
to understand is *eo ipso* suspect.

370. To do away with the construction of the period is
to destroy the individual sentences.

371. In order to answer the question: What is man? one
must of course say everything that he really is and really
possesses, and say it in the right order. But there is one
expedient which is of great assistance, and that is to find out
what, in the whole universe, only man has, and animals for
example and angels do not have. For instance, faith,
laughter and tears.

372. When one is on the winning side one is easily tempted
to believe, in a rationalistic age, that the course of events
follows man's reckoning; but one forgets that the others,
the losing side, have also made their reckoning, without its
having come out right. And then, when one looks at
history—has it ever followed the course of human reckoning?
Can it be otherwise today?

373. In times such as these, to be in the hands of God
means: not to despair. But then, they say, do men ever
despair, or can they be said to be in danger of despair?
Is not everything right in the world since we limit our
thoughts and ourselves to *this* world and to *this* life? No,
my friend, men do despair, many of them.

374. Happiness in heaven means that every man can do
what he wills because he has perfect love. In this æon,
certainly, there is no man who is not horror-stricken at the
thought that men do what they will. For nowadays such
men exist—but they pride themselves upon being good
haters.

375. 20th August. How many nights of writing does this make? I have no idea; I have never counted—They have been the happiness and good fortune of my life. And yet each night I have had to fight against their fatigue before being overcome by their happiness and good fortune.

376. 6th Sept. Now and then I have the most fantastic dreams, though for the most part they are quickly forgotten or else never remembered. This afternoon I dreamed that I sat in front of the Café Luitpold, writing. The sheets of my manuscript lay about on the table just as they do at home, at night, when I am writing. Round about me stood some friends, their faces immovable, staring at me. Suddenly a dark, 'well-dressed' man, rushed up to me and tried to gather up my manuscript. I was astonished and tried to defend myself. And then another man, just as 'well-dressed', came up and shouted: 'Stop! That's not the one!' And turning to me politely, says: Excuse me, this gentleman has commissioned some stories from Moralla. Can you tell us where he lives? Yes, I answered, on the fourth floor. They hurried off into the courtyard, that appeared suddenly from nowhere. In the hand of one I saw a pistol, and in the other one's hand a dagger. I was terrified, but laughed aloud nervously. My friends, their faces immovable, stared at me. After a minute or two, one of the men came back and called to me, beckoning. We can't find him, help us! All at once there was an enormous lift standing ready. I got in, alone. With one swoop and a tremendous noise the lift went thundering up at a terrific speed. It burst through the roof and stopped. I pressed the button again and went down again to the fourth floor. People whom I did not recognise were running to and fro in the warehouse. It was all very sinister, and I was frightened. Suddenly I was standing on a balcony in front of a mansard window, where there were some geraniums. Behind it stood a very old man with ice grey hair hanging down to his shoulders. He was playing the harp; beside him was a little girl about ten years old, to whom he was telling a fairy story; 'And do you know, yesterday Mariele returned to her father and mother as a sound'. Then I woke up, wondering bemusedly how a child could return as a sound. And probably it is thanks to that astonishment that I remembered the dream at all. Gracious heavens, where are we when asleep?

377. How frail and uncertain is man's happiness, even when it is deep and seems invincible! The least breeze blows it from one's brow and extinguishes its radiant light from your heart. And it was night. St. John's Gospel xvii.

378. The world and its overlordship, as demanded by the Germans, is based upon the following principles:

1. There are three kinds of man: (a) Supermen (b) Men (c) Sub-men.

2. In doubtful cases the Führer of the Supermen always decides in which category of man the existing nations belong.

3. The Führer of the Supermen is *always*, without exception, the Führer of the Germans. For it is eternally true of the Germans alone (Germans, past, present and future) that they are Supermen. Of the Arians, who in the widest sense of the word are Supermen, it must be said that until they become Germans they may become decadent, and that on the authoritative decision of the Führer of the Germans they may be degraded for (opportune) political reasons, to the rank of men (if not, as in the case of the English Plutocrats, to the rank of sub-men). This is done by virtue of the fact that the Führer is not only the

creator of the positive law, but also of the
natural law.

4. In precisely the same absolute eternal sense that
    the Germans are Supermen, the Jews are sub-
    men. Close after them come the Poles, and then
    perhaps Negros.

5. There is a God. His name is: the *Herrgott*, or the
    German *Herrgott*, or the All-powerful, or Provi-
    dence. Hence there is a religion, the German
    Herrgott-religion in fact. It has no dogmas. And
    so everyone can think as they please. Only they
    may not act. The theology is simple. The will of
    God, as German *Herrgott*, is that things should go
    well for the Germans and that they should rule
    over everyone. No wonder! German mystics
    have found out that without them, God would
    not exist. But now, since they themselves are the
    products of the German people, it does not take
    much logic to perceive that in that case God
    himself is a product of this same German people.
    And damn me if that's a pamphlet.

379. 8th Sept. We no longer say: 'Gott strafe England'!
Nowadays we say 'Der Führer straft England' and what is
more, with reason. A million and half tons of bombs on
London!

380. Even now, very many people engaged in apologetics
still argue as though God were indeed all-powerful, but in a
world, so to speak, which is not of Him, as though it were
simply foreign to Him as well as to his followers. That is one
form of childishness. For the world is created by Him, it is
His work, His creation. That is a mystery which must be
taken up and thought through in our love of Him and in
His love for us.

381. It does not really meet the case to say that the conception of life as a dream is purely oriental. It is, for example, Spanish, though this might be said to be due to the arab occupation. But in the meanwhile: what about Shakespeare? No, the answer is that it is 'human,' and it corresponds to a reality. Man is created out of nothing, and he could be 'different', like every dream. In a dream everything could be different from what it is. And so the poets say: How often it has happened in a dream that I have seemed to awaken, and have only awoken to a new dream—perhaps my whole life is a dream. To the poet and the metaphysician that is anything but strange. To the religious man it is a distraction—a dream which he rejects.

382. Catholics often confuse themselves with their religion to such an extent that they think people are converted for their sakes, on their account, and not for the sake of Christ and the truth. At times it is grotesquely comic.

383. Men no longer test words to see what truth there is in them. The majority are only interested in knowing what their effect will be.

384. As a rule women are no friends of satire and polemics and that is as it should be; it is not their business. Satire and polemics offer no home and there is nothing 'motherly' about them.

385. The proper order: the individual sentence serves the whole period, which is a building, and it is written accordingly. The spiritual actions of the assertion come first, the innumerable inter-connections of every kind in all their nuances, the foundation, the consequence, the intention, the determinants, and more especially in the case of careful, scrupulous minds, the concession, beginning with the outright ones, and going on to those which are made with difficulty, almost whispered—all these spiritual actions give its form to the classical prose of western languages and literatures. On the other hand, however, there is the stand-ard, pre-fabricated sentence of ready-made material that predetermines the constructions of the 'enlarged' or 'ex-panded' sentence. The semi-colon disappears from punctua-tion; a sure sign of the decay of the period.

386. The great delusion: that mockery is of any use. It does not better the ordinary man, it only arouses his implacable hatred and his lust for revenge. And in certain circumstances it can wound the better man mortally.

387. 22nd Sept. If I should still have many and great sufferings before me, my Lord and my God, then let some-thing thereof be worthy of thy name, of thy humiliation and thy glory.

388. What does it profit thee to gain the whole world and take harm to thy soul? When one thinks that no one has ever gained the whole world, and moreover that none will ever gain it, and that men are willing to harm their souls for a few pence, one may well be staggered. On the other hand, once these words are thoroughly grasped, there is an end to gloria mundi. The smell of it in one's nostrils is as unbearable as the rank smoke of burning straw.

389. In the first instance 'wisdom' needs silence and the spoken word, for the actual 'presence' of the giver is im-portant for the receiver. And consequently the written word only comes second; for then the reader is alone, unless of course he too is wise. And that is seldom.

390. There are prophets who have a 'sympathetic' relation to the horrors which they foretell, they seem half to wish the fulfilment of their prophecies and were it to happen they would fit happily into the scene. I am thinking of Luden-dorff and total war. There are in fact prophets and prophets,

those through whom the spirit of God speaks and then there are .... others.

391. Those who are scandalised say: perhaps God has changed. When those who are 'scandalised' are also religious, they always maintain that some particular dogmatic attribute of God is false. In this case, God's unchangeableness. The 'scandalised' always have too high a conception of their own conceptions and judgments, which have not got the length and breadth, the height and depth of those of the divine. 'Scandal' is the mark of a defective faith.

392. Render unto God the things that are God's and to Cæsar the things that are Cæsar's. That is the division willed by God for this æon. On that point there is not the smallest doubt. The meaning of these clear words can neither be impugned nor twisted. But what has always to be interpreted anew is the content of both commandments. What *is* God's? What is to be given to God? What *is* Cæsar's? And what is to be given to Cæsar? On these matters the bloodiest struggles are possible (even though it may be and should be clear that the conscience of every individual man belongs to God). But this fact cannot continue to be recognised, and will be increasingly denied, and ultimately falsified hopelessly if

1. The primacy of the divine law over human law is not recognised

2. The rights of Cæsar are annulled and everything is brought directly under the Lordship of God or of the clergy, and finally

3. If it is said (the heresy of the present age!) that the only right and the only power is Cæsar's. Everything is given to him, even the conscience

of man, for he is, or at any rate the people are, if not God, then a direct, infallible organ of God.

393. The Prussian-German theology of war is in actual fact: God *is* always on the side of the strongest battalions. The practical consequence of this is, and they draw it and carry it out: we must *à tout prix* make our battalions the strongest, then God must be with us. That is bad theology. Nor will these theologians be converted, even by a miracle.

394. The voice of the 'scandalised': Man proposes, God disposes. But is that not reversed nowadays? Man may not think and propose, but he certainly disposes! And perhaps that will give God to think. Your jokes, my friend, are rather cheap, not even worthy of your despair, and the bitterness of your heart. It is time you looked around for a different way! Be silent, weep, fold your hands and pray; only leave off joking—For nothing has changed and everything is as it was. For God is the Lord. He proposes and disposes differently from man.

395. 28th September. Perhaps it is no longer to be: the association of impure passions with the truth which is Christianity. These impure passions, which in the political life of today turn one's stomach, rend one's heart, and torture one's nerves, unfortunately played a part, at times, in the history of Christianity. Christianity calls for a spiritual society of 'individuals' in which each and every individual in every detail, is formed to the truth. Kierkegaard's category 'the individual' is in fact the Christian need of the day, as opposed to the decadence of man into 'the masses', and in opposition to the glorification of the 'hollow' man without a conscience.

396. I do not think that those who say such things have never happened before are right. Qualitatively they are wrong, for it has all happened before (treason, malice, trickery, lies, horrors). But quantitively speaking they are right: things have never been organised and premeditated on such a scale. And then there is one thing more to be added: I do not think it has ever happened that men have been expressly forbidden to regard what was happening at the time as horrible, disgusting, false and evil, forbidden to long for a better world. In Germany today that is a punishable offence, and surely that is more than even Hell has the right to demand.

397. I am coming more and more to the conclusion that the history which derives from German idealism—a professorial history—is simply *humbug.* In that thin, pale atmosphere, personalities and passions evaporate. And no one could tell from reading it, that Satan was the Prince of this world. The idealistic school of historical writing ends, like idealistic philosophy, with 'as if'.

398. The historian cannot choose his villains like the poet, nor invent them. At a particular time they are 'given'. Given, as it were, perfectly clearly, by a higher power.

399. In addition to his particular knowledge the historian today needs above all to know his catechism, and in addition perhaps a smattering of criminal psychology. That is much more important than a knowledge of German Idealism.

400. 30th September. Kierkegaard's 'Silent despair.' There are many more men in that state than is commonly allowed, not indeed to the same power, and with the same all-pervading reflection. There is, as a counter-balance, a 'silent happiness'. And often the two conditions alternate in the same individual. Fortunately, therefore, Kierkegaard's description of silent despair is somewhat exaggerated. (The world is not Hell, neither is it Heaven). But if it is an almost permanent condition, a 'habitus', it is not always *actual*, and it is often only as past that it becomes vivid and profoundly 'recollected', because it is in fact buried inconceivably deep in the memory. And the same is true, the other way round, of silent happiness.

401. When Plato attained the knowledge and the conviction that it was better to suffer injustice than to commit it, he was not far from Christian ethics—what am I saying: he was at their very centre. But as for the *essence* of Christianity, there I have to believe that Jesus of Nazareth is the Eternal Son of God.

404. Mundum tradidit disputationi eorum. God gave the world to man for disputation, for him to break his head over, and even to break each other's over.

403. 4th October. I once counselled a man in despair to do what I myself did in similar circumstances: to live for short terms. Come, I said to myself at that time, at any rate you can bear it for a quarter of an hour!

404. Even the best that the best have written could be better still. And to that there is no end. If you do not set a limit, and in time a work must have an end, you will never reach the end. And then: isn't that what God did? Might the world not have been better, in spite of Leibnitz?—humanly speaking?

405. There is of course something wrong with a man who is only partly humorous, or is only humorous at times, for humour ought to be a yeast, working through the whole of a man and his bearing.

406. 'Inconceivability' is an attribute of God that rationalism simply cannot grasp at all; to rationalism, one might say, it just does not exist. Neither can it concern itself with any of the attributes of God, consistently or profoundly. It very soon comes up against the contradictions which only exist, however, for human reason. And therefore it is quite unable to risk penetrating to the very foundations, to the ultimate consequences which break the human *ratio* to pieces and render it useless. It looks as though, of the two, irrationalism were better placed, but it only seems so. It is inadequate on other grounds, and unless it transcends itself, it is less dignified than rationalism. They hold that their 'Irrational' is something altogether beyond the intellect and outside it. But it is only beyond and outside the human intellect, though within the divine intellect. Human thought, resting upon faith, means the most fearless and consistent thinking. It says that God is absolutely one, and yet three. It does not fear to say and to hold that man is free, responsible for his acts, and then again to say and to hold that God chooses his own. It does not say this 'as if' it were so, as an 'as if', but says it *is* so. And there is nothing which it so greatly fears as to say one of these truths in such a way as to omit the others.

407. The attributes of God are too many for any one saint to live them all. It is still wanting, it is due to the saints . . . . . . *ab incomprehensibilitate Dei.*

408. Men are really creatures of the middle register, neither altogether good nor altogether bad. And so it happens that when the ordering of the World is good, the wickedness and carelessness of the individuals spoil and slowly bury it, and on the other hand, thank God, the reverse of the medal is that a bad order, or a disorder of the whole, is softened and mitigated by the goodness and the virtue of individuals.

409. What sort of a hellish pretence is it, and what does it mean? Works of love without love, works of light without light! Hatred and darkness as a sign of love and light. What a hellish deception. And men tell the truth in order to lie.

410. Once philosophers have written their principal work, they not infrequently simply become their own disciples. The outstanding example is Schopenhauer. After having composed his system at a very early age, he became his own most admiring pupil. He 'deduced' certain further truths from his own philosophy, which he had conceived and written in an entirely different state of mind, and when the character of his intuition was entirely different. Even the later Plato is not really Plato any longer; he is only a Platonist, his own greatest follower no doubt, but no longer the master himself.

411. A language simply cannot be too rich, and though its wealth may be a danger to gossipy, literary men, it is invaluable where knowledge is concerned. I am always suspicious of the grammarians who are for ever ready to accuse a writer, and particularly one of the ancients, of Hendiadys, as though it were wrong in itself. They are too arid and impoverished (another hendiadys) to perceive that what is spiritually one is not always best expressed by *one* word, and indeed can often be conveyed better by two or even more sides of the 'one', in order to illuminate the whole. They also seem to me to fail in their duty as teachers and masters of language when they hold to a rigid and inflexible order of words in the sentence. It is difficult to say how great is the difference produced by a change in the position of the individual words. In any case, no writer is going to forego the possibilities which this offers for the sake of a rigid rule. And then, language is of the spirit.

412. 'And that too will pass'. How often one hears that said! One has only to think how often one has said it. What a span of time it includes. How much light this fact throws on the human condition!

413. *Nous n'aurons plus jamais l'âme de ce soir*, is of course only a superficial observation, but it calls forth a gentle, almost voluptuous sadness, a melancholy that is also pleasure.

414. 'Passion' is in the first instance a characteristic of feeling, and only secondarily of willing and thinking. To cleanse the passions means to purify the feelings. Is Flaubert altogether guiltless of the fact that so many Germans translate *l'éducation sentimentale* quite meaninglessly, as 'the sentimental education', instead of 'the education of feeling'?

415. The clearest, most transparent relationship of subject and object, and the reverse, is attained in thought. The object of thinking is being, or something existent, even when it is the being of thought, and existing thought, in whatever mode it may be. In willing, the object is not the pure, substantive being of thought, but always being inseparably and most intimately bound up with a verb to do, to act or to possess. I want bread, means I want to have, to take or to possess bread. In thought I may be wholly unconcerned with that about which I am thinking, and to this extent thinking is the most objective activity possible to man, and willing is ob-subjective; nobody who wills a thing can be unconcerned about the thing he wills; but it is outside him, although he may wish to change it; with *one* exception, if he wills the truth. If he really wants to possess the truth, then he cannot wish to change *it*, for in that case he would not receive the truth. And so in this case he can only change *himself.* Certainly a rare case, for who desires the truth? But now what about feeling? Of all three (thinking, willing, feeling) it is without any doubt the most subjective way in which a man may be related to the world. That, it seems to me, is as far as we may venture without treading too near the truth, and disturbing the hierarchy of the orders.

416. There are, in actual fact, men who talk like books. Happily, however, there are also books that talk like men.

F

417. 11th November. Ever and again I am horrified at
the German voices. They betray absolutely everything,
they cry out their own evil. And the fact that this continues unobserved is more frightful still. Today I heard the
voice of Field-marshal Brauchitsch. An empty, hollow voice
rattled out some empty, hollow things: calling upon the
dead in the name of the Führer, and in the name of the
national-socialist *Weltanschauung*. A demoniacal performance. However, the voice of Baldur von Schirach, Gauleiter of Vienna, outdid him and completed this 'German
Requiem'. But what a misuse of the word! And of course
they don't want the dead to rest; they want them to 'arise'
at the call of the Führer.

418. Because, in reality, evil came into the world through
the will, one can understand that philosophers should
regard the will itself as evil; and because power realises
evil—what wonder that, to so many, power itself is evil.

419. The servants of the devil have, by and large, learnt
his most important lessons, and taken over his method.
They dominate man best by teaching clearly and impres-
sively that man is good by nature and that there is no such
thing as sin. They teach man that he is a god, and treat
him like cattle, and as the most worthless *canaille*. As long
as a man can be made to think highly of himself, he will
hardly be able to tell the difference between appearance
and reality. To himself he seems to be a god; and eats dust.
For a time—that is certain: only for a time.

420. The principal cause of the present situation: the
falling away from God, disobedience towards God, is of
course interwoven with many subsidiary causes. One of
these is the mass use and misuse of higher education. Newman warned against it. Why should fathers whose sons
are to go into trade or business have their sons taught
Latin and Greek? Latin and Greek are a violation of the

understanding of the average child, and a torture if the teacher is unreasonable. By far the greater proportion of those of our Führers who studied the humanities were below the average as scholars. They are revenging themselves horribly, full of poisonous 'ressentiment' for the drudgery and sweat and the inferiority complex which a too high ideal of education brought upon them.

421. There is in every man, I believe, a fear of a *Doppelgänger*, of a double in an absolute sense. Even the man of the masses wants to be original. It is naturally the man who has the greatest assurance of being unique objectively who feels the fear most. The height of madness would be to suppose that God has a double.

422. Somewhere or other I wrote that one only knows one's home in homesickness. I really had a home and knew it; I have often been and still sometimes am homesick, but my eternal home is only known to me in my homesickness.

423. It is really appalling how little mankind's consciousness retains of all that has happened in the millions of years of his history, and then how crude, how fantastic and wanting in proportion is the relation between the real significance of the day's events, and the meaning so presumptuously proclaimed by those who comment upon them.

424. I can feel no great respect for those who look upon God as a rigid law, no doubt because I should not have much respect for such a God.

425. 21st November. If one cannot, or does not wish to shoot a man who runs amok, there is only one other way out —though it is a certain one—to let him exhaust himself, and use himself up. The horrible example of the present

day could easily have been rendered harmless at the beginning; now it is only possible by letting him destroy himself. That is absolutely certain to succeed.

426. The general rule is, that a man's spiritual powers are gradually worn down by his body with its unruly demands and its final domination. It is a sad sight. The exception is the growth of the spirit at the cost of the body that is slowly used up. And that too is a tragedy, though a grandiose one, marking the lack of proportion in man. Among the examples in history which we can follow, the greatest, to my mind, is that of Kierkegaard. His body grew weaker and weaker, and at the end there was simply no bodily strength left at all. But there is not a trace of spiritual weakening, of falling off, down to the very last words which he wrote or spoke, not a trace. Anyone with any conception of what writing means must, simply as a writer, be fascinated by the variations on a single theme which are found in 'The Instant'. (Kierkegaard's last pamphlet). Time and again they spring naked and strong, perfectly proportioned and fresh from their author's mind; and over and over again one is moved at the sight. Kierkegaard's *Journals*, that cover almost twenty years, do not contain a single repetition, with one exception, a repetition he himself notes. When one thinks that at the end he had only one theme, and when one thinks of the astonishing productivity of the man during all those years, his power of memory alone is astonishing, and without example. I, at least, know of none.

427. The 'suspension of the ethical', the temporary interruption of the universal law can only be justified, in Kierkegaard's view, as I understand him, by a direct command from God to the individual. And that is without doubt the case with Abraham. But it is not always so. Furthermore, everything depends upon what is meant by 'the ethical', and by a direct command or inspiration from God. The duty to obey authority certainly forms part of natural ethics. But how uncertain all this is, so uncertain that it became necessary to limit the authority that had to be obeyed to 'legal authority' or even to 'statutory' authority, and to speak of an ethic sanctioned by God. This means to say then, that there is also a false authority, a false ethic. Do I really need an extraordinary impulse from God not to obey, in both cases? I think not. If the lawful authority commands me to torture innocent women and children, or a tyrant orders me to perform an action in itself lawful—do I need, in both cases, a special injunction from God within me in order to dispense me from obedience, and to act rightly in God's sight? I don't think so. It is a struggle in man's conscience concerning the *universal* laws of God and the will of a false but temporarily enormously powerful authority.

428. 23rd November. If I write down something which I know full well is valid and true for me, but which sounds presumptuous, or dangerously tempting to those for whom it is not valid, and whom it may harm, then I may not write it down, it remains a secret between God and my soul.

429. 'Three hundred thousand kilograms of bombs rained down on Birmingham today', Herr Goebbels announces through the voice of the 'German Radio Mission'. But really, Ladies and Gentlemen, you ought to listen to the voice! But they have not got 'second hearing', they hear and they do not hear. They have no conception of what is going on in Germany today, nor consequently of what will happen in Germany tomorrow. It is appalling to think that something so transitory as the human voice should have been chosen to reveal the depravity and the curse of a whole people, louder and more unmistakably even than its actions. How simple it looks: you have only to listen, and you will know everything! But the people listen, and when they listen they hear nothing but their own voice—praising and adoring them.

430. A good conscience is appreciated, and it is recognised as being essential to happiness. Men recognise all this, even conscience itself, thinking that no conscience is as good as a good conscience. But they over-estimate their strength; conscience returns, it can only be excluded for a time, but it does not return as a good conscience.

431. Since the world is certainly not completed, a complete system of the world is quite as certainly something funny. But perhaps the plan of the world is finished, like the complete plan of a house that has not even been begun. Perhaps; although that is a very human way of talking about a world which is, after all, so entirely unintelligible to man; and then, pray, who drew up the plan? Man himself, perhaps? That is really too much of a good thing, and man only stammers out his meaning. Nor is it true that 'Philosophy' is gradually building a house that will one day be complete. That is pure nonsense. It is a house of cards that God simply blows away.

432. The comparison between the hitlerian *Herrgott-religion* and Islam seems all right, but it soon wears thin: in spite of everything, the object of comparison is far too exalted, and the present filth does not give the producers and adepts who consume it, anything like the same subjective certainty and faith and assurance which Islam once gave to its followers, and, still does, to some extent. In fact religions, even false religions, come from the East; they do not arise in the neighbourhood of Braunau.

433. Has a single man, in the whole history of the world ever known, and been capable of saying what would happen in his own country, not to speak of foreign countries, in a hundred years' time? I don't believe so. So take care! Now that everything moves so much quicker, one can only say, take care! The cloud will pass, as Athanasius said of Julian the Apostate. But nowadays that by no means implies

a blue sky. Even blacker clouds may come. The nearer the
end is, the more probable it is that the spiritual light will be
darkened, rather than brightened by the passing of a cloud.

434. I consider Karl Krauss to be a great writer, but I
should not like to have written *Die Fackel.* Writing is not
everything. I regard Scheler as an important philosopher,
but I should not care to have taught his changing philosophy.
Philosophy, then is not everything. What is it, then? Well,
perhaps I can make it a little clearer with the following
remark: I do not consider Hilty to have been a great
writer, or a great philosopher—but there are many things
in his works which I should like to have written, for he was
the friend of God.

435. The hardest thing of all for a man to achieve is a
sense of measure, and though it were only a matter of
getting within a hair's-breadth—has any man ever come
within a hair's-breadth of it, in action? For passively, it is
just possible, though very hard and very rare. From time
to time a man is in a position to judge whether another
succeeds where he himself has failed—by a hair's-breadth.
To me, that has always been one of the innumerable direct
proofs of the Godhead of Christ: his rejoinders never stray a
hair's-breadth from the unforeseen and the unforeseeable that
both could and had to be said—the divine sense of measure
is there in all its perfection, the absolute and extreme opposite of man's want of measure, and of his mediocrity.

436. The scandal caused by a false doctrine is often
greater than the scandal given by a deceitful life. As a
general rule people recognise more easily and see more
clearly, that a man's life is deceitful, than that a doctrine
false. It is not enough to say of the priests of the German
Herrgott-religion: do all that they say, but do not do as they
do. One has to begin by saying: whatever you do, do not
believe what they say or follow what they teach.

437. Astronomers tell us that the empty space in the universe defies imagination. But that is surely equally true of time? What is the time of the world filled with since it was created, what fills the time of every individual life? And yet we know that there is a fullness of time. How does it correspond with space?

438. Spirit is autonomous. It is spirit that judges and is not judged by anyone else. If man is a spiritual being, then he is an autonomous, free being. He could never have arrived at the idea of autonomy were he not in himself autonomous. But the path he takes to reach it, in Kant for example, is mistaken. There is only *one* way, and that is the Logos himself, who said himself: I am the way, *and* the truth, *and* the life, in one.

439. Only one man can say *convincingly* what may afterwards prove to have been said by thousands of others at the same time. The mystery of this capacity to impress and convince is not easy to explain rationally, yet this is by no means the same thing as saying that the grounds are unreasonable.

440. There is a specially appointed demon, the particular aim of whose mockery is man's *prayer.* Now, until a man has attained the natural and supernatural point of view from which to see that the only relation of man to God is in fact prayer—and this can certainly not come about without faith—then as long as that does not happen, the more gifted, the more 'intellectual' a man is, the more easily does he fall prey to the 'unanswerable' arguments of the demon.

441. It speaks well, I consider, for a man who is without faith—I consider it a mark of honour, both where his reason and where his heart is concerned, that he should quite simply not wish to discuss eternal life. Those who talk about it all the same, are, in my opinion, thoughtless, empty-headed gossips.

442. There is really too much 'art' in Plato that has not become, and perhaps *cannot* become 'nature'. And how much more true that is of other philosophers and scholars. To that extent science, knowledge and philosophy is a limitation, and a danger where the immediate adoration of God is concerned. Pascal made an express distinction between the God of Abraham, Isaac and Jacob, and the God of Philosophers and scholars, and the most 'scientific' of all Theologians, Saint Thomas, explained at the end of his system, of which his disciples were always more proud than he was himself, that it was mere 'straw' compared with what God allowed him to perceive without the method of human philosophy.

443. God is inconceivable. All that happens in the universe at this very moment, individually and together— how could a man ever conceive it and grasp it all at once. The next moment is already upon him. And to God eternity is there, the before and the after of immeasurable time! God is inconceivable.

444. Generally speaking, man is rarely in a mood happily to desire an *eternal* life, or even to be able to desire it. The mere prolongation of this actual life is a thing so insipid and boring, as to be nauseating, or so terrible as to be a matter of unspeakable dread.

445. Stupidity! Stupidity is the word I wrote down last night when I was tired, so as not to forget what I wanted to say. Can one ever forget the stupidity of the world? How tired I must have been! What I wanted to say was, that the real cleverness of the successful lords of this world consists in their knowledge and use of its stupidity. The nations *ruunt in servitium*, are rushing into slavery, through their stupidity, and a depraved intellect knows how to lead them as it pleases.

446. What is so confusing to man's understanding is that God sometimes quite clearly, one is tempted to say quite publicly, concerns himself with minor, individual and apparently ludicrous things, for example that an old woman's jug should be filled with oil; whereas the fate of things which are all-important in the eyes of men—the destiny of an empire—seem not to concern him in the least. In the one there is a terrifying distance, and in the other a blessed proximity. God is inconceivable.

447. How timely was my reading of St. John of the Cross. He has taught me to see many things, and to understand much, and above all the *Night of Faith.* I have already said once, in this Journal: in times like these I can only live in the Night of Faith; worldly probabilities, not to speak of certainties, no longer enlighten us upon the fact that the God of whom the scriptures write, and of whom the Church speaks, still works his will. Much else, besides, became clear to me. In theology so much depends upon the razor-sharp distinctions of its terminology. Faith, for Kierkegaard, was, after all, almost the same as for St. John of the Cross: *Night*, complete darkness by comparison with all human understanding.

448. The great and dangerous seducer, who does not only seduce a woman or a nation into momentary error with particular consequences, but devastates their souls and turns them away from God is, in Kierkegaard's terminology, an 'extinct' individuality. The events and experiences of these times confirm this remarkable analysis over and over again. It is always the 'feminine' in man that is seduced. The devil, therefore, turned first of all to woman, to Eve. Seduction always aims at the giving up of the individual will, at giving it, or handing it over to another will, to a bad and evil will. Where man is concerned, as man, the devil's tactics are invariably to 'tempt' him to insist upon his own will, and to carry it out as against the will of God, his creator, as against a holy will.

449. History shows that, by and large, the Police or whatever it may be, is stronger, after all, than the criminal, simply because men, in spite of their corruption, wish it so. Even film producers always let the police come off best against crooks and murderers, a thing they would certainly not do unless that was what the public wanted. It is almost a hundred years since Kierkegaard introduced the socratic attitude into Christianity. The importance of the step cannot be denied. And what result did it have in the world? The very opposite. The result was not the indirect *Führer,* always taking himself back, withdrawing out of respect for the individual created in the image of God, so that every individual should have the possibility and the right to be taught by God himself; it was not the *maieutic* thinker, the socratic midwife, helping man to revelation and to the Saviour, to freedom and autonomy that developed out of his work, but the very opposite: the direct *Führer,* born of a criminal and infantile fantasy, an unimaginable product even thirty years ago, born of the putrefaction of the corpse of a rotting nation. Kierkegaard's god-inspired thought, 'the individual', ended in a typically Christian fiasco. It was placed before the world in true Christian suffering, with the suffering of love, and simply vanished in the 'world', as though it were non-existent. But before God it exists! O when will God's hour strike? Is it coming? Why doesn't it come? Art thou *eternally* powerless? O God, you let my faith diminish; leave me my love! Lead me not into temptation! *Me?* Am I then alone? Lead *us* not into temptation.

450. 11th December. 12 o'clock. The Italians will be beaten, and we with them. The fact that millions of

Germans rejoice at the thought, and patriotic Germans what is more, is the surest sign that the world is out of joint. How could I have thought it possible, as a child, that anyone should wish and welcome the defeat of his own nation out of duty and love of God? Is it possible for a child to conceive such a thing? How hard it is, in these times, to be a father, to have children who trust one, and how melancholy it is to be condemned to silence, for one cannot tell them the real situation, because they are as yet quite incapable of understanding it.

451. An Author's rejoinder: I am immune to criticism. Either I am so conceited about what I have written that it is a matter of complete indifference to me what anyone says or writes about it; or I am myself hopelessly convinced that what I have written is entirely valueless—and then again, it is a matter of complete indifference what anyone else says or writes. I am immune.

452. That Christian theology is not solely concerned with 'thinking' is a fact very soon betrayed by theologians themselves. Many of them are adept in developing ideas and in tracing their logical interconnection, and stumble the moment they have to deal with the concrete, or substantially historical, with what is not just 'thought', and often does not seem to resemble it. Kierkegaard is absolutely right: reflection, recollection and turning back to—contemporaneity with Christ, is a requirement of *Christian thinking.* And if that capacity is lacking, a man may be a thinker of genius, where thoughts are concerned, but in the strict sense of the word he is not a *Christian* thinker. The life of Christ among men of every kind and position, is so full, so complete, that in spite of the difference between life in those times and life today, every man can find a situation in which he can in all seriousness ask the question: what should *I* have done in that case? Naturally this imaginary test should only be made with the help of grace.

Otherwise he might despair. And that is certainly not the point.

453. The 'author's rejoinder' does not quite come off. It would be better to let him say: I am immune to both favourable and unfavourable criticism, and what is more by virtue of a *complexio oppositiorum,* which is what I am. I am at one and the same time so conceited about the value of everything I write that I am utterly indifferent to everything that is said, and then so convinced that it is worthless that, again, I am utterly indifferent to anything that may be said. Yes, I am immune—All that, however is unnatural and forced. It was not even the whole, immediate truth in the case of Kierkegaard.—What! And today, 12th December, 'the hundred and fourth day in the second year of the war let loose by Hitler', you still like to entertain yourself with this kind of irrelevant amusement? Anyone reading that in twenty years' time will be indignant, specially with your rhetorical questions. Yet the strangest things happen. Perhaps some former Junker from one of the Ordensburg will be thankful that at the same time that His Saviour Hitler threatened to destroy the world, private matters were still taken seriously in Germany.

454. It is the great privilege of man: he can and may say that a father's, or a mother's blessing, when they are at one with God, is binding, so to speak, upon the angels. But for a man to 'bless' his enemy, must sound unnatural and inhuman to the natural man. The capacity to give that blessing, in all truth and honesty I mean, not simply in the performance of the priestly office, is to my mind by far the highest *charisma*; it presupposes love of one's enemy which to natural man, and this must not be overlooked, is not only un-understandable, but also impossible. A Jewish professor of philosophy, no great philosopher, but an intelligent man, has confessed that he could not understand the command to love one's enemy, given by Christianity, even

as a possibility. (He seems, therefore, never to have come
across it, since what is real is, after all, possible). But it is
honestly said, and I far prefer it to the twaddle talked by so
many Christian pastors who haven't a notion what it is all
about. (On the other hand they must, of course, teach it, by
virtue of their office). The *charisma* of being able to set the
final seal upon the blessing of one's enemy seems to be
reserved to the martyr. The first of these was Saint Stephen.
Some, but not many, have followed his example. It is hard
to realise that Christ, still hanging on his cross, blessed his
people, and not long afterwards St. Stephen did so as he was
dying. What people can compete with this? The English
have something of it in Thomas More. And darkest of all
seems to me the spiritual fate of Germany, for the Germans
have nothing of it. All those whom Germany looks upon as
great have called down devils and demons upon their
enemies.

455. There is no thinking man who does not regard fear
as a restraint and a limitation, as servitude and a degra-
dation of the human 'person', as a decisive lack, in no
circumstances reconcilable with 'perfection'. Everyone
would give a great deal to be free from fear. Christianity
promises mankind freedom from fear. The angels of God
touch man on his weakest spot with their summons: Fear
ye not! The means which Christianity offers is love, or
simply God himself, who is love. Fear is the product of
weakness and guilt. That is moreover why men's efforts
to put an end to fear aim at doing away either with guilt
or weakness. The easiest, the well-tried method, is the forgetfulness or illusion produced by some kind of narcotic. But
experience soon shows how superficial the effects of the
remedy are, in one sense, and how profoundly harmful in
another. This short-lived strength is soon dissolved into a
weakness that is all the more real, and into fear which is
only so much the greater; a momentary forgetfulness of
guilt in some illusion or other is replaced by a recollection

all the more clear, and consequently once again by fear
and dread. That is not the right way. Work is a better
way, but by no means more certain . . . . . 'work and don't
despair' is really a sort of despair. But both, in the last
resort, and that is what I must have in mind, if the rule of
thumb is not to be just a makeshift, or mere twaddle—in
the last resort, neither the power to work, nor the strength
not to despair are in my power. In the last resort, the cure
must fail; it does not correspond with the facts of the case.
The saying is certainly not Christian; it is the old pride of
stoicism expressed in terms of modern bourgeois society.
Between it and the Benedictine saying—*ora et labora*—there
is an enormous gulf—But just a moment; can a man pray
at any given moment, in any circumstances, always? I
admit it is easier to pray than to work at any given moment;
for that, as you have already said, is not always in our
power. But now is prayer really *absolutely* always possible,
at every moment?—That is the very question I was asking
myself as you said it. Let us see! What, in the last resort,
can prevent a man praying? Only two things really: his
free will or death. In the first case man alone is, so to speak,
guilty, in the second case, if he has not killed himself, then
God alone—That, once again, is stated in too extreme a
form. You are really incorrigible, as a writer you always
want to write 'pointedly'. A man does not have to be dead
in order to lose consciousness. And surely an unconscious
man cannot pray.—No doubt it would be hard for a man
who had never prayed—And what do you mean by that?
Are we to understand that some men pray unconsciously?

456. *Midnight: Half-time.* The news and the voices!
God! Listen! listen to the voices and the news! O
Listen and avenge mankind and the Germans who still pray
to you!

457. 14th December. *Continuation:* Lord, help me! As
an average man of prayer I do not think it impossible,

nor even improbable. Think how much the men of today admit they do and can do *unconsciously*, that the men of yesterday would have considered it impossible to do, or to be able to do unconsciously, regarding it as absurd and ridiculous. Only I do not want to digress into protracted discussions. The most important thing about the Benedictine saying is the order it implies, which lies beyond all the psychological difficulties, the hierarchic order where the first thing is, that in order to live, and so as not to take flight, not to take refuge in 'escapism', *conscious* man must *consciously* establish a relation to God who is 'omnipotence', in whose hand he is *absolutely*; this conscious relationship can only exist in *orare*, in prayer, and what is more in prayer in the very widest sense of the word, so that ultimately just as in his beginning, as a child, baptised and without guilt, so in his end, as a man, reconciled to God, the breath of life itself becomes prayer, the breath which is not in the power of man himself, but is the breath and the power of life itself, which God gives to the individual. Prayer is the first thing I have to do, and the last thing which I can do in my extreme weakness before death. The next thing is work, the thing I have to do as long as I have the strength. And nothing in this aeon, goes beyond that saying. One can only lay down rules for 'carrying it out'. Even the devil can only imitate it. He invents his own rites, and so for the rest, there is forced labour. Prayer and work are the 'proper' weapons against fear and dread of life. And yet I think that fear, in the form of fear of God, and awe before God in all purity, is an element in every 'creature', and even participates in the highest love of the creature for God. The child, and the friend of God, is entirely free from all trace of slavish or animal fear, not to speak of the fear of hell, and consequently of sin and its punishment. The omnipotence of God remains in eternity, and God alone has this power. No creature has this power, and the strength of all creatures combined is nothing to it. Fear of this power is therefore part of the very 'nature' of the creature's being. And this power would still be terrible to those without guilt, and to those who are reconciled with God, were it not for the revelation of God's love, in which they may sink, but cannot be destroyed. And indeed, to say everything, they could not even sink in the love of God were it not that the eternal Son, the second person of the Trinity, became man.

458. 'To make a name for oneself' is the height of ambition in this world, and to this end even the great will deny themselves pleasure. It is the only way in which the world can approach the great mystery of the 'name'. But the mystery of the 'name' is really the mystery of 'the chosen', the elect, and God alone bestows this name without man's primordial consent, and this name is given in the name of the eternal Son, whose name is above all names.

459. There can indeed be no doubt that a certain 'bourgeois' and 'capitalist' order, as a manifestation of a specific period, is ripe and ready to fall, and will disappear. But the masters of the German *Reich* behave as though 'man' as God made him, were to be done away with. They have already done a number of things which makes this, their intention, clear. If they are to be successful, then their last days are near. But I am still doubtful. Restaurations do happen.

460. In the Bible, in the Old as well as in the New Testament, there is a want of compassion that, had we enough imagination, would astonish and even terrify us, at least if we thought it over. The men who are shown no 'compassion' are not extra-special rascals, but just what one calls 'men'. In any case, it is not unchristian to be hard on the rabble. Only it seems hardly possible, except towards 'the masses', because it is a 'mass', because there is such a thing as quantity. Would it be conceivable where only a few were concerned?

461. The way of salvation cannot lie in melting people down into a mass, but on the contrary in their separation and individuation. It is worth noting that Hilty, and not only Kierkegaard, with whom in other respects he certainly had little enough in common, was scandalised by the apostles' mass-conversions.

462. I have noticed that every man, even those who are shy by nature, or timid by birth or by upbringing, is, in a given case, far more likely to talk where he ought to keep silent, rather than keep silent where talking would be in place.

463. Rhetorical questions are not without interest: can one imagine a meeting between Goethe and Hitler?—Why not? Perhaps our conception of Goethe is quite wrong! Time and history transfigure many things.—That is true, but only up to a point. A vulgar swine remains a vulgar swine, and a blockhead, a blockhead. Neither Napoleon nor Goethe was one or the other.

464. The only light upon the future is faith. Knowing is only guesswork, and barely worthy of a man. The future is equally dark and equally obscure to every generation. And those who are not moved by the gift of prophecy should remain silent about the things that lie beyond. The safest course, in the long run at least, is always to prophesy misfortune. And as regards good fortune, to adopt the formula of Napoleon's mother: *pourvu que cela doure.* Only those who have the *right* faith possess the certainty possible and attainable in this æon. Those who have the *right* faith, I say, for those who have a false faith are indeed in a far worse position than those who reckon using the cleverness of this world, its science and probabilities. The greatest destruction and seduction among souls is produced by the success of a false faith, whether it lasts for a longer or shorter period or even perhaps for one or two generations. One cannot compare the fruits by which one recognises true faith with that which is nowadays understood by success. One should rather say that, once again, the fruits themselves, the fruits of the holy tree have no success in the world at all, and only bring contempt, mockery and scorn in their train. The success of a false faith, on a lower and superficial plane, often outweighs its falseness, so evident to man's deeper nature.

465. Rare though it may be for a man to be able to pick out a particularly plump lie among the thousands of daily lies, it does not signify much. The man who leads a really spiritual life is the man who has preserved the pristine freshness of vision with which to see every lie as an individual lie, and to grasp its quality, and to continue in astonishment and horror that life and action should be consciously built upon lies, instead of upon truth. If houses were inhabited by rats, and one were struck every now and then by a particularly plump one, that would only go to show that one did not understand the situation as a whole. The point is that the houses are lived in by rats—and not by men.

466. The fact that at this moment I am completely powerless *vis-à-vis* Hitler—well, no one knows that better than I do—I realise my weakness and know its taste to the full—and yet not in *all* its fullness, for then I should be as near to the all-powerful God as the martyrs and the apostles. Thus I am torn in two; I know my powerlessness and know that I am separated by it from the all-powerfulness of God, which does not permit itself to be mocked, that 'laughs' at that other power, which nevertheless tortures me body and soul—as far as God allows, *for my salvation*. O Lord, my God, have mercy upon me and upon my thoughts, that they may not lose their clarity in thy light.

467. Could anything be more easily understood, than that someone should lose their faith on account of Hitler?— Nonsense! Nothing could be more difficult to understand

than that someone should lose their faith on account of a mere nothing, such as he is.—Well, in the first place, my friend, there are many who have already lost their faith on his account. That is a simple fact.—Nonsense, I say, they never had faith, and one cannot lose what one has never possessed.—Of course, if that is how you put it, then the discussion cannot continue. But let us try to look at it in a different way. Never remain in a *cul-de-sac*. You express your indignation at the possibility that a man should lose his faith in God over a filthy swine like Hitler (and our judgment on this point agrees absolutely). Now I should like to ask you which is easier: to lose one's faith in God when goodness and nobility of mind prevail by and large, or when, as is undoubtedly the case at this moment, and has often been the case before, evil and vulgarity are supreme.—Now you are no longer talking about faith at all (I never maintained that faith was easy!), you are speaking of human understanding and of human probability; and there, of course, you are quite right; it is not very difficult to believe in God when goodness and nobility prevail. But is that what happened when Christ was crucified and his witnesses were martyred?—Well, I admit you know how to defend faith. Faith I have, and I do not wish to lose it; God protect me! But tell me now, is faith possible, even when the devil *alone* dominates, and God no longer shows himself or manifests himself in any way, and is absolutely powerless?—That is a frightful sophism; for faith is this: that God is at all times all-powerful and was victorious over the devil. So you see, you have not yet freed yourself from the 'thoughts' of men.—I feel you are right, well enough, and that you are the advocate of the Most High. But let me be, not the *advocatus diaboli*, but the advocate of man in his weakness, who like me, needs the mercy of God. For the ordinary, average 'good' man, whose eyes are open to the events of this world, surely the most difficult of all things to believe in is the all-powerfulness of God? Is it not conceivable that one might even lose one's faith in the omnipotence of God, the Father, and yet continue to believe in Christ; though, no, that is not quite what I mean: but, to love Christ as the most perfect being, who as 'love' had to pay for his existence with failure, because power does not belong to love.—You are wanting, it seems to me, in balance. A poet always 'exaggerates'. But one should only—and then not always—magnify the divine, not what is mixed and mediocre or even evil. Perhaps the man you describe exists, and he is certainly unhappy, and desperate, and we must recommend him to the mercy of God, as long as he does not come forward as 'teacher', that is as a heretic; for you must not forget that Marcion held roughly those views, and that Saint Polycarp called him a son of Satan. Our faith is that God is the almighty Father, and that Jesus Christ His Son sits at His right hand, to whom is given all power in Heaven and on earth. That is our—'Faith'.

468. Rejoinder: There is one weight which I cannot shake off; I can bear it, but I tremble beneath it. It is after all our faith that our will is free, and moreover even our experience. If our will were not really free, then our responsibility to God would be meaningless. And then man, whose peace is freedom, would be without dignity or worth. On the other hand, our faith is that God determines everything beforehand—Yes, I know, even our freedom as freedom. It is the glory of Christian theology, compared with a doubtful and hesitant theology, that it draws all the consequences of both propositions without the least fear, even though they appear to destroy one another mutually. And so they would, for the rationalists, on a *single* level: they simply collide and cancel each other out. But that is not what happens in true theology, and the unspotted faith of the Church. Here, and here alone, something happens which resembles a miracle of the understanding, to the *gloria dei*. It is, to use Kierkegaard's language, this paradox which is the very truth. There is only one such. All the others, the innumerable others, are only abstruse formulæ or simple absurdities. But there is one formula, which to worldly rationalists without the faith is simply absurd, and only one, though paradoxical in the extreme, which is privileged to be the true human expression of the facts of a Christian truth, which simply cannot be stated otherwise. But I seem to have forgotten the beginning. I began by referring to a weight upon me, to great difficulties and I end by almost losing myself in enthusiasm, as I always do when I touch upon this theme. What was I trying to say? That the idea of predestination always threatens to get the upper hand, to such an extent that the thought of freedom is borne away by it, however much one may try to stabilise it. But perhaps the reason for that is, that the human understanding grasps the thought of necessity much more easily than the thought of freedom.

469. Do you want somebody to read what you write, night after night—you only write at night, don't you, have you ever written anything by day?—do you really want to be read?—Your questions take me by surprise; I never consciously asked myself the question, I write so to speak, because I am a reader and always profit by my writing. But now that you ask me, I have to admit that whoever writes wants to be read, and not only by himself.

470. As a general rule the Germans are far from wishing that God should do too much; they would far prefer to do everything themselves. They would even like to create themselves. And of course make themselves guilty, that too of course, and it does not require a great tempter. And then: save themselves! No saviour, not at any price! 'Self', that's the man for us! And having done everything for oneself, then God *must* give it his blessing, he is morally bound to do so. A German Catholic theologian, following along the same lines, managed to define God as *causa sui*, the most barbarous, plebeian theologumenon that I know of.

471. Any number of thoughts are expressed and written down by their authors in the hope and expectation that the reader of these thoughts will understand them better and more profoundly than he does himself. That is by no means impossible. But a conscientious writer would be shy of doing such a thing. He wants to get to know a thought himself before letting it loose on others. He knows the danger of unknown thoughts.

472. A great many average Christians find it very difficult to form any conception of the meaning to be attached to the saying that in the house of our Father there are many mansions, and that many belong to Him who do not visibly belong to the Church; whereas, on the contrary, those who belong to the 'world' cannot understand the exclusiveness of the words, and the gulf which separates them. Certain forms of Christian existence are normally unintelligible. They hang by a thread at every moment of their lives, and wander in the abyss of despair, and almost at the same moment they feel themselves 'personally' in the hands of the all-powerful God, and *everything* is there just for their sakes, and at the same time they are less than nothing; and all this is not twaddle or a propaganda speech, but the simple truth. It simply *is* so.

473. 24th December. In the night when Christ was born the leaders of the German people spoke of the *German* Christmas. Can God still be God after that disgusting insult to His name? Woe to the sons and to the sons' children. Through it all there ran that horrifying pride, particularly evident in Field-marshal von Brauchitsch's speech: 'The sea is only England's wall as long as it suits us'. God can no longer build walls, if it does not happen to suit Hitler. 'God has blessed us' the Field-marshal said, and continued: 'God will not desert us *if*'—if what? could it be followed by the one clause possible, since man began to pray, the traditional formula: if we do not desert God?

No, that much I knew with deadly certainty, he would not say that 'if'; he continued, *we do not desert ourselves*. And so that is the condition placed upon God, the condition he is bound by: if we do not desert ourselves, which means to say, in their eyes: if we do not desert Hitler, God *must* help us. That is the 'proud German faith'. It is altogether impossible, except to God, to whom all things are possible, to teach this German General, in his pride, even the simplest Christian truth, such as that an all-powerful God is, after all, master of man's will and can lead it like a torrent. No, if these principles and sheer pride so evidently conquer the stupidest eternal essential truths—God has never existed, then all is madness—My friend, your indignation and despair, and your carefully prepared climax, show clearly enough, either that you are incapable of keeping calm and are not wholly without anger, or that you cannot hold out to the end, that you are not old enough to look the last things in the face.   For ultimately, if the prophecies and revelations of Christ are not empty phrases, then nothing will change, things will go on as they are, and they will get worse.   Yes, but God will shorten the days—True, but He and not you will decide the measure.—Well, and what am I to do then?—Hold your heart in patience, my friend, and then: do you not thirst after justice?   And do you suffer for it?—Yes, now I see.

474. *Rejoinder:* My faith is no thicker than a hair, and as feeble, and what depends upon it is so strong and so heavy, heavier and stronger than the whole world.—If only it holds!   Only think, the hair is grace.   And grace is the strength of God, strong enough to sustain the world.— Well now, so you are a poet!—That seems to be your worst insult.—That is an exaggeration, and clumsily expressed. No, but in otherwise good men, the poet is often a danger in religious matters.   The poet always magnifies: *Magnificat anima mea Dominum.*   Certainly! that is natural and as it should be, but the poet is not content to let the matter

rest there. He must magnify the world, in both good and
evil, and, alas, himself, in good and in evil, and in neither
case is that right.

475. We say that the Spirit of God dwells in a man, and
we say that a man is possessed by the spirit of evil, is possessed by demons: we do not say the contrary, and by this
distinction we stress the factor of freedom, which is only
given to man in its full sense through the indwelling of the
Spirit of God, whereas possession means complete servitude.

476. My nights are always the same: at first everything
is dry and barren, and there is not so much as a drop to
wet my tongue and give it life. Then, somewhere or other,
a little stream springs up and soon the waters are rushing
down and the bowl is not large enough to contain them.

477. Never leave hold of God! Love him! And if for the
moment you cannot love him, then fight with him, accuse
him, argue with him, like Job, and if you can, slander him,
blaspheme—but never leave him! For then you will become
very ridiculous and wretched, and—worst of all: you will
not even notice it.

478. Children and young people think of old people in a
way which never occurs to them. When he was ninety
years old Prince Eugène said to a forester as old as himself:
we still feel quite fresh and sound and healthy, and we
hardly notice we are so old.—We do not, Your Royal High-
ness, but others do.

479. It is a puzzle to me to know why it never could occur
to me to see anything great in the men who rule the world
today, and who have 'achieved' so much. Nothing. Nothing
but what is most common, vulgar and plebeian; on an
enormous scale it is true; but that is not 'greatness'. Whether
Napoleon's contemporaries felt the same thing about him,

I do not know. But as far as Hitler is concerned, the most I can produce in the way of human feelings is a boundless contempt. He is everything that most nauseates me. That is one side of it. The other aspect horrifies me, but that is no longer human. It is the voice of the fiend: 'I will take their children from them'. (Hitler, 1937).

480. Whoever looks down upon the freedom of nations and of the person, *must* be the enemy of Christianity. The first, primitive form of freedom is to live according to one's *way* of life. And without thought or reflection, quite instinctively, nations and peoples fight for this right. It is part of nature, and by and large it is right and just. But very soon different 'ways', whether higher or lower, begin to emerge within the nations; they begin to look for their 'freedoms'. If that happens without destroying the whole, there is great progress. But should the development lead to anarchy, there may well be a reaction, setting up an artificial 'norm'—*cum fundamento in re* of course—as being the way of life of the people, to which alone 'freedom' is granted absolutely. That is the case in Germany today. And then every way of life which rises above the ordinary is shackled. Ultimately it is the servitude, the enslavement of *the* way of life of the whole people, for if one thinks rightly upon the matter, one would have to recognise that this way of life could never be determined by a single generation, though it were the richest in geniuses, or even saints—that would always be presumptuous. This would be true of animals, and even of plants, and how much more of man. Wherever there is life there is 'possibility', some possibility remains; and one would have thought that nothing was clearer. But now look around at what is going on today! Spiritually and intellectually how far below the average! Masters filled with *ressentiment* and itching for revenge because they did not satisfy the requirements of a certain educational ideal (false in itself, or falsely applied), because they could not understand the *participium absolutum* or indirect speech:

intellectually, then, all those who were hardly treated, the ones below the average; and morally, not just the average, the crude and brutal, but above all the ones with criminal tendencies, filled with hate against God, Christ and the Trinity: these are the men who lay down categorically what is to be the German way of life, for the whole future. And to this end they must extinguish every recollection of the past, of what is great and dignified, or else they falsify it, or alter it into something base. But one only has to try to imagine what it means, in order to see that it cannot last: the whole undertaking will collapse, and the end is at hand.

481. 30th December. Roosevelt has spoken. It looks as though at last he knew, or somehow suspected what it is about. Though it is by no means absolutely certain. Nevertheless, there were moments when he struck the right note. The thing is that the fight is not just about 'democracy' —it is about 'man'. The question is whether mankind is going to seal the end with a lie, whether man ends up as swine and slave, whether the 'German' is pre-destined to establish the kingdom of darkness in this æon. As yet I do not believe it; or rather I cannot believe it. I am frightened; not always, thank God, and the words 'fear not' often echo in my heart. We are going to suffer unspeakable horrors and misery, but we shall be rid of the worst criminals of Germany. And so I take it upon myself to bear with all that is frightful, out of thankfulness to God, grateful that he did not let it happen. But how long, O Lord, how long!

482. Thoughts and forebodings during the last few days warn me that I still have long to live, and at the same time I have the impression that I am not yet mature. God protect me!

483. I am quite unable to understand a man who merely commands his people, and who does not love them, simply, naturally and straightforwardly. A man like that just isn't natural. Mentally or spiritually he is sick. But there the matter must rest: any emphasis on this love, however slight, at the cost of greater things, of truth, justice or goodness, nauseates me in my inmost heart. For this reason alone Goethe is, to me, immeasurably greater than Fichte or Arndt, and Aristotle than Demosthenes whose chauvinistic clique tried to mark him down as a traitor to his country. Never, in the history of the world, have all the worst characteristics of a people been so thoroughly and successfully mobilised and utilised by criminals as are those of the German people today. And so the German's love of his country today consists in not losing hope that there will be time to turn back to a better 'way'. Love must become fearless: better to be reduced to nothing, be annihilated in temporal, material and bodily things, than to injure one's soul for eternity. I can still remember quite clearly how afraid I was in 1918/19 that we should lose our name and our place in the world. That was a great spiritual weakness. I now know with certainty that for Germany to conquer the world today would spell ruin. Minister Frank, perhaps the most 'extinct' of the German criminals, is said to have said that Hitler was destined by God to be Lord of the World.

484. 'My words shall not pass away', could indeed only be said by the Word of God. No one else, however comparatively great among men he might be. Eternal truths must always receive a new body in time. Newman or Kierkegaard, or Hilty could and had to say things that Thomas Aquinas or Augustine could not say, although they said *the same thing.* And indeed it would be unjust if the fruit of their gifts and sufferings were mere superfluous repetitions.

485. The consequence of human freedom seems to be that my salvation depends entirely upon me, and the consequence of divine predestination that it does not depend upon me at all. The human understanding that only draws one of these consequences, and relinquishes the other, without any doubt relinquishes reality and fails in its task; for man is subject to reality, and may not spin thoughts out of his head, or deduce arguments from mere thoughts, deducing, constructing and decreeing. But the human understanding, which courageously and fearlessly draws both consequences, which is what it must do if it is to remain true to its task— this same human understanding declares its own bankruptcy in face of its particular task: of understanding, namely its incapacity to do that from which it derives its name: *to understand. Man does not understand it.* Where *this* mysterium is concerned, every attempt to take refuge in an approximate explanation is either a delusion or a lie: for man does not understand it. And yet there is something quite unique about it. This lack of understanding has marks of feeling, that no other has. There are in fact innumerable cases in which we do not understand facts or real things or events. But in all these cases they only have a negative side or aspect, so to say, and that is all—*basta*. But the lack of understanding of divine truths reached by natural or supernatural revelation has, in addition to the absolute *absence* of understanding, upon which no one could act, a further position which is altogether transcendental in character. The region, the point of complete absence of understanding is, as it were, clearly delimited, and any false demarcation is immediately felt by a sensitive understanding, and a powerful understanding could always demonstrate its falseness by argument. There is so much that is not understood; but this one thing alone is a mystery of light, and it is the only one in which there is the power of God, so long as man does not abandon it in favour of his own poor understanding.

1 9 4 1

486. We, as a nation, apostatised on the 30th January, 1933. Since then, as a nation, we have been on the wrong road, on the wrong side. Yet even now there are few among us who suspect what it means: to be on the wrong road and on the wrong side.

487. If the Germans alone were to inherit England's world supremacy, *within* the Christian order—what would it imply? That was not a question worth the effort and the work of thinking about. But now it is clearly and evidently a matter of Christ, or anti-Christ.

488. All great poets are androgenous, whether in actual fact, as spiritual and physical individuals, they are man or woman. Rilke translated the *Sonnets from the Portuguese* well, by and large, but Elizabeth Barrett Browning is the greater poet. There are many things which Rilke, a mere man, could only translate in a feminine way, which Elizabeth Barrett's unreserved womanliness interpreted with a manly spirit.

489. There is one difficulty which has bothered me for a long time: Hilty, I consider, was one of the most upright of men and one of the truest Christians of the world, and I regard Cromwell as one of the most mendacious in the history of the world, a great hypocrite, though of course I allow that he deceived himself in many things. Now, how is it possible that Hilty should have been ready to put his hand in the flame, so to speak, for Cromwell's honesty? How is it possible. Now, I am not altogether without fear.

Not that I have deceived myself in this matter, on these two points. O no! But I am afraid that I may deceive myself elsewhere, at another point.

490. 4th January. Moscow Radio. A *Pravda* announcement: Russia led the world in 1940—In art and science it lays down the law for mankind. This will be even more true in 1941, and still more so in 1942. A complete culture, Russian and national in form, socialistic in content and essence. And compared with what is happening in Europe and America perhaps there is some ground for this assertion. The hour of the Slavs!

491. The problem of consciousness, its degrees and its levels—which are not to be confused—is full of difficulties and confuses the mind. With regard to the three faculties of mind: thinking, feeling, and willing, the conception of unconscious willing was the one to penetrate most easily, and therefore earliest—as a result, in point of fact, of a misunderstanding. Will was equated with instinct, or at any rate explained simply as a development or as a specific case of, instinct. But 'instinct' is a biological conception, and is completely unconscious. The most difficult to arrive at, was the conception unconscious thought, and there are no doubt people, even today, who regard unconscious thought, as a *contradictio in adjectu,* like 'wooden iron'! They regard thinking as pure subjectivity, and pure subjectivity as consciousness turned back upon the I, but in neither case does it meet the real facts of the case. Unconscious feeling has never seriously engaged the attention of philosophy, because it has never really bothered about feelings, even those which are conscious. Poets, indeed, and the great psychological novelists have for some time been telling us about unconscious feeling and unconscious sensation. And in fact neither our will nor, obviously, our thought can be so hidden from us, can work in our unconscious and condition our life, as our feelings can.

492. 5th January. Midnight. The Italians have struck
their colours in Bardia. Why have I a feeling of satisfaction?
Is it right? Have I this feeling because I believe that at last
God has intervened? That *His* mills are grinding? That
the house of sin is built upon sand, now as always? Have I
a clear conscience? Are my feelings free from private wishes,
free from *Schadenfreude*, from antipathy and sympathy, *sine
ira et odio?* But perhaps that is a fussy, and an idle question?
Why so? Surely both anger and hate can be sanctified?

493. There can be no doubt, for a believing Christian,
that the *first* rebellion was an absolutely evil action: it was
directed against God, who is *good.* This rebellion knows
neither repentance nor atonement. It is the free act of
beings originally good—originally created good. That is
an absolutely inconceivable *Mysterium.* Agnosticism tried to
evade the mystery which, to repeat, is absolutely inconceivable to human understanding, by supposing that evil
did not arise as the result of a free act, but that it was both
necessary and without cause, from the beginning; that is to
say, Agnosticism assumed, or assumes it as existing 'in the
beginning', for that religion exists today. At the most it
allows good, in some sense, to prevail; and so, to all appearances, they evade the mystery, only to fall into an absurdity,
which makes both silence and prayer impossible, and
encourages reasoning. Man's rebellion is a different matter.
Where man's rebellion is concerned an apparent and
genuine additional injustice plays a part. In any case
every rebellion makes use of it to the full; the more despicable it is, the more it does so. It is not merely that in the
beginning man had to be *tempted* to sin, and so could not sin
of himself, by himself; it is not merely this, but the fact that \
the devil had to persuade him that something was being
withheld from him by God, *unjustly.*

494. Let me distinguish between rebellion against God and
rebellion against men. The latter always implies guilt on

both sides, and indeed very unequally. Naturally, the rebel always tries to make it appear that what is right and honourable in him rebels against what is wrong and ignoble. In doing so he at least concedes the existence of an objective order, independent of him, namely that what is wrong and ignoble has no right to rebel against what is right and honourable. Now in point of fact we live in a world of continual rebellion, of rebellions moreover which ought to be, and again ought not to be; rebellions, or let us say revolutions, which more and more take on an inevitable character. And they assume this character more and more, because revolutions from below combine rebellion against what is often undoubtedly wrong, against the guilt of those above, the rulers, that is to say, a rebellion more or less justified, with an unjustified 'evil' rebellion against right itself, against the rights of the natural order and the supernatural order, against the natural and supernatural hierarchy—we believe in hierarchy! (*Nota bene.* Is disorder a greater evil than a wrong order? 'Anarchy' than the *organised* dominion of evil? It is far from easy to decide.) Nevertheless, although these revolutions appear to involve the relation between man and man and human things only, they do actually in fact involve divine things and ultimately even the relation between man and God. The most frightful and most confusing things imaginable may then follow, and that is what is actually happening today: entirely separate and distinct natural things which had been hopelessly confused and overturned may be restored to their natural order as a result of a revolution, at least in some measure; and *simultaneously* the relation to God, both natural and supernatural and revealed, is fundamentally and diabolically perverted. For that is what is happening. The excesses of individualism which are harmful to the community, and the absurdities of an outworn formalism which interfere with genuine rights, are done away with, but *simultaneously* all true religion is persecuted, suppressed and done away with—what may that signify? That is, when the very principles of the supernatural order are overthrown, turned upside down, or denied? But I am in danger of getting off the point. For this is the thought I want to stick to, and which grows into a thesis: every purely human rebellion bases itself, or claims to rest upon a wrong inflicted upon the man in question, or upon man in general. Is that correct? I should think so! That is the meaning of the great Promethean myth. Is it not true of the experience of man, who is and ever will be called Job? But is that all there is to say? Is it the most one can say? I believe not. Let us look more closely! 'If God existed, how could I bear not to be God' Nietzsche asks, expressing a rebellion against God that goes much deeper than any historical revolution; moreover, the motive which he gives puts every other motive in the shade. It is of so spiritual a nature, that it almost seems to have been the motive of the fallen angels themselves. Superficially and at first sight it almost seems so, but a more careful examination reveals the whole difference between man and the angels. Nietzsche's hypothetical 'if', 'if God existed' is human, and what is more, relatively late in date, impossible in a pure spirit like Lucifer. The devil can never be an atheist; he can only use sophistical arguments to tempt to atheism men of a specific intellectual culture and of a certain power of reflection moreover, or strengthen them in it; men of a special type, to whom religion in its original and immediate sense is something quite foreign. Adam could certainly not have been seduced with atheistic propositions. Nothing was so certain to him as the existence of God. Adam could not have fallen into the sin of Atheism. But: *eritis sicut Deus* (You will be like God)! That fetched him. And why? Because man is formed by God: to long to be like God. Man always wants to be like God, and when the cloud of madness is upon him, he wants not only to be like God, he wants to *be God, he himself* wants to be God. And so it was with Nietzsche, who was already going mad when he proclaimed that 'God is dead'. The fact that man can go mad is connected with the fact that he can be saved. The final escape is not granted to pure spirits; the devil cannot go mad. More frequently than is generally believed, madness is a last, avenging grace, at the same time that it is a punishment. Some men know this; they beckon to the awful guest, and throw themselves of their own free will into his strong arms.

495. It might be instructive to carve up a classical period into fashionable little sentences and to illustrate what has been lost. There are still a few readers who would understand, but it could only be a pastime. Their slips of sentences are like slips of plants; there are no longer any real sentences, sentences like trees.

496. I was very early struck by the thought, and it has never deserted me, of how little I myself could contribute to my existence and nature. And I drew the conclusion that it was far more important for me to meditate on the power which created me and sustains me, and can certainly dispose of me as sovereignly in the future as it has done in the past, than upon the little which I can do, or can do merely in so far as that power demands it of me. That is the limit. That is certainly connected with the fact that from childhood I was of a contemplative nature!—What does that mean? Surely you will agree that all children are contemplative; and that the gift is only lost or buried after a certain age.— Undoubtedly there is something in what you say, although even among children the gift is unequally bestowed, and even at play, for example, the distinction between practical, theoretical and even contemplative holds good.—You are no doubt right there. Some States even display their hatred of the contemplative life in the games which they make obligatory for children, by forbidding those which invite contemplation. —But then the contemplative life too has its dangers and its forms of degeneration. Isn't it better to be active in reality than to invent fairy stories, or listen to them?— 'Brooding' is not by any means contemplation! More often than not it is just gazing into space, 'star gazing'. And it is

only the demoniacal counterpart of real contemplation—
which grows in fullness and does not concentrate on a single
point, losing itself in space.

497. 14th January. There are signs that firm believers in
the infallibility of the 'Führer' are beginning to consider
him mad, particularly those who have to do with him
personally. And in the end the Germans will be the most
deceived of deceivers among the nations, and each man
individually will point at the other in rage and contempt:
how could you, you fool! It *must* have been plain to everyone that this *must* happen. But not one will beat his own
breast.

498. Men who themselves still respect the invisible
boundaries which belong to the idea of man, and believe
that they still exist in others and must be respected, can
allow themselves to be liberal in the maintenance of outward laws and to mitigate punishments. The man who has
torn down the invisible boundaries within himself, the
nihilist, will always be a 'fanatical' adherent of capital
punishment. There is a certain lack of discipline within
the limits of discipline, that is the first stage; and there is
a certain discipline within indiscipline, and that is the
second, demoniacal stage of indiscipline. That is the mark
of the 'Kingdom of Antichrist' that has not yet come.

499. The German *Herrgott-religion*, as I like to call it, is
not, of course, the 'personal' faith of our 'Führer'; to maintain that would be a great error. He is a nihilist, who does
not know what he believes. As far as he is concerned,
religion is just another instrument, the best way of managing
a certain German thoroughness. Among Germans that
frightful proclivity seems hardly to be touched even by the
water of baptism. The German *Herrgott-religion* was set up by
the Prussians. There is only *one* people that was chosen, in a
supernatural sense, by God, the Jews—*salus ex judaeis*, in the

words of the God-man himself—though there are of course
many peoples who, as a people, have a mission and often
an exalted one, but there is only one that is chosen. But if
nevertheless others imitate or try to imitate in this sphere,
then the result in general and naturally in the individual,
is a grotesque caricature. Look at the Prussians and their
prophets.

500. It lies in the very order of nature, and is a maxim
of experience, that 'leadership' should belong to a minority,
for the best and the most gifted are always in the minority,
and the best and the most gifted ought, after all, always to
lead. But that is no longer the meaning of the sentence: a
minority should and always will lead. Cynics interpret it
abstractly. The decisive thing is to be without scruple and
determined to stop at nothing, to have a specifically criminal
intelligence, and to use it. After all the criminals in any
nation are a minority. Germany is led by a few criminals,
and the German mind is represented by a few low types.
Thus we have the very reverse. But a country ought to be
governed by a minority which is above the average.—Is that
really so, my friend, is this country not led, to a large extent,
by exceptionally capable people?—*Technically*, yes! That is,
morality, ideals and the spiritual life apart. Mentally and
spiritually, technique, 'the machine', is a difficult problem,
that I allow. There is at this point a demoniacal *interregnum*;
the spirit and soul of man *can* be devoured by technique,
and owing to certain other qualities, the German of all people
is the most capable of living and dying 'like a machine'. It
is possible to reach the summit 'technically', and to touch
bottom *qua* man, as God intended him to be. That is the
fate of Germany today. There is no thought which gnaws at
man so surely as technical thought, and yet on the other
hand it is the most human of things. Abstract technique
is the pure invention of man, and is certainly as far as possible
from godly thought and from that of pure spirits. Action
and contemplation can be thought of in terms of polarity,

so that the one conditions the other, and the being in question needs both, and nothing without both: no action without contemplation and no contemplation without action. But technique is possible without contemplation. Technical thought is all-too-human thought, and must therefore never assume command. It is an extremely useful and usable servant, but it *must* serve. One must never give it the upper hand for a moment.

501. There must always have been Nazis, or how would it be possible for the Bible to be so full of warnings against them.

502. How the tower of Babel must have impressed men, before it fell down! How they must have hated, despised, persecuted and done to death those who expressed doubts or warnings, or even openly declared it an offence against God! But the attempt to build the tower will continue to the end.

503. There is perfect tragedy in Vergil's Dido. Shakespeare and Racine, to whom the material was so suited, must have seen that there was nothing new or better left to do.

504. To the Germans 1941
Your fame is without lustre. It sheds no light. You are spoken of because you have—and are—the best machines. And in the world's astonishment there is not a spark of love. Without love, there is no lustre. You regard yourselves as chosen, because you build the best machines, the best machines of war, and serve them best. What grotesque inhuman men! Another race! Not these men, oh my friends! Let us create others ..... But how? From the Christian point of view there is only *one* way: to turn back; an active remorse. Outwardly perhaps, God intends to recast everything on a grand scale, using a new mixture of

races and peoples, which is the exact opposite of what the Nazis want and are doing; the artificial purification of an inhuman race, and of a people without sense of measure. Can anyone believe in the Christian regeneration of the German people? On the basis of *human* possibilities and probabilities it can only be considered impossible. Were it nevertheless to happen, it would be a miracle.

505. Man cannot think himself. He is God's thought. And 'My thoughts are not your thoughts', is also true of this thought.

506. When the dead bury the dead, the funeral is often very quiet. One hardly notices it, and only few know how illustrious is the dead man being buried at this very moment. But sometimes it occurs to the accompaniment of stupendous noise, and the cost to the mourners is in hecatombs of blood offerings. A noise like Beelzebub driving out the devil.

507. 13th February. I write almost every night now. At the very time when I neither know why nor for whom I am writing! Except: for my own instruction and for myself. Now, that I can only read with the utmost difficulty, the only way for me to learn is to write. I get to know things that I have never known; I acquire knowledge that I should never have grasped by mere thought, and that writing makes possible. And so I write for myself, and my own improvement.

508. The man who acts at once, on first thoughts, will make many mistakes, both in theory and in practice; it is seldom that first thoughts are best, though then indeed in quite a different degree—when it is a matter of doing something good. One should do it on the spot! The man who acts on second thoughts, the careful man, lives more securely; he will have fewer disappointments. Second thoughts can of course include an indefinite number of

thoughts. Decision really lies then, in the third thought, that outweighs all the others, the first and the second. And so right living implies three thoughts. Might they not be distinguished by the fact that first and second thoughts are almost always 'inspired', and only the third follows upon a conscious, logical judgment? Far from it, the third thought may well be 'inspired'.

509. I am a good listener and a good hearer: I understand at once, and clearly. But usually I only know the right answer later. And so, with certain exceptions, I am not cut out for discussion, and least of all for conversation. I can very well remember that one of the most painful experiences of my youth was when I had the absolutely certain feeling that an assertion made by someone was false, and I could offer nothing in reply, or only the most ridiculously inadequate reply, because my tongue was paralysed by my inarticulate thoughts. On the other hand it was this very impotence to answer on the spot which occasioned my endeavours to attain clarity, and to break up the solid rock of my feeling of certainty, to carve out of it logical arguments.

510. The fame and the historical influence of the schools and the schoolmaster belong to the culture of the West; they do not belong in the same degree to the East, where they do not have the same significance. Naturally, they are known in the East, they belong to man, to a certain stage of civilisation. There is a certain difference and a certain tension between a Master and a schoolmaster, for a good schoolmaster need not be a 'Master' and a 'Master' certainly not a schoolmaster. But sometimes they are united in a single person, and that is the glory of the West. Sometimes the perfect 'Master' is a 'master of the Schools', the perfect schoolmaster. The greatest example is St. Thomas.

511. At times the power of the *Zeitgeist* is overwhelming. Rationalism for example was so powerful that it even

compelled men who were in essence anti-rationalists, to think and speak rationalistically, at any rate up to the point beyond which it was no longer possible or permissible, for example Pascal, and still more so, St. John of the Cross, whose mysticism, in so far as he renders an account and a justification of it, is the end of rationalism, exhausts it.

512. Music and poetry are very ambiguous. Our masters, the first absolute apostates of Europe, have Mozart, Beethoven and Bruckner performed at their rallies, and the poetry of Hölderlin, Goethe and Schiller recited. They do all of these geniuses more or less of an injustice, though few notice it. But after a certain point the apostates themselves dare not, even for the sake of a momentary political purpose, use Christ's words. At a certain point the divine is protected, but not so genius.

513. Since the fall of man the method beloved of criminals who need accomplices, because they want to commit crimes on the greatest possible scale, has been to involve 'conspirators'. By giving them a share in the crime, they prevent them from turning away, or turning back. That can be learnt from the great historians, Thucydides, for example. People are so glib nowadays with the excuse that 'they were not there at the time', in regard to anything that happens, so proud of 'unbelievable achievements'—and in this they are right: unbelievable—and not to have been present is the correct expression for a conspiracy in evil. What an awakening, when the German people awake to the knowledge: to have taken part, to have taken life, to have conspired and lost.

514. As a rule, it is the simplifiers who are the most dangerous and the most mischievous seducers of men. God and the good are simple, but the world and the good things of the world are not. The simplicity of God and of the good contains in itself the fullness of all being and of the possible.

In one sense Christ is the greatest simplifier, for he teaches that all the commandments depend upon one: on the love of God and of one's neighbour. This commandment contains everything, and the saints can live according to it if they are perfect, else they too must distinguish. Whoever is even one step behind this commandment, as for example the man who teaches that everything depends upon justice: to each his own—even he, a just man, sends the world off the rails, for man cannot live without mercy. But true love is both: justice and mercy. Mankind is one, as the idea and creation of God. Upon the basis of this unity, men are both equal and unequal. The pathos of this distinction lies, naturally, in the eternal. What is more unequal than the chosen and those who are not chosen? And yet both are men. The whole truth is very much more exhausting than arbitrary simplifications. The one calls for Masters, the other is the part of bunglers, and the vehicle of power for evil men. The world has experienced the consequences of both simplifications: 'all men are equal', and 'men are unequal'. A false simplification is intellectually degrading, and because it is an impoverishment, it is a perversion of feeling and leads the will astray.

515. Properly understood, the business of a don is: knowledge, to bring knowledge of every kind on to the level of indifference. Things only become awkward if he wants to be the equal, or tries to be more than the man who has had to gain or to use his knowledge on the summit of decision.

516. There are authors who always write pointedly, even when they write about things that have no point; and that is very wrong, and thoroughly unnatural. The world is round, not pointed. Perhaps someone will say: yes, but that too is a point.

517. When men are no longer in a condition to regard death, objectively, as something frightful, as a violation of

the spirit of man, then although they may be able, nevertheless, to build machines, they can no longer use the Bible;
neither can they think Plato's thoughts; why, not even
Kant's.

518. There can hardly be any doubt that in essential
respects the Church will be driven into a situation which
will resemble the earliest Christian times. It will be very
similar—and not identical. There will be great differences,
ruling out any simple copy, and calling for meditation rooted
in the times, and needing to be illuminated. I mean of
course the political weakening of the Church. Christians
will no longer gain any advantage from belonging to the
Church, on the contrary! And that is a good thing. They
will also be without influence, like the early Christians.
They will be so far removed from the world that they will
not even be noticed, and so not even despised, for in order to
be despised, one must first of all be noticed. But as in the
first ages of Christianity, they will be just as close to the
world, so near that they will be hated, persecuted and put to
death for Christ's sake. And that will probably be the case
on a great scale, for today, in the end (at the end), Christ
is more hated than in the beginning.

519. Lies have their day. If after a certain time they
are not driven out by the truth, then it is by another,
and perhaps a greater lie; but they are always driven
out.

520. They love power, above all for the sake of power, and
in order to do harm to their enemies, and the heart of their
pleasure, is *Schadenfreude.*

521. 1st March. Believe it or not! The German *Herrgott-
religion* already has its hymnalist. Lehar, the dear man,
has written a song: 'O Herrgott, lass mir meinen Leichtsinn'
(Deprive me not, O Herrgott, of my thoughtlessness).

522. A completely mature, thoroughly reflective man will not, ultimately, wish to have written anything but his own work, not even the words of a master.

523. Immortalia ne speres .... (Horace), is a magnificent poem. 'Humanism' can reach no further. But the perfect form is touched by a breath of insipidity, of inadequacy, of untruth.

524. Hitler, Goebbels, Himmler—just imagine them! You know them after all, you have seen them, before and behind, from right and left. Just try to imagine it: they dominate Germany, they dominate Europe at this very moment . . . . . and you may not—at the risk of your lives—laugh. Could you have imagined such a thing? But, believe me, you cannot do so even now, at this moment, when it is a reality. It can only end in blood and squalor, otherwise . . . . . . otherwise? Can anyone doubt that it will end in blood and squalor? Could my heart or my brain conceal a thought capable of doubting it? Come forward then, you monster, come out of your dark hiding place! Show yourself. But nothing appears. An erroneous suspicion. Otherwise? What did I mean by otherwise? O, I know: otherwise there is no God and God is not God, and the non-existence of God is proven. Otherwise all is confusion and madness.

525. Bürkel, at that time the Gauleiter (the God Baldur, of the line of Schirach is Gauleiter of Vienna now) is said to have referred in Vienna to 'the son of a whore of Nazareth'. There is hardly any doubt that he was referring to Jesus Christ, the second Person of the Trinity, and that the whore was the Mother of God. The matter has never, I think, been put so bluntly except by a Jew, which might give Herr Bürkel to think, if that were possible. On the other hand it is to be noted that Houston Stewart Chamberlain also put it bluntly when he said that the Father of Jesus Christ was a German Legionary! The only difference is in the language, the proletarian language of a Bürkel and the more aristocratic language of Chamberlain, and so in a matter of taste.

526. A kingdom for an idea, that would bring Europe under one hand! But where is the kingdom, and where is the idea? The Germans of course think that Europe without England amounts to an idea. And who dies for it? Germans, of course, who die for everything, for trash and filth, as they prove daily; but where are the others? Is it possible for the racial idea to unite Europe? As though a doctrine which divides, could unite. A Negro is *capax dei*, and can eat the body and drink the blood of the eternal Son, can go to heaven; a Jew or a Pole, however, can never share in the rights of a German, even though he be of the quality of Herr Goebbels or Himmler. Where is the idea? Socialism, the equality of man? It is a great idea, certainly, which will equally certainly play its part. Without any doubt, it is superior to the German racial ideology, which is simply the idea of a proletarian romantic. 'Europe without England' is the German political solution, at the very moment when it is explained that England is no longer an island. How absurd it all is! Where does England belong, if there are no more islands?

527. It is not simply the case of a man maintaining his family by robbery and theft, about which his wife and family are in ignorance; it is more nearly the case of—a man who makes 'his' people 'great' through criminal and evil deeds, and makes the people increasingly aware of their guilt and complicity. And if in the first case it could hardly be said that the family were blessed, in our case there is certainly a curse on the nation. And the nation itself must demand expiation through 'conversion', for its salvation.

528. The fact of possessing power gives a man so many of the desirable goods of this world into the bargain.

'Power' not only has whatever it desires at every moment, wealth and material pleasures of every kind at its beck and call, it has the favour and the art of this world, and its beauty, and if it so desires, and has the sense thereto, the leadership of 'culture'. It can decide which philosopher is to teach or rather, if there is one about, whether he should teach or not. It even has a pale shadow, a phantasmata of the three Christian virtues: faith, hope and love. They are the insane images of the deceit: men believe in this power, hope in it and love it. And that is not all. The devil is capable of still more terrifying deceptions. There can really no longer be any doubt that the dominion of evil involves a *simulacrum diabolicum* of the martyrs. And their blood fertilises the earth of evil. Their frightful oaths call the spirits of the dead to resurrection, and they possess the living, shout their songs, increase their strength tenfold, and are visible in their every look.

529.   Men are more jealous of their sorrows than of their joys. As far as I'm concerned you may have been as happy as I have been, and have had as many and as great joys. But don't dare to say that you have suffered as deeply as I have! 'Whose sorrow can be measured with my sorrow?' It is right that the highest mark of the elect should be given to Mary, the Mother of God.

530.   Faith and opinion. Faith is concerned with the End, and in time it is not possible, without divine inspiration, I mean where temporal things are concerned. I believe in the trinitarian God and his promises. But these are concerned with the End. I only have opinions about the immediate result of temporal occurrences and struggles. I am astonished that so many people talk of a firm, and unshakeable, and unbending 'faith', and can only think that they are either lying, or hypocritical, and do not understand their own words, or that they are possessed. Get thee behind me, Satan! All that is simply stupid, an

impertinent lie, and the purest nonsense—as if I could believe that Christ is the son of God, and also believe that Germany or England would be victorious. I am indeed firmly convinced that at the present moment the government of Germany is profoundly evil, and that the German people is exposed to an unbelievable religious and moral danger; I am firmly convinced that it will have to bear the responsibility and punishment for its actions, but I consider it possible that it may be *immediately* victorious in time, according to the higher intentions of God's will. I consider it to be possible, and I would not despair of God's justice, I would not lose the 'faith'—I consider it possible, but not probable, for even fallen nature has and recognises limits to evil, which I hold have been overstepped in the present thoughts and actions of the German people. Moreover, fallen nature also has and recognises powers which are good, and they are, I believe, called to full consciousness among the enslaved and threatened peoples. It is said that the world does not change, and there is some truth in this, nevertheless there is a difference, which is heavy in the balance: this difference is consciousness. So much and so great evil has never been committed so consciously. It is the first, definite apostasy in Christendom, or let us say: the second, raised to a new power, if we reckon 1789* as the first—in the west.

531. It has often been loudly maintained by modern humanism that the good *must* always be victorious, even in time; and it is in no sense a Christian belief. Where is there a single word to this effect in the Gospels? Where is there a trace of this belief in the symbol of the faith? It is the opinion of modern humanism, itself a heresy, and is one of the most dangerous of heresies. The notion is simply a distortion of the Christian faith in the victory of good in an absolute sense, and in God as the Lord of the world.

*In case this should be misunderstood I would refer the reader to *494.*

532. There are nations who have the political gift of making the yoke which they lay upon others seem much lighter than it really is. The Germans have the opposite gift, of making a yoke weighing ten pounds seem like one of a hundred pounds. An unfortunate gift, when one wants to conquer the world.

533. The feeling of the nihilist is one of perpetual sinking and drowning, that of the Christian is of perpetually being carried, and lifted up (or uplifted) even in the lowest depths.

534. 27th March. Revolution in Jugoslavia. After the crisis, the awakening of the virtues of citizenship, which in the west, and in such a form, were sadly lost. The words freedom and patriotism and honour have won back their honour. They were hardly recognisable beneath the crust of dirt and disgrace and lies.

535. I am the master of everything I can explain.

536. A myth need not, of course, be literally true in order to be true, in the sense in which myths can be true; but when it is literally a lie, like the German contention not to have been defeated in 1918, then the term myth is also a lie.

537. A genuine, essential patience is a divine virtue, but it may contain a sort of reflection of impatience, which has something attractive about it, and that must not be confused with a rebellion against God. On the other hand, there is also a caricature of patience, made with a will to evil and destruction, which out-devils the devil, who is fundamentally impatient, the spirit of impatience.

538. The relation of man to his creator is of clay in the potter's hands—the comparison has not ceased to be the cause of scandal and offence. There is also much to be said against it. But the meaning and the passion of the prophet can be understood. Still, man is not clay, but neither is the potter God.

539. In face of the true believer, the unbeliever has, nevertheless, a sense of inferiority, a feeling that the other has something which he has not got, and something which he cannot take from him. That ends easily in hate and persecution. But when a society dogmatically excludes the faith of the Christian, the forms of hate surpass imagination.

540. It is a dangerous conceit to think that one can have a 'religion' of humanism and of this world, without the co-operation of the devil. He is the Prince of this World, and refuses to be excluded, although one may only mean to be concerned with this world, and not at all with him, who does not—exist.

541. Let there be no mistake; and it ought to be said with all possible clarity and calm: to hate Christ, is to hate God. John, 15, 23: Whosoever hateth me, hateth also my father. The German *Herrgott-religion* proclaims a God who is certainly not the father of Jesus Christ, and from whom the Holy Spirit certainly does not proceed. And so is not God.

542. 6th April. Entry into Jugoslavia and Greece. Grandiose proclamations. Belgrade declared an open town by the Jugoslavs and by us 'Fort Belgrade' (sic!) and bombed three times successively and 'most successfully' by Stukas. The German heart rejoices. It is Easter! The twelfth Psalm was written thousands of years ago, but it is just as though it were written today, today, the 6th April, 1941, shortly after six o'clock in the morning, immediately after Goebbels had read the proclamation, and having been written, was recited: the wicked walk on every side, when the vilest men are exalted.

543. God is not an image of anything, therefore one must not make an image of him, nor any representation. God is spirit. He is neither image nor representation, and his will is that one should pray to Him, in spirit and truth *only*.

544. Time always moves on. One can take a step back in space, and in other similar things: but never in time. One deceives oneself easily, in great and in small, over this curious fact.

545. If there were no truth in the saying *anima naturaliter christiana*, if there were nothing in man's nature which answered to and called for Christianity, then considering how much in Christianity in fact goes against man's nature, it would be quite impossible for any man to make a prolonged effort, a lasting attempt, freely to live according to it, not to speak of his being actually able to do so. But in fact the position is rather that the more harshly and violently men lay aside the Christian religion, the more they cease to be 'men', as God created them, the more corrupted their 'nature' becomes.

546. There can be no religion without eschatology. What is the End? Eternal pleasure, eternal peace, eternal struggle, eternal repetition, eternal progress?

547. The German is not creative where religion is concerned: that is sometimes the complaint of the apostates, who are on the look out for a better *Ersatz* for the Christian religion than they themselves can supply. That fits the facts. Before one can be creative in this sphere, one must be humbled, one must give oneself, and through a complete annihilation of oneself, pass through a 'death'; and as a rule, the German is much too proud.

548. In times of danger such as these—and I may certainly boast that I live in dangerous times—the art of life consists in being able to circumscribe short periods of safety, so that the knowledge and impressions of the danger which is quite certainly at hand attains no power upon the soul, *within* these narrowly circumscribed boundaries. For the next eight hours I need fear nothing except God, and that is a fear full of love: so let us live and enjoy the next eight hours in peace, perhaps even in peaceful sleep.

549. If one is responsible for every unprofitable word that one has spoken, how much more so for every word that one has *written!* There is, what is more, no saying where I feel so strongly that I am placed before an unfulfillable command. There is no saying to which man's reaction, I would hold, is so certain: he can only remain numb and motionless, he can only keep *silent.* But Christ will answer: with God this too is possible. That is to say, not to speak unprofitably. A saint, then, will not use a single unprofitable word.

550. For a hundred years no one has known how to build a church. All the recent attempts are really miserable failures; hollow and empty or strained. Perhaps it is simply a sign that no more churches are to be built. The Christian Church is entering upon a new form, the mark of which is not, as it has been for nearly two thousand years, churches. The Church lives already, and will continue to live *in partibus infidelium.* And the Church may exist *in partibus infidelium,* but one does not build churches there.

551. In the year 70, five thousand Jewish Christians left Jerusalem together, in order not to take part in the national rising. Traitors to their land and nation, every one of them! To a national Jew the spirit of this rebellion could have been none other than that of Maccabeus. What did the five thousand Jewish Christians see standing between the Maccabees and the new patriots who rebelled against the foreign yoke? The crucified Messias, the new faith. The

Jews are the chosen people. As a nation they rejected the messias and even crucified him. But those who accepted, accepted him to the full. Where is there an example of such an agonising break with one's 'country' among the gentile Christians? No-one will surely maintain that these five thousand Jewish Christians hated the Jewish nation. They must have loved it like Paul, or rather as Christ loved it. The first martyrs too were Jews. The gentile Christians only followed later. Why God chose the Jewish race is naturally inscrutable, and why the Eternal Son took flesh and blood of the Jewish people. But once this is said, one is not completely in the dark. And so through the reckless, boundless sacrifice of national pride, and what a national pride! There is nothing like it, when awakened—it sometimes slumbers—except the German. Who can hate like the Jew? And the Protomartyr, Stephen: how perfectly he fulfils the new law, how brightly he carries the mark of the Christian martyr, that marks him out distinctively: to bless one's enemy instead of cursing him, to love him instead of hating him. There are some who have the stuff of martyrs in them, so to say, by nature, in modern times Kierkegaard for example, and in a more brutal form, Bloy. But the latter would have hated his enemies in the very act of martyrdom, the former would probably have despised them, which is also not right.

552.   I have spoken in these pages of a heavenly impatience, as of a treasure within the great virtue of patience. But there is also a hellish patience. And really great and evil works cannot be achieved without it. An ordinary, natural man, even though he may wish to attain evil, and desires to possess it, simply cannot summon up the necessary patience. Long before it is over, he sickens of it. Face to face with really evil men, an ordinary good man can avail nothing, though an angel were to come to his help. Who can hold his arms up for eight hours? Moses could not do so without help. Who can shake the hands of ten thousand men, one

after the other, not because he singles them out before God, but because, on the contrary, he degrades them into the 'masses'? Who can endure the roar, not of animals, but of herds of men, at all times? Except the man who hates God and the Son of Man and the Spirit?

553. The most significant event in the twentieth century is the rise of the Catilinian power-state. Nihilism spread among individual, theoretical minds, will construct the 'bonds' which the Great State will take over when 'the hour of evil' is at hand.

554. The 'spiritual' understanding of man understands that there is a qualitative frontier vis-à-vis the divine understanding. It is perfectly possible for such a frontier to exist without human understanding knowing it, or being able to know it (and that is very often the case in actual fact); but the 'spiritual' understanding, as I shall call the understanding which has made its submission to faith, hope and love, the characteristic of the 'spiritual' understanding is that it *knows* this at the decisive moment. That has nothing to do with the quantitive measurable frontiers of the human understanding, with its greatness or smallness, that is. It even seems as if at times the greater the understanding the greater the difficulty in recognising the frontier and of living according to it. Among these one would have to include the great rationalists, and above all Kant, who was certainly one of the greatest intellects. Kant's transcendental understanding, and his 'reason' are certainly no longer the individual human understanding, they are *human* understanding, *human* reason in purified and sublime form. What are 'contradictions' to them are *absolute* contradictions and consequently are also contradictions for a divine understanding. The great rationalists and Kant, too, as can immediately be seen, were wanting in any sense of perception for the mystery. There are not x mysteries in God, but a quite definite number. There are not an indefinite number of contradictions and opposites for the human understanding which find their solution in God, but a quite definite number, for example predestination and freedom, justice and mercy. The spiritual understanding stands absolutely by the principle of contradiction and will always declare the absurdity and wickedness of saying that God is good *and* bad, whereas, he will maintain that certain contradictions which are absolute to an autonomous rationalist are resolved in God (for example predestination and freedom, mercy and justice), and what is more that it is a solution which does not abolish the principle of contradiction. That is certainly a mystery, but not any number of mysteries it is, on the contrary, within a definite divine revelation.

555. The final expression of an absolute despair would be: it has always been so, and it will always be so. That would be the despair of God, for the individual man would always be released by death.

556. A Christian society is not complete without those who 'have made themselves eunuchs' for the sake of God's kingdom, and even outwardly this is true: it would be lacking in one of the signs and marks of Christian society. Monasteries, certainly, may be the form conditioned by the age; but those who defame 'monks' and 'nuns', as has sometimes been the case among Protestants, and nevertheless want to possess the 'true' doctrine, are simply castrating Christianity. They deny the spiritual strength which makes it possible for a man, even in this life, to live as all will live after death. It is not possible to remain unmarried supported by 'ethics' and 'morals' alone; it is a vocation and a grace and only upon this foundation can it become the expression of an ethic and of an asceticism. The words of Christ: He who can grasp it, let him grasp it, leave no doubts upon the matter. Everyone can 'grasp' the ten commandments.

557. The fact that language does not permit of calling machines 'wonderful' and 'divine' rests upon a generally accepted feeling. It is clear that these words cannot be used to describe the products of the machine, unlike so many products of man's hand, and in particular, works of art. The human hand is a wonderful instrument by means of which the spirit, and at times even the Holy Spirit, with an absolutely immaterial intention, creates the difference between a mediocre mechanical work and a work of genius.

558. The way from God the Saviour, to God the Creator is difficult, hard to see, and hard to understand. The identity of the two has been denied from the very beginning of Christianity, sometimes by men of outstanding talent, founders of sects and heresies, and there are many men at the present time who feel the same way. That Jesus Christ, the Saviour, is at the same time the creator of the world, of the milky way, of the earth and the lion, is an unfathomable mystery that many do not so much as notice, and *may* not even notice, without running the danger of losing their reason.

559. Certain rites among magical religions create an effect of being mechanical. And is not the effect of some great smooth-running machines almost magical!

560. To do something for 'God's reward' means, in this world, to do something for 'nothing'. In the world 'God's reward' is—nothing. In the eyes of the world whoever does something for God's reward is a fool, and in the eyes of the same world, the Christian who hopes to be rewarded by God for his good works is a common beast, because he does not do good for the sake of doing good. That is the sort of contradiction which the world swallows.

561. The really fruitful paradoxes grow on the frontier between 'being' and 'nothing', and they are the only adequate expressions for things and conditions which cannot otherwise be grasped. Movement is the mark of life. What can move so fast as a machine, and yet it is dead, a 'dead life' compared with the smallest plant, which may seem motionless—but in which there is the mystery of life. 'Dead life' is not 'wooden iron'. The devil, significantly enough, is described as 'living death'. He is spirit, and spirit is life, the most living life. But he is also furthest from God, and nearest to nothingness—to death that is.

562. All our victories are won 'according to plan'. It is all worked out 'logistically'. And yet gradually it is becoming clear that very much that unquestionably happens, is not 'according to plan'. Or is it, after all, 'according to plan'? A fraction, certainly no more, of another plan, of the plan of quite another? Supposing, now, this very different plan were to be carried out, and it were the plan of our defeat!

563. Even in nature there are so many animals whose origins one does not understand. 'That worm-like creature you say, will turn into a Red Admiral? You must be mad'. But it will; and so a criminal can become a saint of God. Not by nature, of course.

564. 7th June. The Germans who are trying to uproot Christianity entirely and are being enormously successful in quantitate, seem to think that Christian theologians will die out at the same time. But that is a feeble-minded notion. The Professors, the professors paid by the State: yes, they will of course die out. But the theologians? Good heavens, one would think the fathers of the Church were salaried professors. On the contrary! Then we shall once again have some great theologians.

565. When someone is successful, he always likes to think that everything was planned in advance. But that is always

an error. The devil was successful, but he had not calculated that God could become man.

566. Leibnitz would have stared open-eyed at anyone who told him that he, Leibnitz had received his intellect from a God who himself had none.

567. In rationalism the only sign of freedom is the fact that events cannot be calculated and are in fact 'incalculable': a purely external view of things, and false at that, in so far as 'freedom' most unquestionably lies beyond the calculable and the incalculable. It belongs to a different order.

568. Men can very profitably be divided into those whose field of vision is dominated by the things which cannot be altered, and those to whom the things which can be altered occupy the front place. That marks one of the profoundest differences. Great political wisdom consists in rightly distinguishing the things which one can change from those which one cannot change. As it is, however, things are appallingly and terrifyingly muddled.

569. Abraham must have loved Isaac more than anything in the world, loved him so much that he was in danger of loving him more than God. And so he had to be tried. If Abraham had preferred Isaac to God, Christ could not have been born—over and over again sacrifices like this one are required. If Stephen had hesitated or weakened, Saul would not have become Paul, and the gentiles would not have been converted.

570. The notion that the argument of some philosopher or other against Christianity could be above my head, that I could not understand it, has really never crossed my mind; on the contrary as far as the moderns are concerned, Schopenhauer, or Nietzsche or Scheler, there are many

things which I could put better than they do. No! No! No!
I may suffer from almost anything else, but not from an
inferiority complex in this matter. Neither Paul, nor
Augustine nor Thomas Aquinas, nor Newman nor Kierkegaard are 'stupid by comparison with the others', but crudely
and brutally put, exactly the opposite is the case: though
indeed I know well enough that the real difference is grace.

571. 'Scientifically', it would certainly be preferable to
state the truth without stating it paradoxically. But then
science is not man, nor the reverse. Science ultimately is
there for man's sake, and not the reverse. It is human and
even divine to talk in paradoxes, and to stress and exag-
gerate one part, at the expense of another part, so that the
whole can be better perceived. And it is with similar
methods that a painter brings a landscape nearer to one
than the 'scientific' photographic lense.

572. The pain I had was unbearable. What does that
mean, my friend, since you bore it? You bore the pain, and
so the pain was bearable. When does pain become unbearable? When you die or lose consciousness; and so it is not
you who decide when pain is bearable, but nature and
ultimately God.

573. 15th July. Since the 22nd June the Russian earth
has been drinking blood, and nothing quenches its thirst.
Alas, is there any sense in asking what sense there is in the
world? Where is the peace of God, the *requies aeterna?*
What is it, if it is not in life? If it is in death, then it does
not concern the living! Peace, eternal peace, is in God,
our peace is in God. In the world there is no peace. The
'little mother' the Russian earth goes on drinking rivers of
blood, drinking like a drunkard. So God is not in the
world. But what do my stammerings signify? How does it
concern me; what have I to do with what goes on in the
world, so long as my soul is not saved.

574. Plato considered a certain music, a particular mode, harmful. Who knows, and who is to say how far this music was merely the expression, or how far the cause of the decadence of the Greeks? The fact that a particular music *accompanies* the decadence of Europe, and to musical ears actually *is* that decadence—who can fail to hear that? one would like to ask—a rhetorical question the wrong way round; for no one seems to hear it, except a few whom nobody hears.

575 The basis of the German *Herrgott-religion* is a fundamental pride that will not let itself be broken by God. Every nation is proud; but there are differences. The national pride of the French is to a great extent vanity. It is not for nothing that the cock—*gallus*—is the national symbol. The cock is proud, but perhaps even more vain. There is something delightful about the way in which French national pride reveals itself, it is so open, frank and free, like the cock-a-doodle-doo and the fine feathers of the *gallus* and like the direct sensual appeal of the *clairons.* German pride is gloomy, hermetic, self-isolated and like all self-imposed reserve that is not sealed with the seal of God, it is terribly dangerous. It must also be remembered that the French, more than any others, by nature express analogically, the *gloria dei.* The French *are* by nature the nation of *la gloire.*

576. One can divide the great minds of the nineteenth century into those which had and those which did not possess the spirit of prophecy. Kierkegaard, Newman, Dostojewski had it, Tolstoy did not have it, though his natural genius was certainly no less than theirs.

577. God is in all truth mysterious enough, but the fact of his predilection makes any understanding even more hopeless than it already is.—I can't say I agree. I, too, love this or that more than other things! Why? Well, simply because it is worth more.—But my friend, you are missing the point. You are not the *creator* of the things you prefer, or love more. *But God is.* You don't mean to say that just as I prefer this or that work that I have written, so God prefers this or that. For how can one of God's works be unsuccessful? No, at this point anthropomorphism is wicked folly.

578. How can I have dreamed such a dream in August, 1941? I, who do not even know what *The Myth of the Twentieth Century* looks like externally, not to speak of having read a line of it—what made me dream that I was interrogated by Rosenberg, and then because I utterly refused to answer, because I remained *silent* (Magnificent! as a rule in dreams I am, alas, a coward) was condemned to be executed in a most curious manner. By night, in the middle of a field, and surrounded by SS men, I was asked how it is that I write as I do. I remain silent, contemptuously silent. Then followed endless tirades on the role of the Christian religion as the enemy. At first they said that it was a purely *spiritual* battle. But in the end nevertheless it was decided that I had merited death. I was put on to a sort of hand-wagon which started to move at a single shove, rolling faster and faster towards a precipice, without my being in the least afraid. Just before going over the edge I woke up, still not afraid, but astonished at my dream.

579. 10th September. A year ago today the official propagandist, Fritsche, talking on the wireless, said of the bombing of London: 'Once upon a time fire rained down upon Sodom and Gomorrha, and there only remain seventy-seven just men; it is very doubtful whether there are seventy-seven just people in London today'. I already know many reasons why Germany will not win the war. Fritsche's speech is one.

580. 11th September. On the psychology of the German people. People are asking impatiently when the new gas

will be used, and young girls talk about the 'chocolate factories' that are being put up everywhere—they mean gas factories. We shall need very many just people if there is to be anything left of our people that can still bear a 'name' before God and the world.

581. How capable the German Fieldmarshals are. And then they get themselves well paid. They are supposed to have received a million each. In addition to all the honour! Not to mention the Cross, with the hooks on it. 'The world belongs to the capable', an old German saying. But they are just that much too capable. And the saying then, is no longer true. The world will not belong to them.

582. The devil was in a good mood and said to the soul that wanted to break its pact with him: Tell me a good story, make me laugh, and you can go scot free. The soul answered: If I were to tell you a story that made you laugh, I should lose my blessedness a second time!—and was free.

583. Today it was announced that as from 19th September every Jew must wear a yellow star on the left side of his coat, the star of David, the great King from whose stock the Son of Man, Jesus Christ, was born according to the flesh. It is not impossible that the day will come when every German abroad will be obliged to wear a *Hakenkreuz* on the left side of his coat, the sign of the anti-christ. The more they persecute the Jews, the more the Germans resemble them, and their fate. Today they are crucifying Christ *as a people* for the second time. What is improbable about their undergoing similar consequences?

584. It may seem very much the same, superficially, whether a man has nothing to say, because he has no thoughts to express, or because his thoughts are too great, too mighty and too rich. But what a world of difference between them.

585. Is it madness to assume that mankind might have taken quite a different direction, and that it might have been much happier than it is today? When one thinks that in the life of the individual the possibility cannot be denied, then why should it not be true of mankind as a whole?

586. Good Friday, 3rd April. My God, My God, Why
has thou forsaken me? How can a man be *God* after uttering
these words? That is how the question is sometimes put.
The son of God in a human sense—then certainly, a father
can forsake his son. But that is to bring everything down to a
very human level. Is not this Son of the same essence as the
father? Are these words meant to be heard by the ears of
man? Since man cannot understand them? Nevertheless
they were spoken and they express, as it seems, nothing less
than despair. But a quite definite despair. Some un-
believers interpret them to mean that with these words,
Christ gave up God, and His faith in God. But there is
nothing of that in the words themselves, they are not
atheistic, they say nothing about there being no God, or
about God being dead. On the contrary: *God is.* But he
has forsaken me! And that indeed leads us out into a
restless sea of thoughts which only the power and the peace
of God can still—and the Resurrection.

587. Easter, 1942. In all their impenetrable mystery they
remain the most human words: My God, My God, why
has thou forsaken me? The most divine are: Father,
forgive them, for they know not what they do. The first
words I can say at times in all truth and honesty. The
others I can, up to the present, only look upon with astonishment and wonder, recognising of course, that they express
the *novum mandatum,* and the new order, here lived, expressed,
realised and natural. To be a living stone in the building
of this new order is the aim and end, but that I can never
become of my own strength. So there only remains the
complaint that God had not given me a new heart newly
ordered; though God knows I long for it.

588. 29th April. One must begin with the *equality* of men. Then one can and indeed must go on to speak of the inequality of men. The reverse order is full of dangers, and leads in practice to frightful catastrophes. To the Christian, the thesis is perfectly plain.

589. 1st May. Cold and snow! The weather is not joining in. It is even against us. Science tells us that sun spots are the cause, without telling us however whence they come or why. How many battles and campaigns have in the past been decided, lost and won by the weather. The conquerors of the future must see to it that they also have command of the weather. And if they succeed in doing that then where can you be, poor God! Then what will all the superstitious men do, the men of darkness who so impudently and stupidly, or stupidly and impudently dare to say they see the hand of God in such things?

590. 2nd July. Power and weakness are mysterious things. They may exist in created being without sin, that is to say in the innocent and the good, before the fall of man, and after his redemption, after the coming of Christ and after the judgment, by virtue of the being and the will of God, the creator, who is good. St. Thomas says of woman, after the resurrection: *similiter etiam nec infirmitas feminei sexus perfectioni resurgentium obviat. Non enim est infirmitas per recessum a natura, sed a natura intenta; et ipsa etiam naturae distinctio in omnibus perfectionem naturae demonstrabit et divinam sapientiam omnino cum quodam ordine disponentem commendabit.* (In the same way, the weakness of the female sex does not detract from the perfection of the risen body. For it is not a weakness arising from the non-fulfilment of nature, but is intended by nature. And this is precisely what will demonstrate the perfection of nature in all its varied dispensations, and make manifest the divine wisdom which everywhere creates according to a gradation of orders. Thomas Aquinas: Summa against the heathen, 4, 88). Thus the marvel of

power and of weakness, of strength and weakness, will
continue to exist in a perfectly and indestructibly good
world, not merely united and harmonised, but separate and
distinct. It is one of the divine mysteries of the creation,
and one of the secrets of the beauty of the 'eternal feminine'
—*tota pulchra es!* How beautiful thou art! The core of the
mysterium iniquitatis is a very different matter: the power of
evil and the weakness of good in the world and the history
of man. Certainly it is related, in a manner obscure and
impenetrable to us, to the everlasting mystery of the
separate existence in creation of power and weakness. But
at the bottom of this mystery, the mystery of evil, there is
pain and despair: the prince of this world with great power
and its rightful 'king' hanging powerless upon the Cross;
il sera en agonie jusqu'à la fin du monde. At the very beginning
of the incline or of the decline, there is the Will to Power, the
power before and against God. The will of the healthy and
ordered creature before God or where God is concerned, is
the will to weakness: not my will but thine be done. Even
the pious pagan desired to be without power before God:
cede Deo! Make way before God! 'Who is like unto God' is
the name of the most powerful angel, Michael. Why yes,
of course all that is true, but it does not really begin to
approach the mystery, for God is omnipotent. Just try
and think what that means. Only he must have given
Satan and certain individual men of today power, must have
given it consciously and wilfully, to bring about all the
horrors and the desolation of these times. Indeed, it is
true: the omnipotence of God is not difficult to conceive,
one might really say, that it is naturally assumed. What is
inconceivable is all that God allows. My God, My God,
let me be weak before you, let me be in the wrong!

591. 3rd July. *Nemo enim simul miser et felix esse potest*, no
one namely, can be miserable and happy at the same time—
a sentence taken from St. Thomas, the logic of which is
surely self-evident, incontrovertible. And no doubt it is,

H

where *concepts* alone are concerned. But where a human being is concerned—then it is quite a different matter. One might even say that this is the point where the man and the Christian of today, differs from the man and the Christian of the middle ages. Hölderlin, always so incomprehensible to himself, is not the only one who saw himself in a state which he thus describes: *Wie so selig doch mitten im Leide mir ist*—How happy I am, nevertheless, in the midst of my suffering'. Even Kierkegaard, so much more transparent to himself, understood himself at moments *simul*, as simultaneously the most miserable and unfortunate man, and also as among the happiest, at different levels of the hierarchically ordered strata of man's being, naturally. And that is the explanation which helps us to reach agreement once again with St. Thomas. Max Scheler's recognition of this stratification, and his thorough discussion of it, is among his finest work. In the sense in which he meant it, St. Thomas is obviously right. But men are no longer so 'whole' and 'complete' as in his day, they are dismembered, disintegrated—precisely because they lack faith, and consequently they perceive the dismemberment, the disintegration more easily, though of course it *always* existed, for there is no such thing, essentially, as a new man. But this disintegration is one of the problems of our time, and what is more a painful one, and one, consequently, very fruitful in knowledge. The really astonishing thing is that St. Thomas's philosophy is the only one which provides the principles with which to dominate the problem; and it almost seems as though schizophrenia were a universal disease among modern men. The different realms of man, who is *quodammodo omnia*—in a sense all things—are rebelling against one another. The band which unites them has been broken—by the fall of the hierarchy of the orders. But in spite of everything, St. Thomas's words *nemo enim simul miser et felix esse potest* seems to me to show that he himself was Angelicus—angel-like—in a degree which the Apostle Paul, for example, was not. Thomas had no thorn in the flesh. And to some extent that explains why he is so strange and foreign to modern man who more often than not has not one, but several, thorns in the flesh.

592. It is the impertinent, as well as the thoughtless use of the words 'eternal' and 'unending' which embarrasses and repels the philosopher in me. In created nature there is no such thing as 'eternal' and nothing is unending in the strict sense of the word. The creation is finite—and that is recognised by the natural sciences in so far as they can think philosophically; there is an *indefinite*, but no *infinite*— which comes from God alone.

593. 7th July. As I wrote the date, I was struck by the 7, and how dark and mysterious everything is, and alas, how the Light itself is at times darkest of all. Has the immediate future of nations ever been so dark and hidden from all and each individually as it is today? That is what I meant to ask when I wrote the date 7.7.42. I think one can answer the question with 'no', for they have not even a Promise with which to see vaguely into the future. Everything has fallen about our ears. There is nothing left but the Christian Promise, and it does not refer to this world, but to the new world *before* which comes death. Century after century Christians have deceived themselves about this truth.

594. 8th July. Nothing that is good in this world can claim eternity and immortality. Everything here is destined to perish. If there is not something eternal in the very being of man, then it is ridiculous to postulate or to expect an eternity.

595. The belief in God includes belief in his attributes. No one of his attributes lies altogether easily to hand, in such a way that it cannot be questioned or has not been called in question. To believe in every single one of them

varies in difficulty from age to age. Nowadays, for example, the most difficult is: that He is all powerful or that he is love.

596. The *Verbum* for the sake of which language and all other *Verba* really exist, is the verb 'esse', 'to be'. The German language has a very unfortunate way of calling this verb a 'Zeitwort', literally a 'time-word', a word indicating time, or else a 'Tätigkeitswort', literally an 'action-word', indicating action, whereas it is in reality the word of eternity, and of being. But it reveals much of the German genius.

597. The fact that the spirit of Christ outshone his body perhaps helps to explain the curious circumstance that the disciples at Emmaus did not at once recognise the risen Lord, not until their spiritual recognition once again revealed the whole appearance to them.

598. In a really common, evil man, vices which seem at first sight to be mutually exclusive and contradictory often grow together, or at least tend to do so, for example hypocrisy and shamelessness. It is not merely that he is at one time a hypocrite and at another time shameless—sometimes the same action manages to be both hypocritical and shameless.

599. 4th October. It seems that we cannot live entirely and absolutely without God. As long as we are successful, and above all as long as we spread-destruction 'on a scale hitherto unknown', then of course it is all our own work, our strength, our intelligence, our incomparable genius, our planning, our logistics, the home front and the battle front; for the dominion of the world, the hegemony of one nation, is not God's matter, it does not happen by his permission, but is 'the work of man'. Thus, when it comes off, when the success is there, the merit is entirely ours. But if, for instance, the weather is bad, if the cold weather

comes much earlier than usual, unexpectedly early—then it
is Providence behaving to us like a step-mother.

600. How immensely thankful I was in Church today,
4th October 1942 to hear the Cardinal's decree read out—
as a consequence of the shameless treatment of the last
air-raid victims by the Party—that, in future, ten minutes
after the sirens go, a general absolution will be granted to
everyone who makes a perfect act of contrition. What
consolations the Church has, my God, that thou hast
given her! And almost as though with the intention of
showing us the gulf which separates thy Church from the
German State, Göring made a speech, to give us courage.
Hell was opened, like the heavens at dawn. A nasty mess
of infernally stupid jokes and empty threats the summit of
which was supposed to be the expression 'then God have
mercy on them'. But that, and that alone will be fulfilled:
God will give us grace.

601. 21st October. The mysteries of Christianity excite
various feelings in us or difficulties of feeling (or relating
to feeling) apart from, and yet related to their intellectual obscurity. The mystery of the Trinity is the most
exalted, the mystery of the Incarnation the most disturbing
and the most moving at the same time—it touches us so
nearly, so intimately. And I can never consider the
mystery of the predestination of the Saints without a profound sense of anxiety. Nothing, I think, could alter that.
And a theologian who was to tell me that he could contem-
plate this mystery with the same feelings of solemn calm, as
he would have in contemplating the other mysteries would
be as sinister and almost demoniacally foreign to me as a
man without dread.

602. If Eros is the only power that draws a man up to
higher things, to higher and higher union—then he either
remains proud or becomes proud: 'my name will not

vanish in ages'. How true! But what about eternity? And
God himself, the highest, he can never reach. He remains
so frightfully certain. Suffering is a better way, perhaps the
only one, for it *can* make a man humble, whereas Eros,
whatever its form, can *never* do that. And one only attains
the highest, one can only remain on the heights through
humble love. The 'fall' and the 'pride' of the angel are one
and the same thing. Neither comes before the other.

603. *Short dialogue:*   I do not wish to be on the losing side.
I want to belong to the victorious party.

That is a very human desire, but there are times when
it is more honourable, and therefore more human, to be on
the losing side.

You misunderstand me. I mean that I want to be on the
side that wins in the end, to belong to the party that is
ultimately victorious.

Why do you suppose that I misunderstand you? My query
is still the same: may it not be more honourable, perhaps,
to be on the losing side?

That is a question arising from the despair of unbelief.
For in the end, Christ is victorious. And where is there
greater honour than in Christ?

604.   The majority of men find no difficulty in always being
themselves, that means to say they are always their middling
selves, and of course middling men. And nevertheless they
are probably all created quite differently by their creator.
When one sees them as children, one is convinced of the
fact; when one sees them as grown ups, it is easy to be
vexed and scandalised at the thought that God has created
a very middling, not to say mediocre world.   One of the
principle sources of the slightly contemptuous attitude of
experienced men towards others. When a man 'pulls himself together', not merely for a particular work, or for a
school task or for a game (though even that may very well
get him out of his indifference) but when he does so in

every respect: his whole *self*, in prayer or devotion that is,
then he is never 'middling', 'indifferent' or mediocre. But
then how rare it is! Just as rare, naturally, as the exceptional.

605. If God is 'changeable', then man must despair; if the
world is 'unchangeable' he would also have to despair, or
rather he would be in despair. That is one of the relations
between despair and the changeableness, or unchangeableness of being that Kierkegaard might have treated in
Sickness unto Death. It is, however, a metaphysical question,
and not primarily a psychological one. Only the being of
God is unchangeable, the being of the created world is just
as essentially changeableness. 'The Eternal Recurrence'
(Nietzsche) is therefore despair, because it is based upon the
unchangeableness of the world.

606. There is some life in the German Idealists because
they not infrequently contradict their own systems, and as
a result, say something true.

607. Is time a child of eternity? Even as an analogy it is
difficult to conceive. In time itself, in our time, parents die
and children live on. But if the mother herself is eternity,
she cannot die, and the situation is certainly reversed: time
can and does die. Time may be taken back, or what is more
probable, a new time can be created. One of the promises
made to us is that a new earth will be created, and that is
hardly possible without a new time, however unimaginably
different it may be. But if one can imagine a new earth,
then why not, after all, a new time, more in harmony with
God's eternity.

608. One can always talk best with God. With men, even
with the most trusted friend, I am always conscious of
coming up against a misunderstanding or a failure to
understand, and I even believe that I can understand that
it is more or less inevitable; almost as confidently as I

understand that misunderstanding and failure to understand are ruled out where God is concerned, because He
knows who and what I am.

609. The mark of the poet, his gift of being able to express
his suffering, has degrees and grades of quality; the highest
degree is to be able to say more by not saying it, than by
expressing it, and consequently to introduce the right
proportion of silence: the mystery of wisdom and of beauty.

610. No one likes to be deceived, and everyone is more
or less in dread of it. But only too often this dread
deceives man and robs him of valuable things and
experiences.

611. Fundamentally, metaphysics, in its two pure forms:
that there is only absolute being without becoming, or only
an eternal becoming without an absolute being—fundamentally, both are foolish. But an absolute being, without
becoming is nevertheless more respectable than the philosophy of becoming. The curious thing, in all this, is that
the founder of the pure philosophy of becoming, that has
become the philosopher of the 'common man' in our day,
Heraclitus, was himself, in all probability an aristocrat,
proud, disdainful and contemptuous.

612. Impressionism, not only in painting, but in all the arts,
was the exact expression of the contemporary philosophy of
becoming, a philosophy of the surface, and of the dissolution
of the concept substance. In painting the task might be
set of painting 'running water' as one thing. Disregarding
for the moment, the different gifts, the different capabilities
of the individual artists, and the varying degrees of success
consequent upon these, then in a period when philosophy was
healthy, no artist would think of trying to separate the
unity 'running water', and painting water only, or 'running'
only. This was, nevertheless, the ideal of the impressionists.

The water that flows is only an appearance, it is really—well, it *is* superfluous, an unfortunate remains, that art, and 'ability', cannot quite get rid of, which it could not quite dissolve, unlike 'flowing', the principal thing, since Πάντα Pεῖ everything flows—but that, as Hegel very quickly perceived, meant: *nothing* flows. Everything and nothing, being and non-being are the same; they are identical, and consequently inter-changeable. There is only 'flowing'. To paint 'flowing' alone, is an insane attempt to paint the absurd: the attempt to paint the change without the thing that changes. Nor did even the greatest impressionists succeed in doing so.

613. 21st December. If a man can say in all honesty that he loves God with his whole heart, then he may be sure that he is loved by God; for *only* the love of God can make a man do this: make him love God, the invisible. And when was God so invisible as in these times.

614. It is very humiliating for a man who can do great things, when it is made plain to him that he cannot do the lesser, the ordinary things that almost *everyone* can do. But perhaps that is one of the fundamental principles of this world: in this world the spirit *must* be humble, for without matter it cannot carry on. The pride of the pure spirit in its own realm is lack of love and a betrayal of God; in this world it is, so to speak, materially ridiculous and a lie.

615. The fact that an idol was somewhat ridiculous, that there was something ridiculous on both sides, in allowing oneself to be honoured as a divinity and in honouring another with divine honours, belongs—or belonged!—among the distinctive characteristics of Europe; it marks the difference of quality, its humanism, and that is what made its 'humour' an essential part of its culture, differentiating it from the East. It appears that even nowadays, in Japan, most intelligent men do not even faintly perceive the objective ridiculousness of their religion. It is surrounded by an impenetrable wall of animal solemnity. That a monstrosity, at very first sight so supremely ridiculous should not, nowadays, be laughed to death, and reduced, by ridicule to the nothing which it is, is inconceivable humanly speaking, and inexplicable in Europe, unless one assumes the concurrence of demons, and the fact that the whole nation has previously apostatised. The catastrophe announces itself in advance, of course, in the appearance of such utterly humourless, bestially solemn minds as George, Klages and Spengler. Once a monstrosity, and inhuman behaviour ceases to strike human wits as ridiculous, and is not treated accordingly, Europe is at an end; and the only judgment left is that of the Psalms: 'God laughs at them', and that is certainly not comic in time; but it has an eternal pathos.

616. 31st December. I am still tempted to preserve or to write down the more exotic and revealing blooms of official speeches and announcements. As I hear or see them the impulse is almost irrisistible, there is a real compulsion behind it. But fortunately neither pen, nor paper, nor scissors were to hand. And a few minutes later my desire had passed. Why? What is the point of it? How does it concern me? 'Satires and Polemiks' was written more than twenty-five years ago. I am much too old. Satire, when the talent is there, is not the work for a boy, but for a man, but not for an old man. Not to mention the fact that I think this war transcends the individual man's subjective satire.

1943

617. 1st January. One can already hear the howls and the whines of the demons more clearly in their dread-filled phrases. It is the last breathless gasp of the crazed man who runs amok, just before the end. An official, public call to hate! The hate will certainly be found all right, but it will not be the hate they intend, and want today; it will be different. Hate is the last revealing phase of the fallen spirit, and the very logic of dissolution. But it is also the dissolution of logic, so astonishing that one hardly believes it possible. For example, whoever plans everything will win. We have planned everything, *ergo* we will win. Or: if we do not win the party is lost. The party must not lose, *ergo* we will win. Or: we embody the highest virtues, God gives victory to the virtuous, *ergo* we will win. Or again: for three years now, God has let us win; it would be senseless not to let us go on winning, *ergo* we will win. Or simply; we *must* win, *ergo* we will win. Or, simplest of all: we have already won, only the enemy hasn't noticed it yet. It is our business to strengthen him in his illusion, in order that he should exhaust himself more and more, and then our final victory will be all the more complete.

618. Some Protestants get very worked up about Litanies, Our Fathers and Hail Marys as being in *every* case mere babbling. Even Hilty is sometimes caught napping. But although I see the danger here quite clearly, there is another side to the question. Hilty will be astonished, in the next world, when he discovers how many men have been saved by Our Fathers and Hail Marys apparently just recited by rote, and by the number of sins that were not committed

187

simply as a result of 'grinding out' Litanies. Someone may perhaps object that any meaningless rigmarole would have done just as well. But that is a great error. Every word of our great Litanies has an objective, inexhaustible meaning, an incomputable possibility of contemplation: on each one of these words there is a great blessing granted by God, through those who have prayed them with a pure and burning heart.

619. 3rd January. Once the whole deceit is over—and the beginning of the end is already at hand—then the thing will be not to make a false move. Astonishment and respect, even though negative, would be a fundamentally false move. In addition to the feeling of horror and revulsion that one feels for the inhuman evil that lay, and lies, beneath it all, there is only one possible attitude: *riguarda e passa*, look and pass on. One can look at it, despise it and—pass on. But above all: *pass on!*

But supposing the manifest loathsomeness were only the mirror mercifully held up to us, reflecting with exceptional clarity and without shame exactly how we look in truth and before God? What then? What about our contempt in that case? Perhaps the best thing is reserve. *Le mois est haissable.*

620. In the natural (as opposed to supernatural) history of the creation, we are almost involuntarily driven to the idea of a 'cul-de-sac'. Certain lines of development suddenly reach a point where every prospect of further 'development' and 'progress' appears to have been lost. They seem to be excluded from all fruitfulness—they are 'cul-de-sacs'. The same mysterious method seems to play a part in the spiritual life, in the life of freedom; though here guilt is among the causes of the 'cul-de-sac'. One has to turn about and begin a new life from the beginning. Hasty conclusions crowd upon one at this mysterious point of the 'natural creation', which seem to contradict the plan of God the Creator, all-knowing and all-wise. But be careful! We do not know his ways. If he is the creator, and the 'cul-de-sacs' in fact exist, then of course he is the creator of these 'cul-de-sacs', but it may well be that the term, which is ours, is only a clumsy makeshift for something which we are far from seeing fully and correctly, or that we simply interpret falsely, like a bent stick in the water, that is not bent.

621. The unnatural style of some writers is the result of a secret dread of being banal. But in order not to be banal one must not set oneself the task of being original at all costs, as they imagine, but merely write as clearly and as truthfully as possible, after having first of all overcome a certain natural laziness and tendency to scattered thoughts— for one should of course never write in a mood of 'go as you please'. At the present time language is in a condition which requires the utmost watchfulness on the writer's part, in order that he should not fall victim to it. That was not always so, nor will it necessarily be so in the future.

622. The personal *and* good style of a writer is the natural unity of two natures—often the fruit of the very greatest art: the nature of the writer and the nature of the language at the time he is writing. For these two natures are not identical, and the unity is most often to be reached by mutual concessions and compromise. A man may write an original and personal style that is bad when viewed from the point of view of the language, because he uses violence upon the nature of the language, in general and in particular; and a good pupil may write a 'good' style without betraying anything personal, which he has not got. The great writer, however, is the one in whose style both natures have become a single unity, which it is not possible for anyone ever to separate again.

623. 6th January. Since there can be no doubt that the way to all best higher forms of being is suffering, and that in

certain cases it is the only way, it is not difficult to understand
that some people make it an end in itself, at least as far as
this world is concerned; whereas, eternally speaking, it is
only intended as a means, and even as a means there is
something about it which stirs up man's abstract understanding and is always absolutely un-understandable and
mysterious. To make a means into an end always involves
perversion, and this is particularly so in this case. The end
is God alone, which is to say happiness alone. On the other
hand the significance of suffering as the way to perfection
is so great that whoever withdraws entirely from suffering,
if the choice is given him, assuredly forfeits the highest end,
but whoever choses suffering *for God's sake*, even though he
might avoid it without guilt, is a hero and one of the
'chosen'.

624. 'Human honesty', is something very imperfect because, among other things, its principal object, the '*I*' is so
inadequately known. Who, in fact, knows what his own
'I' is at any given moment, or when it is in its 'fulness'. The
illusions and disappointments that a man meets with at
this point are very great and very painful.

625. 'Paradox' and 'Absurd'. When I say that as a
literary medium the paradox is the result of the poverty
of human language, that is an unequivocal statement, but
not the whole truth. In other circumstances, however, it
might be said with justice that it is the outcome of the
richness of language. Both are but half truths. But if I say
that the paradox results from the poverty *and* the richness
of language, then I merely explain one paradox with
another—and to this there might be no end. Of course it is
paradoxical, but it is not absurd; for when speaking thus
of poverty and riches, they are not referred to in the same
sense. If they were it would be absurd nonsense, which can
neither be, nor be thought. The paradox belongs to man
alone, though as a means and a way, and not as end or aim.

If he thinks that, his mind is diseased. A means and a way!
Whither? To what purpose? To simplicity and harmony.
And man, here, is confronted by grades and degrees. There
is greater simplicity and harmony in man's thought than
in his words and sentences; the natural gift of intuition
possesses greater unity and harmony than his thought which
grasps and deals with it, and the supernatural revelation
which has been given him, indeed his real Christian faith, is
simple and harmonious in the highest form possible to man.
In God, of course, there is neither the absurd (that is
nothing—Nothing) nor the paradox, because he is absolute
simplicity and harmony. Human science, as idea and ideal
is the part of man which does not love the paradox and tries
to exclude it as far as possible. It is essentially rationalist.
Wherever a paradox forces its way to the fore unexpectedly,
as it does nowadays in theoretical physics, in the theory of
the atom and of light, science feels thoroughly uncomfortable
and will not rest until the rational harmony and simplicity
of the principles is restored. At least that is the case with all
the individual sciences which aim at the most complete and
closed system. But in metaphysics, and still more so in
theology, man cannot get on without the paradox. There is,
for example, 'becoming'. What is 'becoming'? Being that
does not yet exist, non-existent being, or an existing non-
being? That is a genuine paradox and what is more unavoidable to the human mind, as to human language. There is a
philosophy, it is true, the philosophy of Heraclitus, and all
its followers in history, for which 'becoming' is a simple and
harmonious conception, because there is no such thing for
them as 'being.' But this philosophy does not in fact strike
the whole truth and reality, simply because there is 'being'
in truth and reality. This philosophy, if it were true, would
not be paradoxical but simple and one, if it were true,
true that is according to the classical definition, according
to which intellect and the thing are completely assimilated.
But neither, on the other hand, would the Eleatic philosophy
of being be paradoxical, but perfectly simple, if it only

expressed the *res*, the facts of the case, if only it were *adequatio rei et intellectus*, when it held being, but not becoming, to be real. But now becoming simply *is*, and must therefore be defined intellectually. That was the task before platonic and aristotelian philosophy. And it has no other means than the paradox of existing non-being.

626. It is very easy to explain the paradox with a paradox, and thus to define it, but it is not absurd. On the other hand the absurd is not to be defined paradoxically, but perfectly simply; it is not the least ambiguous. In one dialogue man has been defined with the words, that his 'non-being' is part of his 'being'. But that is not absurd. Ultimately it might be said somewhat paradoxically of God, that it was of his 'being' to be more than being, and one might say 'super-being', which to man is a paradoxical thought. And indeed non-being and 'super-being' are both incomprehensible to the mind of man, the deep which calleth unto deep—and moreover only something more than being, what we have called 'super-being' can fill 'nothing'.

627. If the comparison with leaven has any meaning, then it can only mean that the world could be Christianised, that progress in goodness is possible in the ultimate meaning of the word, in goodness and love; one cannot really restrict the comparison to the individual merely, where of course it can always be observed, again and again. There is no sense in denying the effect of the leaven in the wider sense. The Christian life of the individual, however, cannot become a habit in the sense of it becoming automatic (it is the exact contrary!) and if this is true of the individual, then it is still more true of a whole nation, or even of the masses. A fresh inspiration is always necessary, and 'the enemy', with his unexpected attack and his new conception of man, (as well, of course, only men in appearance), calls upon the individual to make new decisions, to renewed (or new) use of his free will. All comparisons taken from the

physical and biological sphere and applied to the life of the
spirit, only apply up to a certain point. And 'spirit' means
that one knows and marks up to what point the comparison
is valid.

628. 14th January. From the point of view of the will,
evil is an attitude, a position resulting from an omission,
a want or a deficiency. In metaphysics, therefore, the essence
of evil may be defined as a lack. But in religion that is not
really true. In the last analysis evil is always defined as the
wilful exclusion of the divine by the creature. The wilful
exclusion! And then the cause of evil is created freedom, for
uncreated freedom, God himself, *cannot* produce evil out of
himself. He is one, and 'three-personal' love. Evil cannot
be in matter without life and without spirit, if matter is the
instrument of a free spirit. The summit of God's creative
power is that he can create a *free* being, that can even be
free in relation to him, even to its own mischief.

629. Unless the mystics receive a direct commission from
God to communicate something, or to speak of themselves,
they are wont to remain silent. It is only if they happen to
live on the frontiers where poetry and philosophy meet that
they sometimes regain the power of speech. When Thomas
Aquinas left the realms of philosophy far behind him, he
became silent.

630. You said that 'evil' was a limitation, an amputation
and that it was 'closed', 'finished'. Would you be prepared
to say that 'good' was always 'the whole', 'all'? And if
not, then would it not have to be limited, closed, cut off, in
this finite world?—Certainly it would have to be limited,
but I should not care to use the words 'closed' or 'cut off',
not even 'wanting', though I should certainly say ' limited'
and 'formed individually', yet marking the difference
between life and death, between light and darkness. For the
'good' is always in communion with being in its fulness,

which is God, however little and poor it may be. And that
is precisely what evil does not do, however great it may be,
and outwardly magnificent, like the *Reich*, the Kingdom of
this world, which belongs to the Prince of this world.

631. Justice is a far better maxim in social matters than
'liberty, equality and fraternity'. If all men were equal by
nature, the social problem would not be too complicated.
And they are of course, equal, that is the first point, but they
are also unequal, and that is where justice comes in, and
where the difficulties begin.

632. 17th January. If God were love, indeed, but at the
same time, or rather eternally powerless, would one not
despair? But he is omnipotent. His saints have never
doubted that.

633. 20th January. Human understanding is so easily
angered to find that things only add up very roughly.
Goodness is rewarded and evil is punished, true enough,
that is the simple childish rule. And woe to the nation or
the individual who does not acknowledge the truth of these
words and who does not simply accept them as an unshakeable foundation, in such a way that it is a crime to
assert the contrary: goodness is punished, and evil is
rewarded. But at times a hasty, superficial look at isolated
cases: and everything adds up wrong. One can only see
deeper, and look beneath the surface again with the eye
of faith. Things only become confused before the understanding, as in the opening verses of the seventy-third
psalm.

634. A path that does not lead to the goal, goes to rack
and ruin, becomes a waste: a means that does not attain
its end and perishes, and is soon forgotten. In the life of the
spirit and of freedom, the ways and the means that do not
attain their goal and their end, and often do not *want* to

attain it, put up resistance, for they are often living ways and living means, and even the most insignificant form of life resists death and extermination most tenaciously. The final way out for a way that does not lead to its goal is to declare itself the goal, and the last way out for a means that does not attain its end is to make itself into an end. And that is what is happening to mankind today in such a horrible manner: in its ways, which are the races and nations, and these once again in their means, which are the States and the Parties. Where the spirit is concerned, nothing can happen without freedom, and the half of all the destruction is self-destruction.

635. 23rd January. Literature passes away, and not one of the words which she commands does not pass away. Even the most famous have their limits, and their effect is at last at an end. What is Hecuba to us? What would Hecuba be to us without Shakespeare, who gave the word and the name a few centuries more life? But the time will come when Hamlet will be no more than Hecuba. 'What is Hamlet to us?' someone will perhaps say. And only the learned philologist will discover what it means, and be pleased at having understood it.

636. I much prefer absolute silence about things which with the best will in the world I do not understand, to the semi, forced explanations that leave a bitter taste in my mind. It is so easy to say God permits evil—and what evil!— in order to bring good out of it. I confess that while I understand that, it has never *entirely* satisfied me. And so I prefer to be silent in the abyss of my ignorance, and to pray. I fight shy of the famous paradox: *felix culpa*, the happy fault. It was literally only possible through its 'success'. It is hard to imagine someone encouraging Adam before he committed the decisive sin, and shouting 'Go on! The guilt will bring even greater happiness with it, than you yet know of'.

637. The prophet is a seer and a speaker, he is not a doer. He sees, and declares what will happen, but he does not carry it out.

638. God is so very much, and so essentially an artist that there must be something wrong with those who despise art, even when they are pious and believe. There is absolutely nothing in the works · of nature that is not created as a work of art; even the 'repetition' is the highest form of art: every leaf is a work of art. The curse of the machine!

639. 6th June. There is something soothing and calming about scientific work, latent in its object. It is, so to speak, an innocent science of the works which are *wie am ersten Tag,* 'as on the first day'. Stars and Atoms. And they seem to be so closely related. It seems as though guilt had no part in this marvel. The only delicate point is that the scientist who participates in life which is itself stained with guilt, is not as a rule spiritually pure and purified so that he can perceive the divine connections within his special sphere of knowledge. Even if he is not predisposed against the faith through some prejudice or other, against the true faith I mean, he is nevertheless cold as a rule, and that does not make a man fruitful. On the other hand it seems to me that the more intelligent among the scientists, those who have some slight philosophical leaning, and in particular the theoretical physicists, in their understandable enthusiasm for the discoveries in the field of atomic science, overestimate the possibilities and their consequences to a degree which is very nearly comic. They behave as though these discoveries were not, from the very first, bound within the 'order' in which they were made, at least as far as the *direct* consequences are concerned. However wonderful the atom may be, and however mysterious in spite of its clarity—it will never teach us anything about the greater mystery of life. It may, for example, be a good thing that the physicists

should approach, in this way, to the *prima materia*—and the
antinomies and *a priori's'* which thought on these matters
reveals, suggests that such is the case—but it is another
matter to imagine that: one day, and no one can say whether
it is near or far, perhaps a *new* man will open his eyes and
look upon a *new* nature—the disciple of the *philosophia
perennis* and the believing Christian can only laugh in his
astonishment at such things.

640. We are in God, and God is in the Saint, to a degree
which the pantheist simply cannot conceive because he
does not know the meaning of the transcendence of God,
of the Trinity, in relation to created and creating nature.
On the other hand, to us as nature, the 'Deitas' is foreign and
distant to a degree that an agnostic cannot conceive because
he does not know what is knowable about God.

641. We live in an age of great mystery: divine and living
impotence, barely concealing its power—worldly power
already decaying into lifeless impotence.

642. That is the mark of the great writer: with a single
sentence he establishes the spiritual level, his level, and
remains there. Whether he descends to comedy, or rises
to the height of the ideal—it all happens on his level, and
every word is borne aloft by his fire.

643. 4th July. The sceptic: 'Really, one can only admit
and admire how successful your God is in concealing himself!
You seem indeed to be aware of the fact, and to perceive it,
which is why you like to talk of a hidden God. Only isn't
it carried just a little too far? He conceals his existence so
well that quite clever men simply deny it. One might
almost say that the cleverer a man is nowadays, in the eyes
of the world, the more likely he is to deny the existence of
God. He conceals his omnipotence so well that from the
very beginning men have looked for power elsewhere

(everywhere in fact, except in God who is supposed to be spirit), and clever men have even called him powerless. But without a doubt his masterpiece in the art of concealing himself, is shown by your contention that he is love. No one feels it in the slightest degree. Love, after all, must be suspected and felt before it can be known. I know people who have been in the fighting, they were in Russia and had their eyes open, and their hearts too. They even believed in God, believed that he could be known, believed in his wisdom, in his power, in his Will and in his works, but his feeling, his compassion, his love and his mercy—no, at that point they became indignant and hard, then they grew angry: at least don't come to me with that story, they said. Love is an internal matter, it is rare, and is found among exceptional men—there is not even a distant analogy to it in God.

*   *   *

I let the man talk, I did not have the answer ready beforehand—although I have one—to which I could then preface the question—suiting it to the answer—the usual rhetorical trick of all those who write dialogues, and which puts the passionate enquirer out of humour.

644. All that I know and my whole work rests on my faith. To such a degree is that the case, that at times I am terrified. All my knowledge falls to pieces and becomes incoherent, meaningless, empty, unless it coheres in the faith.

645. There is a tendency, and God does not seem to be averse to it, for the things of this world to be explained almost 'totally' and purely from the immanent laws of nature, from the causality of the *causae secundae*; and what is more, on the *whole* field of created being, from physics and chemistry to politics and metaphysics. And never by halves. And in a sense that is a good thing. And then, moreover, does that not make natural theology a matter of quite tremendous importance?

646. The writer's passion is sometimes very great. Even in the pale night of dread, he is still anxious to safeguard the accuracy of his expression: It is a pale night, not a dark night, nor an impenetrable, nor a black night! It is a pale night. And even while feeling the abyss open under his feet, the frightful feeling for which there is no comparison, of falling 'in itself', falling without hope, falling into the bottomless pit, he is still impelled to save the description with the true expression : Such and nothing else, is dread: a pale night.

647. Apollo and Christ: that was the synthesis for which Hölderlin longed. Then came Dionysus and Christ, less noble, indeed. And corresponding to them the madness into which they both, Hölderlin and Nietzsche, fell. But how astonishing the synthesis is in the Turin picture: Zeus and Christ!*

648. 'The apocalypse of the German soul' is even more painful than Sörgel's bilge; it has very different pretentions! To compare Stefan George with Isaias, yes indeed, Isaias, is a horrible blasphemy; or rather it *would* be a blasphemy if the man could reach the necessary level; but he doesn't. And so it's bilge. It cannot even be called 'literature', for that implies a sense of quality. And that is what fails him. He cannot write a 'sentence'.

649. Short Dialogue: 'We have gone to war for the sake of peace'—How I love the archer who sends his arrow into the plumb middle of the target! You may have hit one of the inmost circles, but not the centre of the target. No, everyone, listen to this, everyone goes to war for the sake

---

* Haecker is referring to the impression of Christ's face on the Holy Shroud in Turin.

of victory. In war, they want victory, and only in the second instance all the other things, and even something as good as peace. Even Michael wanted victory in the first place. I think one must stick to this precise definition, otherwise one very easily gets among half-truths and lies that weaken and corrupt thought. Very soon one ceases even to notice one's own mistakes.

650. In the name which God himself gave himself, God is not 'paradoxical'. He is majestically simple: 'I am who am': that does not allow of any 'interchange and reversal of concepts', nor of any of the nonsense and falsehood of idealistic philosophy. In his revelation God is Father, Son and Spirit. What could be more clear and simple, universally intelligible, unalterable in its being and meaning, incapable of being confused.

651. If the purely human conception of our æon is prolonged indefinitely, or only the human aspect of our æon is pursued in a straight line (what might be called radical humanism) it leads to an ultimate despair. If God is only man magnified, as we meet him in history and in life, then he cannot save himself or God from ultimate meaninglessness, and the meaninglessness of the world is absolute, and the absolute is meaningless. The argument indeed goes further: If being itself is radically and eternally meaningless, the fact remains that the spirit of man nevertheless *has* the notion of meaning, quite radically and eternally as it seems. Why? Why ever ask the meaning of anything? And that is the objective madness of the whole thing. When we say: we do not otherwise ask about something which does not exist. The fact that we ask at all about meaning, already presupposes meaning; and this in the sense, moreover, that we could not raise the question if it had no sense. Meaning there is, somewhere or other, and in fact in God, only we do not know him—when we say all this, then the usual answer is: But aren't we talking about Nothing— and then does it exist? Nothing? And if that is so then it is like being. Satan is the Lord, and lies and pain. That is the seasoning, the salt of despair that burns for ever in the wounds of man: the fact that he seeks for a meaning that does not exist. That is *objective* madness.

652. For almost a hundred years the function of literature has been understood to consist in describing, as exactly as possible, how the world looks without God. One after the other they have surpassed each other in the art of portraying the frantic flight before God. Even when their art itself was not recognised as a flight from God—that is what it was. For it only held to God, at best, in the shriek of dread and despair, in its hopeless homesickness, in the unlimited disgust that was eating their souls away. The tone was irremediably false. None of them believed in the 'victory' of God. How could they believe, then, in their own? And yet it would be untrue to say that none were loyal to God, in even those times. But when they appeared and spoke, they were often already in a sense beyond the world. Where the world was concerned, they were curiously weak, mediocre, inadequate, and the literature they produced was actually *sham*. The one exception was perhaps Hilty. There there was strength, strength from above, a mission, joy, certainty, truth and victory. Keppler was only well-meaning literature, and the Rembrandt-Deutsche* were all too German. They were never consumed by the eternal flame. They could only relate how once upon a time . . . . .

653. The qualities in man which make him a soldier also serve to make him a Christian, because the soldier

* Keppler, Bishop of Rottenburg. *Rembrandt als Erzieher*, published anonymously " von einem Deutschen ". Its many admirers were called " Rembrandt-Deutsche ". The book sought to counteract the "scientific culture" of the period, and was vaguely Christian, though owing much to Nietzsche.

understands better than others, by nature in fact, and by training, one particular element in the service of God: *obedience*. In the creature's relation to God, his relation as being and as acting, there is no substitute for obedience, except the perfect love of God's saints. What a show of sentiment the poet in a man puts up, how many intellectual difficulties the philosopher in him thinks he has to solve before obeying an order from God! The soldier in a man may be a great help towards Christian obedience. Women do not need it in the same way; by nature and out of love, women are closer to obedience: woman is humbler.

654. Sic transit gloria mundi—transit yes, but the *gloria mundi* is not nothing. Nothing that is the symbol of a divine being, is nothing. We are not nihilists but 'hierarchists'.

655. In recent times it seems as though the Germans had chosen madmen, men who quite simply went mad, and consecrated them, raised men like Nietzsche and Hölderlin to the level of prophets, heroes, saints and wise men, and made idols of them. Are the Germans blind to the fact, or do they think it perfectly normal? Have they no after thoughts? Has it ever happened before? Even in Germany? Does it occur among other nations? I know of no other example. In recent times other nations have at the most acclaimed a number of staggering idiots as great men. But have they made lunatics into founders of religion? Surely only the Germans do that; and they are mad themselves, they are mortally sick.

656. The spiritual man is indeed something other than the intellectual man, though naturally presupposing and including him: he has a whole dimension more, he is the complete man, according to the idea of God, a perfect unity, an incomparable totality, desired by God, and, as *anima naturaliter christiana*, longed for by man. The spiritual man is the opponent of the gnosticism and 'idealism' in German

philosophy, after all only a sort of watered down gnosticism.
Only the spiritual man understands the 'holiness' of the
body. An embrace can never be holy to the gnostic. And
those who do not want to insult the creator, should be careful not to insult his creation. The Christian is the 'enemy'
of the 'world', the world in inverted commas. And that is
by no means the 'pure' creation of God, but the product
of fallen man and fallen angels. The world in this sense, the
'world' in inverted commas, and the man who belongs to it,
one might even say 'man' in inverted commas, the ambiguous fudge of good and evil, wanting in all decision, and
incapable of saying 'no' to anything, is consequently dangerous: this 'world' and this 'man' have evil in them, metaphysically speaking, as nihilism. The 'man' corresponding
to the 'world', sometimes impertinently called natural man,
as though he were the product of uncorrupted nature, which
exists only in the Immaculate, this 'man', outside Christianity, necessarily has in his Art a certain nihilism of
feeling. Even love sings and murmurs a melodious Nothing,
like *Tristan*; he has a nihilistic, devastating philosophy once
away from the privileged philosophy of being of Aristotle
and Plato; he has a nihilistic politics, an apostate politics,
because his will is nihilistic and does not will the true end,
which is God alone. And it is perfectly normal, perfectly
in order that the three faculties proper to the spirit of man,
thought, feeling, will, should each have their part in the
dangerous, almost mortal illness of being in this 'world',
this 'world' in inverted commas.

657. 5th November. We, too, smile at the arguments of
our natural reason for the truth of our supernatural faith;
we can, and of course do smile at them, though not quite
in the same way as others may do, for we do it with humour.
We see the point. It is not as though we simply regarded our
arguments as worse than theirs, or as though we thought
their arguments better, or *unanswerable*. That would be a
great mistake on their part. O no! And in the end, after

much has been said, we have our faith, and not by virtue of our own reason. *That*, you see, is our secret, the secret you do not understand. *That* is our transcendent, eternal superiority.

658. 'We want eternal life', you once said, solemnly. But I think there are times when you have no wish to live at all, and certainly renounce an *eternal* life, for what more voluptuous consolation could there be than the fact that there was no eternal life—if all were over? Why do you lie?—Take it calmly, my friend, I am not lying.—What? Are you denying that you have such moments?—No, I don't deny it. But I am a man and weak; in fact I am not always I, and I might almost say that I am seldom I, I am only half, or a quarter or not at all myself. I am often tepid, worthy of being 'spewed out'. And then I have neither the right faith, nor the right hope, and anything but the right love. But when in truth I love God with my whole heart, and with my whole mind, how should I not have a burning desire to live eternally? How should I lie when I say: 'We want an eternal life'. Is God not eternal, and is love not eternal? But God is love. And He is *unchangeable.*

659. Why has dread now departed, the frightful dread? As I knew: I myself could do nothing against it; it could only be taken from me.

660. There is an art which is evil, but even then it is 'Art', art that comes from God.

661. If the designation 'spiritual man' means, in the first instance of course, that man is 'planned as spirit', which means to say that he has within him the life of the spirit, and of the Holy Spirit, and acknowleges its primacy, it implies here, in all its fulness, in its totality, the man who has a *body*, in the original, real sense of revelation, so that in eternity, in the fulness of his spiritual life he will not be without a body.

662. Even in the West, Christian theology has shown a certain cowardice, and a wretched want of understanding of the munificence with which God has endowed created and creative nature and the world with power and energy of its own; and the testimony of history to the fight of the Church against the natural sciences, and its representatives, and their great discoveries is one that shames us. It arose from a great fear that the natural laws might lead to a proof of the non-existence of God. That is its only, all too human, excuse.

663. God alone is eternal. God alone is all his attributes, but certain ones belong to him absolutely alone. He alone is Creator. He alone is all-powerful. God alone is eternal. He *can* annihilate. He can annihilate after aeons. His majesty is terrible. He is eternal. He alone.

664. Without time, humour is unthinkable; yet it belongs to the things that are unthinkable without eternity. And that is saying a great deal, for most things belong to time *only*. Humour in eternity is hardly conceivable, but in eternity faith and hope will also cease to be.

665. There are some liturgists so rabid that they are idiotic. They really behave as though Christ came into the world to found a liturgical movement.

666. Hail to the glorious, happy voice of the announcer of the 'German Mission': it explains everything as a victory, or at least as being like a victory, even defeat.

667. It is by no means so simple to establish *error invincibilis*, and accuracy, here, is essential. It is only valid *absolutely*; the slightest trace of relativity annuls it and brings it within the possibility of guilt.

668. The relation of eternity to time is simply not to be expressed in essence in human speech, because language, even more than thought, is temporal.

669. I saw in secret a man flowing with the tears of thought and repentance, and inwardly he shone like a young tree with all the blossom of May upon it.

670. ad Temptations . . . . .* and finally the image of all images, of all worlds and æons and of eternity itself, that must always be spoken of, that all must speak of since the Revelation, because it is inexhaustible in its being, and indescribable in its meaning: the cross.

671. Suddenly woken from sleep, I remembered—a rare pleasure—an interrupted dream: it was an interesting discussion of a theological theme that had bothered me the previous day. I was delighted to have dreamed of such things. My Lord and my God, if I think of you night and day—am I not in your hands? Is it not a sign that you think of me?

* 'The Temptations of Christ', Haecker's meditation on the temptations of Christ as the symbol of history. Published 1944.

1944

672. Whether they are really the *horrifying* scoundrels they undoubtedly are, or the *unimaginable* and for ever indescribable blockheads that, equally undoubtedly, they are—has always been, and still is a tormenting dilemma which it is hard to answer clearly. Now we know, in point of fact, that they become quite disproportionately more excited and angry at being called the unimaginable, and for ever indescribable blockheads they undoubtedly are, and can be proved to be, than at being called the horrifying scoundrels they quite as undoubtedly are, and can be proved to be. This fact would appear to lead to the conclusion that they are the unimaginable blockheads they are, rather than the horrible swine they nevertheless continue to be, and in a far more profound degree, and to a much greater extent. And this conclusion corresponds to the last aspect of the Saviour on the Cross: Forgive them, for they know not what they do. Their desire to rend to pieces anyone who calls them the unimaginable blockheads they undoubtedly are, cannot be accounted for by the fact that they really are blockheads, for if this were so, then we should, on the contrary, have to conclude that they were horrible scoundrels. But no, they are primarily unimaginable fools *because* they do not see it, and regard themselves as unbelievably clever, always preferring a criminal act to a folly. Their general teaching, which can hardly be kept secret any longer runs thus: cleverness means to do evil and go unpunished, and what is more this holds good metaphysically, before God. And the fact that they believe it, is the ultimate source of their ultimate

unspeakable stupidity. There is not a single soul praying for them, and they do not know that their cause is consequently lost irretrievably. They cannot pray themselves, that I can understand, and it is understandable, for in the first place they do not want to. But not have a single soul praying for them, not one soul before God, praying for their cause, not one who dares to pray for it even—well, that is their death sentence.

673. With the help of the axiom that the love of God is always greater than the love of man, the love of the creature, I can master the difficulties which the eternity of hell presents to me. I include belief in the eternity of hell, so to speak, in my belief in the love of God, in which I believe unshakeably. Belief in the eternity of hell does not offer my understanding any difficulty, *the* understanding, I would even say, as long as it recognises everything impersonally, and above all the essence of freedom and of obedience, and of justice; it is not contradictory—But where love is concerned! There are very many who have never got to the end of it, and nor should I, without the axiom in question. The axiom is incontrovertible, logically, intellectually and, of course, to love. What could be more true, more clear, more just and blessed, than that the love of God is always greater than the love of man?

674. The gate to the *knowledge* of our salvation, too, is a narrow gate, as long as one is *in via*. And unless the Angel of God leads you, you will go astray. *Self*-faith, *self*-confidence, *self*-knowledge, all these are bad and dangerous leaders. You must learn to curb your curiosity.

675. Men are so often made unspeakably unhappy by looking in the wrong direction. They make the great sacrifice that their eternal salvation, that is God, requires. But they fix their gaze upon the sacrifice, as though hypnotised. And in that way it grows to giant proportions, and

becomes unendurable. But God is surely 'more' than any sacrifice, however great the sacrifice may be, and one look at God, in exchange for that almost hypnotic gaze, will often save a man from torture.

676. How thoroughly mediocre is the rationalistic notion that man's sacrifice to the Gods, or to God is man's discovery, an invention prompted by his fear and dread. Oh no! Sacrifice is primarily God's idea, and even that is saying too little, it is a mode of God's being, so to speak, for ever and ever, and therefore *had* to enter into time. God's sacrifice of himself is the overflowing of his Being.

677. Quite openly, God works in secret; and without deceiving, He deceives His enemies. That has always been so, and it is also always true of men that they see without seeing, and that they hear without hearing and understand without understanding. And anyone who sees and understands that for the first time thinks he is the first to do so—the impression is so immediate and overwhelming.

678. What a curious change of scene: to make doubt the starting point of philosophy, instead of the sense of wonder. A revolution, not only in thought, but also and perhaps primarily, fundamentally, in feeling. And probably too, a revolution in the will.

679. More than half of life consists in waiting—for a particular moment in time, often purely abstract—waiting to be twenty years old. For an uncertain, insignificant accomplishment in time. And finally for death. Waiting for an ephemeral fulfilment that does not even fulfil its name, and quickly disillusions one, and for the nothingness of death. That is almost the rule for the man of the present age. But waiting only becomes significant for the spirit of man if it means waiting for the absolute and the eternal. All else is an illusion, *vanitas vanitatum*.

I

680. Those with a well-founded expectation of suffering a martyr's death can perhaps endure the far greater agonies of dread in imagination, beforehand. For in the reality of martyrdom God helps a man; in his own fantasy, in the possibility of his imagination, unlimited by factual reality, that is not so. Even Christ, the Son of Man, found the momentary dread of anticipation in the Garden indescribably more agonising than any subsequent moment of definite torture in the unavoidable suffering. For then, instead of a boundless fantasy, it was the concrete suffering that determined the unsurpassable measure of the real limit of suffering.

681. Nowadays, the East interprets its art in western terms, because it has none of its own.

682. Christ always speaks in the last, and absolute, spiritual sphere, of man's salvation, that is to say the salvation of the spirit, the soul and the body of man in relation to God and his neighbour.

683. The unquestionable dignity of the contemplative life is stained as though by the ugliest sin, by every disregard of the practical command to love God and to love and help one's neighbour, so absolute is the command to love God and one's neighbour, on which everything depends.

684. Love alone knows no measure, and yet when it is immeasurable, it is measure itself, the divine by which we shall be measured.

685. The corruption began when the dominating idea in the hierarchic order ceased to be 'the good', and was replaced by 'the beautiful'—what is called the Renaissance—and the result was not a harvest of evil, but the profound ugliness of the souls of today.

686. To be able to say of a writer: whether his adjectives come from thought, and are strictly relevant, or from the will, expressing wishes and intentions, more or less, or come from feeling and are consequently subjective, sub-objective.

687. The fact that God remembers everything is human, and perfectly intelligible; but that God should be able to forget, that is what is really inconceivable, for ultimately a complete forgiveness of sins means to forget in eternity.— But then what, if you please, of the existence of an eternal hell?—What has it got to do with those who are blessed and happy?—What it means to the blessed? O but, my friend, can you really imagine one of the blessed looking at hell?— For myself, I can't, but there ought not really to be any difficulty. God sees it after all, and God is holy. But perhaps the blessed will not see it at all. Have any of those who have been blessed in time seen hell? Blessed in time only, and then in eternity! Will he see hell?—Perhaps not, but I do not know. But one thing I do know, there *is* a hell; and could one, then, call someone blessed and happy who did not see a part of reality, and consequently of truth, at all, even though he himself were satisfied?

688. One of the principal instincts in man is towards 'pleasure', in the body and in the spirit. Even while he suffers, he enjoys in advance, the pleasure of one day relating his suffering, and even the poet who *can* say what he has suffered, gets the fullest pleasure from avoiding suffering. I think men would be less willing to go to war if this natural thirst for pleasure did not express itself in subsequently relating great sufferings. Very often the most melancholy man is the most pleasure-loving. That is what makes him so hard to understand, so ambiguous, so difficult to heal. Does he belong among the good? Is the melancholy man a good, a kind man? That is not I think the way to set about it. Is he bad? Is he guilty? That is not quite right either. Rather, he is a man who feels guilty.—Without a

doubt, that is right. But he is, you say, pleasure loving.—
Yes, I really think so. He enjoys his misfortune. And then
he is vain. Still, that does not prevent his misfortune being
real, and not something imagined. How deep down the
instinct for pleasure goes, how unbelievably deep. There is
however a melancholy that is sheer poison.

689. The endless chatter about Nietzsche and Kierkegaard is quite hopeless. Outward similarities set up a superficial sphere of comparison that is utterly meaningless, for
they are localised and limited by a decisive difference at a
deeper level; the one prayed, the other did not. And
people are quite satisfied, and the radical difference is no
longer perceived. An example of the growing 'blindness'
of which I spoke.

690. Those who are spiritually blind, are not only blind
to the object they want to see, but blind to their blindness.
And that, ultimately, is the motive of the words: Forgive
them for they know not what they do: that indeed, is not
'blind' love, but love which sees. Love that sees the fact
of this 'blindness'.

691. Historical writing since the Reformation, on the
Protestant side, is all tendentious, a matter of propaganda.
History and the truth of history is decided by 'the
truth' of Revelation, whose guardian on earth is the holy,
Catholic, apostolic Church. There is nothing to be done
about that; nothing can alter it. Even men of Ranke's
nobility of mind, striving for pure subjective honesty, *must*
fail and make mistakes if they fail to strike the target of
truth in the centre through their own, or inherited guilt,
and are led astray from the light of revelation. Not all the
human virtues put together can attain the goal, which is
the spotless perfection of true doctrine. The Roman-
Catholic Church has *lacunae* because it no longer has within
its totality the Germanic element, nor has it any longer the

Greek and Slav elements, nor as yet the Chinese or the Indian element. Those are really great *lacunae*, a great lack of fulness and of completeness, but its supernatural core is spotless and without *lacunae*. And those who do not see that—well, they are blind. Spiritual blindness differs from physical blindness in this, that it is not conscious. That is the essence of *error invincibilis!*

692. The written language must continually be refreshed by the spoken language, that is by great writers, whose living soliloquies (monologues or dialogues) are spontaneous and lead directly from the heart of feeling to language, without going a roundabout way, avoiding the usual worn-out, conventional lines, avoiding the old pipe lines, choked with old phrases, so furred-up that language loses all its *élan*, all its strength and all its purity.

693. 'The discerning of spirits', in any sphere, is a gift that makes the possessor lonely and, from a worldly point of view, unhappy. In a higher sense it is the source of profound happiness. He cannot communicate himself and his certain knowledge with success. Discussions and argument are, as he knows, useless. But there also exists, nowadays, another gift, 'the discerning of voices'. Those who have it, have it; it cannot be communicated. And yet how needful it is nowadays, for voices today are so significant. The 'announcer' 'reveals' politics and even religion to us, is a political functionary, and his function is incalculable in its effects upon the feelings of men and of the masses, far more decisive than thoughts. Thoughts in themselves are far more independent and more abstract than the voices that express and announce them, than the feelings that are voiced by and fused with certain voices. Today on the wireless I heard Kayssler making his fine and in itself 'expressive' voice the vehicle of hollow lyrical idiocy. And I had the familiar experience, that alarming impression which can be made upon one by a discrepancy between things which ought to belong 'together'. Why is it that men have the power of dividing up what is living as though it were dead, and exchanging the parts, or separating them just as they please? Of handling the inner as though it were the outer, and the reverse? That is one of the principal reasons why life does not 'add up'. There is a 'true' disorder in this æon. And moreover the inmost things can be torn apart in a way in which outward things cannot be.

694. Sufficient understanding for the day—but no, that never satisfies us, even though the day were an æon. We want the absolute and nothing else. The 'fame' of this world only makes the pilgrim of the absolute all the more melancholy; the more fame he has or can have, the greater his melancholy, the longer it lasts. And isn't the insipidity and worldliness of Faust due to the fact that he is satisfied with 'æons', a bourgeois hero of this world's progress. The ordinary Christian who believes is beyond such childish notions, and has a further sense of quantity.

695. There is something cassandra-like and almost sinister in not being able to communicate one's most certain knowledge, what one sees and hears immediately, not just deductions reached somehow or other, among which one can so easily go astray—but ones immediate intuitions. And then one cannot communicate them to others, not even to those one loves, and who aren't stupid, simply because they neither see nor hear! It is a very strange and very painful condition to be in. I can hear something in the voice of the official announcer of *Deutschlandsender*—and what an ominous double-meaning the word contains in German, with its play on the word 'sender' and 'sendung', a mission—to me absolutely evident, something I could not shake off with the best will in the world, a stupid infernal pride that inevitably and freely calls down a curse upon itself, the incurable, hopeless condition of the soul of the nation that takes pleasure in the voice that is identical with it—and not even

the better people notice it. Sometimes I am tempted to beg
God to spare me so painful an insight and so agonising a
spiritual hearing. What am I to do? Over and over again
I try to communicate my despairingly clear knowledge
spontaneously, I point, as it were, to the tone, the quite
unmistakable tone that cannot be misunderstood or not
heard, the tone that is identical with the whole thing and
the catastrophe, and again and again I am stunned by the
astounding fact that the tone in the voice is not heard, and
the sense not understood. What am I to do? Say nothing
at all? Keep silent? Or speak too late?

696. 1st May. The 'cul-de-sac' referred to in evolu-
tionary theory—particularly in Bergson—gives me no rest.
The spiritual 'cul-de-sacs' that certainly exist, are formed in
the realm of 'freedom', for spirit and freedom belong
together. There is always some guilt involved. In the philosophical systems that lead to cul-de-sacs the intellect
naturally plays the chief role: error and illusion. But that
is not all. There is something existential in it too, based
upon perverted feeling, something ambiguous in the will.
Intellectually it is always false principles that lead to a
cul-de-sac, and they are more or less easily demonstrable.
If the principle behind a statement, whether clearly recognised or half unconscious, or only darkly implied, includes
the proposition that the difference among men is greater
than their equality, and not the reverse, which in my opinion
is the truth, then that philosophy leads theoretically, and if
anyone lives according to it, existentially, into a cul-de-sac,
however broad and however beautiful and fruitful the
prospect may seem at the outset. Nowadays that is an
instructive and topical example of how 'guilt' is always
involved, and not just the 'error' of the 'pure' intellect.

697. There is a great difference between saying something
differently, or saying something different. And there are
three kinds of men, all dangerous, who bring about

confusion at this point. First, there are those who do not see the difference at all. They are not much good at thinking, which does not however hinder them from writing, and often writing quite a lot. The result is the type of doctrine known as 'liberalism'. The two other kinds are more dangerous. Those who denounce any and every different view of the same object as the description of a different object; they narrow and confine all that is vital. The most dangerous of all however is the man who merely pretends to describe an important object differently, but in fact describes something quite different. That has done great mischief in philosophy and theology.

698. The Germans tend *by nature* to the heresy of Pelagius and of Arius, by nature, that is by their own ability, that makes them proud, and by their own pride, that makes them intellectually shallow.

699. Warf er nicht höher den Ball in die Luft als jeder andere? Und flach traf sein Kiesel die Fläche des Sees und hüpfte zehnmal. 'Did'nt he throw the ball higher into the air than any of the others? And his pebble struck the surface of the sea so smoothly that it bounced ten times'. That is well told, in every respect, though of course its content is unimportant. And nevertheless the sentences remain stuck in my memory on account of their rhythm. I cannot remember or whistle a melody, not even the simplest, but even the emptiest sentences remain in my memory simply on account of their rhythm . . . . . Of all delights the noblest is surely the delight in language, language which as a symbol is so entirely different from the object, and from the 'being' to which it corresponds—and then again it is indescribably one with them!

700. 29th May. 'Einmalig', unique, though literally it means 'happening but once'. A word that ought not, properly speaking, to be used more than once, and that has

become the most worn of old clichés. All the throat clearing
and the spitting that goes on is 'unique'.—Perhaps, but the
absurdity of it is surely *'einmalig'*?

701. All that I write down tends, quite by itself, to grow
into a dialogue. My mind always tends to fall at once into
conversation with another, with a 'you'. And what of my
soliloquy! There indeed I am alone, and that only places me
all the more absolutely before God. My partner then is the
eternal 'You', the transcendent You, my Creator, my
Lord and my God.

702. 4th June. My sixty-fifth birthday. The entry of the
Allies into Rome!
The President of the State Literary Bureau writes to me
as follows 'On this your sixty-fifth birthday, on the 4th
June, I wish to convey to you the best wishes of German
Authors (deutschen Schrifttums!) as well as my own'. What's
that? What's that? Has Herr Johst the faintest idea who
I am? In that case he certainly knows nothing about this
letter. And if he knows of the letter, then he cannot know
anything about me. There remains, however, the well-
founded suspicion that the letter is the automatic product
of a well-ordered card-index system where the number
8814—that is my number—gives out the name Theodor
Haecker, my birthday and my address. That is the only
possible way of giving the thing any kind of meaning,
although of course there are still a number of other possibilities. But why bother.

703. I know a tragic man whose writing is tragic and who
regards God as the most tragic person of all. He cannot get
away from that. He is eternally enveloped in tragedy. And
that gives his writing a terrible reality. He is capable of
talking of the silent jubilation of the mystics with the
unmistakable note of the silent despair of Kierkegaard's
father. He possesses the language and the being of an

objective, scientific melancholy that is absolutely impenetrable. Now Kierkegaard did not have that, although his
melancholy was unlimited; for at times he did break
through it, did really break out of it, so that he could really
breathe freely, and let his reader breathe freely.

704. 9th June. Friday morning towards ten o'clock. In
the cellar. High-explosive bomb. The house and my flat
destroyed. Unbelievable destruction. Some good people,
helpers, people who console me by being what they are and
by helping! Scholl. And also some *crapule*. Upright souls.
And miserable souls. God is merciful! God is great! God
is precise, but magnanimous. What has happened to me
is no injustice.

705. Even pride has its justification and may be valid in
God's eyes, if humility has acknowledged it. But it must
pass before the judgment seat of humility. Otherwise let
no one believe it! For pride is insidious, and sometimes it
even apes humility. The one certain court of humility is
the Cross, on which one hangs with Christ. And the pride
that is justified after that—that one should have! For one
can have it without danger!

706. 22nd December. It makes a difference whether a
writer can suddenly surprise a reader with an unexpected
turn of phrase or whether one expects something unexpected to occur. It also makes a difference whether one
can read the unexpected passage twice, or only once.

707. 30th December. The passionate endeavour to paint
the picture in which H. shall go down to history has recently
given Goebbels the cramp. But today he surpassed himself:
he is not only the greatest genius of the world, he is its
'saviour'; the apocalyptic cretin is not only without shame,
he has even lost the cleverness of the 'world'. The fool
thinks that because no one any longer accepts his base and

fulsome flattery except a few imbecile fanatics, he can write
his enormous cheque to be drawn on posterity, as though
it would be honoured with enthusiasm, and brass bands;
in fact they will not even protest: the cheque will not be
presented.

708. 31st December. This afternoon at three o'clock it
was announced on the wireless that tonight at 'five minutes
past midnight' the Führer would make a speech. The
manager of this sensation did not of course suspect that
this only happens in order that the words might be fulfilled:
'I shall only stop five minutes after midnight'.*

* The reference is to a speech by Brunning and is an example of the
senseless ' symbolism ' employed by the Nazis.

1945

709. 1st January. The first broadcast I heard was: the Führer spoke 'shortly after midnight' . . . . no longer 'five minutes after midnight'. So they have noticed something—only too late! *De nominibus est curandum* (one must be careful of one's words), and in time, otherwise it is too late. The announcement on 31st December 1944 at three in the afternoon: The Führer will speak to the German people tonight at five minutes past midnight, is of such appalling symbolic power that it simply must bring reality in its train in 1945: I shall only stop five minutes past midnight. *Fiat voluntas tua.*

710. 2nd January. It seems nothing worse, nothing less desired could happen to the German people than a miracle. It is true that the ghastly individuals who give us the news and disguise their wishes as statements, have not tired for the last fortnight of describing the German offensive as a miracle, as a 'German miracle', though they continued to insist that nothing would be more mistaken than to regard the German capacity for resistance as a 'miracle', for on the contrary, it represents the perfectly understood power of the German people, their fanaticism, the genius and the thoroughness that explain everything, the careful plans, and the natural fact that they are unconquerable. At the last moment, it is true, Goebbels spoke of 'a miracle of the German people', of the only one, and this miracle is: the Führer.

711. History teaches us that no one feels so disgustingly certain of victory, or is so unteachably sure, and immune to reason, as the fanatic, and that no one is so absolutely certain of ultimate defeat.

712. 23rd January. One ought to, and may reproach one-self alone for not being a saint; on no account anyone else.

713. No, the practical demonstration of the non-existence of God will fail too, just as the theoretical attempt failed and always will fail. But the practical attempt is far more dangerous and makes a much greater impression on far more people than the theoretical. I must admit that the victory of the Party in world history, to speak like a fool and *per impossibile*, would have exposed me to the great temptation of believing that the non-existence of God had been proved or at least—but God forgive me for a madman, tortured almost to death, forgive me the fog of blasphemy! Forgive me daring to understand that 'falling away' and that despair. But the practical demonstration will not come off.

714. 30th January. The glory of Europe, its high point, and the sign of its election, is that a sentence in Plato, which says that it is better to suffer injustice than to commit it, should touch from afar the divine revelation of Christ. If there is injustice in the world, then the greater worth belongs to him who suffers the injustice, not to him who commits it. That is astounding, and belongs to another world. Injustice! Not power be it noted, for the good and the wicked can use power, but not injustice.

715. 8th February. The unmistakable mark of the false prophet, of the prophet of this 'world', is that openly or hiddenly he tells men that the way of salvation is broad, and the gate wide, whereas in truth and according to the will of God, the way is straight and the gate narrow.

716. In very many cases faith in God is no longer much more than faith in a last, saving, straw. But what does it matter, if the straw is really God, for God is all-powerful.

717. 9th February. Man will be judged and sentenced according to the order of reason, not according to the order of the senses, to which in the first place he also belongs. The idea of man, his ideal, is given to him by God, though in such a way that it is man who freely gives it to himself, and must give it freely to himself, if he is to grow up out of the sensual, animal world, in order that he should spiritualise his body and his senses, and not destroy or treat the body with contempt. The union of the sensual and the spiritual that alone rightly deserves the name of man, raises many difficulties: for example a being that is purely sensual, an animal in fact, that is not planned as spirit, cannot sin when according to its sensual nature it demands and enjoys the pleasures natural to it, for that is just as it should be. Every nature that fulfills itself in pleasure does the will of God.

Lightning Source UK Ltd.
Milton Keynes UK
171670UK00001B/151/A